D1171872

Presidential Visit. John F. Kennedy was the first President to visit Internal Revenue's National Office and address Service officials. Commissioner Mortimer M. Caplin is shown with Mr. Kennedy.

First Commissioner. The first Commissioner of Internal Revenue was George S. Boutwell who took office on July 17, 1862. A lawyer from Massachusetts, Mr. Boutwell had been governor of his state and later was Secretary of the Treasury during the Grant administration. This portrait now hangs in the Internal Revenue Service building in Washington.

THE AMERICAN WAY IN TAXATION:
Internal Revenue, 1862-1963

Every man who knows how to read has it in his power to magnify himself, to multiply the ways in which he exists, to make his life full, significant and interesting.

—Aldous Huxley

THE AMERICAN WAY IN TAXATION:

INTERNAL REVENUE, 1862-1963

Edited by Lillian Doris

PRENTICE-HALL, INC.
Englewood Cliffs, N.J.

LIBRARY OF CONGRESS
CATALOG CARD NUMBER: 63-12128

PRINTED IN THE UNITED STATES OF AMERICA

03205—B&P

FOREWORD

Our federal tax system can be understood only with full appreciation of the administrative aspects of tax collection. Knowledge of the Internal Revenue Code—its constitutional and legislative history, its judicial development—will not suffice by itself.

Historian or political scientist, student or practitioner, each needs to study the evolution as well as structure and practices of the agency which administers our federal tax laws, the Internal Revenue Service. Without this background, the flavor of the American taxing process is not captured. Without this appreciation, court decisions cannot properly be evaluated nor tax advice soundly rendered.

The dynamics of federal tax administration was underscored recently in the 1962 liberalization of procedures for depreciation deductions. New legislation was not required. Instead, by administrative action alone, liberal and flexible rules were adopted sharply affecting business accounting procedures, equipment replacement practices and income tax liabilities.

Administrative ingenuity and initiative are also found in the development and expansion of the private rulings procedure. No other nation has been able to parallel the American system of issuing to taxpayers binding written rulings on the tax consequences of prospective transactions.

The story in this book begins in 1862, with the establishment of what is now the Internal Revenue Service, and moves on to major developments in our tax laws and tax administration up to the present time.

Attention is focused on the operation and procedures of our unique self-assessment tax system, which in 1962 raised some

$99.4 billion to finance our defense and other important domestic and foreign programs. Included is a description of the current installation of ADP—automatic data processing of tax returns—and the master file of taxpayers' records maintained on reels of high-speed electronic tape at the National Computer Center in Martinsburg, West Virginia.

Also prominently treated is the Service's "new direction"—a philosophy of tax administration which, parallel to vigorous enforcement efforts, emphasizes reasonable administration of the tax laws, concern for the rights and conveniences of taxpayers, and programs aimed at attaining higher levels of voluntary compliance.

Students of law, accounting, government and related subjects will find this book a valuable adjunct to their academic work. It will be enlightening, too, to tax practitioners, lawyers, accountants and businessmen interested in the practical operation as well as legal basis of the administrative process.

Compiled in the Centennial Year of the Internal Revenue Service, this is a highly readable account of where we have been and where we are going in tax administration. I welcome the contribution it makes to our increased knowledge of the most effective tax system the world has ever known.

MORTIMER M. CAPLIN
U. S. Commissioner of Internal Revenue

Washington, D. C.
January, 1963

CONTENTS

THE AMERICAN WAY IN TAXATION:
Internal Revenue, 1862-1963

Chapter One

THE U. S. TAX SYSTEM

THE TAX SYSTEM of the United States of America is considered the strongest and most effective tax system in the world. People in general recognize the vitality of a system that has demonstrated year after year its ability to raise the vast funds needed by the Government.

During fiscal year 1962, for example, gross receipts amounted to $99.4 billion—an all-time record—and the Internal Revenue Service collected this sum at the small cost of less than half a cent for every dollar raised. Businessmen generally agree that this represents a high return per dollar invested.

The remarkable aspect of this record is that the nation's tax system is based on individual self-assessment and voluntary compliance. It is, in the words of Supreme Court Justice Jackson, "a system of taxation by confession. That a people so numerous, scattered and individualistic annually assesses itself with a tax liability, often in highly burdensome amounts is a reassuring sign of the stability and vitality of our system of self-government."

Voluntary compliance is the heart of the tax system.

Self-assessment and voluntary compliance are the very heart and strength of the tax system.[1] It is a striking tribute to the

[1] At least partial self-assessment has been a feature of American taxation since 1862 when the law stated it was the duty of anyone liable to pay a tax imposed "to make a list or return" of the items on which the taxpayer was to be taxed. At that time, however, an Assistant Assessor checked these returns and figured the amount of tax due.

people of this country that they paid voluntarily $91 billion of the $94.4 billion collected, either through self-assessed returns or through excise taxes.

The self-assessment feature is based on the good faith of the people and their continued willingness to report income and deductions accurately. In turn, this good faith is largely dependent upon the public's general confidence that the tax laws are operating fairly and impartially and that all are paying their proper share of taxes.

The entire Internal Revenue Service has been oriented to see that this public confidence is sustained and strengthened. In its program to improve tax administration, it has been focusing its efforts on three major objectives:

1. Better service to taxpayers. This objective means service to all—wage-earner, farmer, small proprietor, professional man, the corporation—through public information programs, taxpayer assistance and education, and improved procedures.
2. A vigorous but more reasonable enforcement of the tax laws;
3. Curbing of abuses in the reporting of income and claiming of deductions, where remedial action is needed to reaffirm public confidence in the tax system.

These objectives are part of the "New Direction" of tax administration that got under way in 1961. The implementation of the objectives will be given in some detail in other chapters of this book.

Where federal and state revenues come from.

The collection of $99.4 billion by the Federal Government in fiscal 1962 came from the following sources:

Income tax: $71.9 billion
Excise taxes: $12.8 billion
Estate and gift taxes: $2.0 billion
Employment taxes: $12.7 billion

This total does not include the additional $8 billion contributed annually by the public for the federal old age and disability insurance program.

The income tax is obviously the chief source of federal revenue, accounting for about 72 percent of all tax receipts. Excise taxes return about 13 percent of the revenue, while all other receipts bring only 15 percent. Of the total income tax, almost two-thirds comes from individuals, the other one-third from corporations.

The state governments, which raised about $19 billion in the fiscal year 1961, do not lean heavily on income taxes. States rely more on other taxes, in the following approximate order of importance:

General sales, use or gross receipts taxes
Motor vehicle fuel sales taxes
Individual and corporate income taxes
Motor vehicle taxes and licenses
Alcoholic beverage sales taxes and licenses
Tobacco products sales taxes
Property taxes
Severance taxes
Death and gift taxes

In addition, states require sizable payments for unemployment compensation taxes.

County and city governments have traditionally relied on property taxes, both real estate and tangible personal property, as the mainstay of their revenues. In recent years, however, there has been a marked growth in non-property taxation by local governments—license fees, municipal sales taxes, gross receipts taxes, amusement taxes and occupation taxes.

The tax dollar becomes the budget dollar.

Under federal fiscal administration, the tax dollar becomes the budget dollar and as such is apportioned to planned government expenditures as determined by Congressional study. Forty-three cents of each budget dollar comes from individual income taxes, 31 cents from corporation income taxes, 16 cents from excise taxes, 6 cents from customs and other incidental taxes, and 4 cents from loans.

Of the outgoing budget dollar, two-thirds—68 cents at latest figures—goes to the national defense program with its manifold vital requirements. Certain charges fixed by law account for about 22 cents of the budget dollar. These include the interest the Government must pay on its bonds and other obligations; the expenses incident to its many programs in behalf of veterans; its grants to states, and numerous smaller but necessary expenditures.

Taxation has some secondary functions.

While revenue raising is obviously paramount in the American tax system, the Federal Government recognizes that taxation may have many subsidiary effects. In fact, it has experimented in varying degrees with these secondary functions of taxation.

Taxes have been used to discourage the use of child labor, and the sale of certain products, like oleomargarine, firearms and narcotics.

Estate and gift taxes have at times been increased to prevent the perpetuation of large estates.

Income taxes have been recognized as a weapon against fluctuations in the economy. When inflation threatens, high taxes may prevent excessive consumer purchasing and encourage investment and savings. In contrast, during a recession, lower taxes may encourage spending and discourage savings, thereby increasing demand for more goods and services.

Taxation has been recognized as an effective means for providing incentives to different businesses and groups of individuals. For example, various extractive industries—oil, gas, different minerals and ores—are encouraged by providing special deductions for drilling and mining costs, as well as for depletion. Investors are given special rate privileges for long-term capital gain. Timber and coal operators, investors, executives, and others are also given certain capital gain benefits.

In the 1962 tax legislation passed by Congress, one provision calls for a 7% investment tax credit which is designed to act as a stimulus to plant modernization and expansion. A credit against tax equal to 7% of new investments in plant equipment may now be taken by business.

How tax laws are made.

The Constitution grants Congress a broad power to "lay and collect taxes." Under the 16th Amendment to the Constitution, Congress may specifically tax "incomes, from whatever source derived, without apportionment among the several States."

The House of Representatives originates all tax legislation, although the Senate is free to propose amendments. This amendment power may be broadly exercised, and the Senate often becomes the moving force in new types of tax legislation.

After a tax proposal is introduced by a member of the House, it is referred to the Committee on Ways and Means. Often such legislative proposals result from Presidential requests for new legislation which are framed by the Treasury Department into a proposed tax bill.

Details of the tax bill are thoroughly discussed in hearings held by the Committee on Ways and Means. The Secretary of the Treasury usually testifies as do other Treasury and government officials. In addition, representatives of business and labor as well as all groups and individuals concerned with the tax bill have the opportunity to express their views. After the hearings, the Committee returns to executive session.

Based on the testimony received during the hearings, the Ways and Means Committee approves, amends, or rejects the proposed legislation, or may write an entirely new bill. It then refers its version of the tax bill, along with a Committee report, to the House, where it is approved or rejected after debate. No changes or amendments to the Ways and Means Committee bill may be made from the floor without Committee approval.

If approved by the House, the bill is referred to the Senate. There the bill is sent to the Senate Finance Committee, which schedules hearings.

Following testimony on the proposed legislation from Treasury, government, business, labor and private groups, the Finance Committee accepts, rejects, or modifies the House-passed bill. If it approves the measure, with or without change, the bill is referred to the Senate. Here, contrary to House procedure, amendments to the bill may be made during debate by individual Senators.

Should the House-approved tax bill pass the Senate Finance Committee and the Senate without change, it is sent to the President. If any changes have been made in the House bill, either by the Committee or on the floor, differences between the two versions are ironed out by a Conference Committee. This Committee is composed of leading members of the House Ways and Means Committee and the Senate Finance Committee. Its proceedings are conducted on a give-and-take basis.

Traditionally, a compromise bill reasonably satisfactory to all parties emerges, and it is referred back with a Conference Committee report to the House and Senate for a final vote. The legislation is then transmitted to the President of the United States who usually signs the tax bill, which then becomes law.

What the Joint Committee on Internal Revenue Taxation does.

Although it has no direct legislative function, the Joint Committee on Internal Revenue Taxation provides valuable assistance to both houses of Congress on tax matters. Membership of this Committee consists of five members each of the Ways and Means Committee and the Senate Finance Committee.

The Joint Committee, set up in 1926, has two main functions. It reviews refunds and credits over $100,000 proposed for payment by Internal Revenue, and it makes studies and recommendations to the two Congressional committees on tax matters. This second responsibility helps coordinate the tax activities of the two houses of Congress and provides a source of technical tax information that the committees can draw upon.

Congress places great reliance on the staff of the Joint Committee. In practice, this committee gives Congress a group of tax experts who can supply studies and analyses of tax proposals submitted by the Treasury Department and from other sources.

Although the staff of the Joint Committee works closely with its Treasury counterparts, the fact that they represent different branches of government, the legislative and the executive, may lead them to adopt varying points of view on specific issues. Disagreements are particularly marked when control of Congress and the White House is divided between the two political parties.

Internal Revenue Code contains all the tax laws.

From the adoption of the nation's first modern federal income tax law in 1913 until 1939, each major revenue act contained a complete set of income tax provisions which superseded the preceding revenue act. This process of complete re-enactment was ponderous and unnecessary. To simplify it, early in 1939 Congress enacted an Internal Revenue Code applicable to the years 1939 and thereafter. This single code contained all of the then currently applicable revenue provisions, except those relating to tariffs and customs. Future revenue legislation was thereafter cast in terms of amendments to this basic code.

In 1954, Congress undertook a major revision of the tax laws and the Internal Revenue Code of 1954 replaced the 1939 Code. The 1954 Code introduced a great many changes in the various taxes: rearrangement of most provisions, changes in terminology, revision of the income tax treatment of partnerships, trusts and estates, and corporate distributions, and many other technical changes reflecting the recommendations of a number of research groups, principally the American Law Institute.

Since then, various additions and corrective amendments have been made to the 1954 Code. The latest of these is the Revenue Act of 1962 enacted by the 87th Congress and signed into law by the President on October 16, 1962. This new law provides a great number of additional comprehensive changes. However, reference in any tax matter is still to the Internal Revenue Code of 1954. The precise words of the applicable provisions of this statute are always the point of beginning and the controlling factor in any tax issue.

Characteristics of federal income tax reveal its uniqueness.

The major characteristics of the federal income tax law are:

1. *Self-assessment.* The federal income tax is collected under a system of self-assessment, by which each taxpayer files a statement, called a return, setting forth his income for the taxable year and the tax due thereon. The normal filing date for individuals is April 15 of each year, and the normal filing date for corporations is March 15. Every individual whose gross income during the preceding year amounted to $600 or more must file a return unless he attained 65 years of age before the end of that year. If he reached 65 years of age, he is not required to file a return unless his gross income amounted to $1,200 or more. Certain deductions are al-

lowed from gross income to produce the net taxable amount, which is referred to as "taxable income."

2. *Graduated tax.* Beginning with the 1913 statute, the United States has always used a graduated or progressive tax. Under the 1954 Code, for example, the first $2,000 of taxable income is taxed at the rate of 20 percent. This is called the "first bracket." The next bracket, $2,000 to $4,000, is taxed at 22 percent; between $4,000 and $6,000 at 26 percent; between $6,000 and $8,000 at 30 percent, etc.

These rates then rise rapidly. Thus, between $16,000 and $18,000 of taxable income the rate is 50 percent, reaching the highest tax rate of 91 percent on all taxable income above $200,000.[3] As a small solace for taxpayers with most of their income ranging over $200,000, the Code provides an over-all limitation to the effect that the total income tax shall in no event exceed 87 percent of the total taxable income for the year.[4]

3. *Pay-as-you-go.* With the high tax rates effective during World War II, Congress felt it advisable to adopt a pay-as-you-go system for collection of the federal income tax. Consequently, instead of a taxpayer paying his tax at the end of his taxable year, he is now required to make advance payments during the year on income that he is currently earning. This is accomplished in two ways: (1) by withholding, and (2) by estimated tax payments. Under the first, employers deduct from the earnings of their employees an estimated amount of the tax due. Under the second, persons having income other than from employment are required to estimate their tax at the beginning of the year, to file advanced estimates, and to pay in quarterly installments the tax estimated to be due for the year. Hence, when April 15 arrives, the average taxpayer will have already paid most of the tax due on his previous year's income, either through withholding or estimated tax payments. Any balance must be paid with his April 15th return; any

---

[3] The income tax rate reached its highest level in history during the closing years of World War II, 1944 and 1945, with a normal tax rate of 3 percent on income over $500 plus a surtax rate of from 20 to 90 percent on income over the exemption of $500 each for taxpayer, wife, and dependents.

[4] In the case of an individual other than the head of a household, the 87 percent limitation applies only if taxable income exceeds in round dollars $629,500; for a head of a household the figure in round dollars is $938,000; in case of a joint return, the figure in round dollars is $1,259,000.

CHIEF CLERK
FEB 25 1913
DEPT. OF STATE

PHILANDER C. KNOX,

Secretary of State of the United States of America.

To all to Whom these Presents may come, Greeting:

Know Ye that, the Congress of the United States at the first Session, sixty-first Congress, in the year one thousand nine hundred and nine, passed a Resolution in the words and figures following: to wit--

"JOINT RESOLUTION

Proposing an amendment to the Constitution of the United States.

Resolved by the Senate and House of Representatives of the United States of America in Congress assembled (two-thirds of each House concurring therein), That the following article is proposed as an amendment to the Constitution of the United States, which, when ratified by the legislatures of three-fourths of the several States, shall be valid to all intents and purposes as a part of the Constitution:

'Article XVI. The Congress shall have power to

16TH AMENDMENT. With income taxes declared unconstitutional in 1895, Congress in 1909 prepared a resolution to amend the Constitution. After ratification by the required number of states, the income tax law of 1913 was passed.

lay and collect taxes on incomes, from whatever source derived, without apportionment among the several States, and without regard to any census or enumeration.'"

And, further, that it appears from official documents on file in this Department that the Amendment to the Constitution of the United States proposed as aforesaid has been ratified by the Legislatures of the States of Alabama, Kentucky, South Carolina, Illinois, Mississippi, Oklahoma, Maryland, Georgia, Texas, Ohio, Idaho, Oregon, Washington, California, Montana, Indiana, Nevada, North Carolina, Nebraska, Kansas, Colorado, North Dakota, Michigan, Iowa, Missouri, Maine, Tennessee, Arkansas, Wisconsin, New York, South Dakota, Arizona, Minnesota, Louisiana, Delaware, and Wyoming, in all thirty-six.

And, further, that the States whose Legislatures have so ratified the said proposed Amendment, constitute three-fourths of the whole number of States in the United States.

And, further, that it appears from official documents on file in this Department that the Legislatures of New Jersey and New Mexico have passed Resolutions ratifying the said proposed Amendment.

Now therefore, be it known that I, Philander C. Knox, Secretary of State of the United States, by virtue and in pursuance of Section 205 of the Revised Statutes of the United States, do hereby certify that the Amendment aforesaid has become valid to all intents and purposes as a part of the Constitution of the United States.

In testimony whereof, I have hereunto set my hand [illegible]d caused the seal of the Department of State to be [illegible]xed.

[illegible]ne at the city of Washington this twenty-fifth day of February in the year of our Lord one thousand nine hundred and thirteen, and of the Independence of the United States of America the one hundred and thirty-seventh.

Philander C. Knox

overpayment is refunded by the local District Director of Internal Revenue.

4. *Split-income provision.* In 1948, Congress sought to place taxpayers of most states on a parity with taxpayers of those few states with community property laws.[5] Married couples throughout the country are now permitted to compute their tax on a split-income joint return method, which results in their total tax being equal to twice the tax on one-half of their combined income. The effect of this provision is to treat the total income as being earned equally by each spouse. Under the graduated tax there is a resulting sharp reduction in the total tax due.

5. *Annual accounting periods.* Income must be reported by each taxpayer on an annual accounting basis, which normally means a twelve-month period ending on the last day of a given month. Most individuals report on the basis of the calendar year. Once an annual accounting period is selected it usually may not be changed without the consent of the Commissioner of Internal Revenue.

This annual accounting concept often results in hardships, particularly where a person receives fluctuating amounts of income over a number of years. A lawyer, doctor, athlete, or entertainer may earn low income over many years and then realize high income in a comparatively few years, only to find himself severely taxed in these later years through the sharply graduated tax system. Or a business profitable over a number of years may incur losses in one year which wipe out all of its prior earnings.

To alleviate the hardships encountered on receipt of irregular and fluctuating amounts of income, Congress has considered a variety of proposals for averaging income over a number of years. To date, no satisfactory averaging provision has been adopted. However, the tax law does contain a number of special provisions giving relief from the burdens created by the annual accounting concept.

One such relief provision permits lump-sum compensation

[5] Where the community property system exists, all earnings of either husband or wife constitute a common fund of the husband and wife. The property is known as community property. The central idea of the system is the same in all community-property states (Arizona, California, Idaho, Louisiana, Nevada, New Mexico, Texas and Washington), but the statutes and judicial decisions have directed the development of the system along different lines in the various states.

earned for services rendered over thirty-six months or more to be prorated over the period of employment, with certain limitations. Similarly a lump-sum income from inventions or artistic work created over a number of years can be prorated over the period of the work.

A very important relief provision for business is known as the net operating loss deduction. Under it, losses of one year are permitted to be carried back three years to be offset against the profits of these prior years, and thereafter any remaining unabsorbed losses may be carried forward five years as an offset against income earned in this later period. In effect, taxpayers are thereby granted the opportunity to spread any loss over a total period of nine years.

6. *"Realization"—severance.* Another basic doctrine of the income tax law is that of "realization." In brief, the law does not tax an individual on the mere unrealized appreciation of his property. Nor does it permit him to deduct a loss for mere unrealized depreciation of property. This is sometimes referred to as the doctrine of "severance," under which gain or loss is given tax recognition only if there has been severance from the underlying asset. This makes it unnecessary for the tax administrators to examine each asset of a taxpayer at the beginning and end of a year to determine fluctuations. Instead, the Internal Revenue Service need consider only identifiable events which gave rise to a realization of gain or loss, such as sales, exchanges or other dispositions of property.

7. *Capital gain.* One of the outstanding features of the income tax law is the special provision for the taxation of capital gain. Where a capital asset has been held for a period of more than six months and is then sold or exchanged, the maximum tax payable on the gain so realized is 25 percent.

Capital gain treatment has been justified as an averaging device for accretions of capital over a number of years received as income in a single year. It has also been defended as an incentive provision for investors and other taxpayers.

Congress has used the capital gain approach to provide relief for a wide variety of taxpayer groups, usually in the belief that their incomes were being taxed at too high a rate. In this category fall many transactions which normally would not be regarded as capital in nature. For example: long-term capital gain treatment is given to royalties from patents; to sums received by lessees from cancellation of leases; to amounts received by distributors of goods for cancellation of distributors' agreements; to total distributions within one year from pension funds on an employee's death or other separation from service; to certain employee stock options, etc.

Re-examination is underway to improve the system.

For several years Congress has been making a comprehensive re-examination of the entire federal tax structure. Extended studies and hearings have been conducted over a period of many months. The stated goal is to strengthen the tax laws, to correct inequities, and "to obtain a revenue system which is fair, equitable, neutral in impact between similar dollars of income, responsive to changes in economic conditions, and capable of compliance and administration with a minimum of taxpayer and governmental effort, and which will produce the needed revenue for the Government."

Although many of the aims of this ambitious program *may not be attainable,* nevertheless numerous legislators and private citizens are devoting themselves to this project. Their hope is to achieve at least a number of basic improvements which will *strengthen the tax law.* The undertaking is regarded as of major importance, for a sound federal tax structure is vital not only to the nation's well-being but also to the continued freedom of the world. Without the revenues produced by the tax laws, the United States would not be able to provide the services and security required by its people, and would not be able to meet its commitments to its friends in the free world.

Chapter Two

HISTORICAL ROOTS OF TAXATION AND TAX ADMINISTRATION

EACH OF THE MAJOR WARS fought by the United States brought about drastic changes in taxation to provide the revenue required to meet the heavy demands of national defense and the successful prosecution of military, naval, aeronautical, and—more recently—outer space activities.

National growth and development also brought about new government activities that increased the need for revenue and gave rise to new taxes.

How the tax laws have varied from the founding of the nation to the present time is traced briefly in the first part of this chapter. The second part is devoted to the Commissioner of Internal Revenue, who for the past hundred years has been the chief revenue officer of the United States, and to the early development of the Internal Revenue Service.

The Tax Laws of the Past and Present

The Internal Revenue Service was born a century ago, with the major changes in taxation that occurred as a result of the Civil War. Prior to that time there were intermittent long periods when the Federal Government imposed no internal revenue taxes at all.

In the beginning there were few taxes.

Few taxes were collected in colonial days, and those were mainly excise and poll taxes. A "faculty tax," which might be considered an ancestor of today's income tax, was levied in New England in 1646. It required "every laborer, artificer and handicraftsman" to pay a portion of his earnings to the taxing authority.

The controversy with the mother country over taxation without representation, and the general distrust of central government that prevailed when the nation was founded, led the states to withhold from the Continental Congress the power to collect taxes. The Congress had to ask the states for whatever funds were needed. They were then collected by the states through taxation and turned over to the central treasury.

Having experienced the difficulties of financing the war for independence with heavy borrowing and paper money, and having realized that lack of taxing power was one of the weaknesses of the Continental Congress, the states could not deny the central government the power to levy taxes. The Constitution was therefore ratified with a clause that gives Congress power to tax and spend for the general welfare. It is Article 1, Section 8, which reads:

"The Congress shall have power to lay and collect taxes, duties, imposts and excises, pay the debts and provide for the common defense and general welfare of the United States; but all duties, imposts and excises shall be uniform throughout the United States."

Internal taxes were imposed from 1791 to 1802.

The first period in which internal taxes were used to support the Federal Government was from 1791 to 1802.

Alexander Hamilton, the first Secretary of the Treasury, pushed for a system of excise taxes accompanied by proper collection machinery. The thought of federal revenue agents abroad in the land caused consternation among some members of Congress, but Hamilton won approval of a rather broad tax program with the Revenue Act of March 3, 1791.

Taxes during the period from 1791 to 1802 were levied on dis-

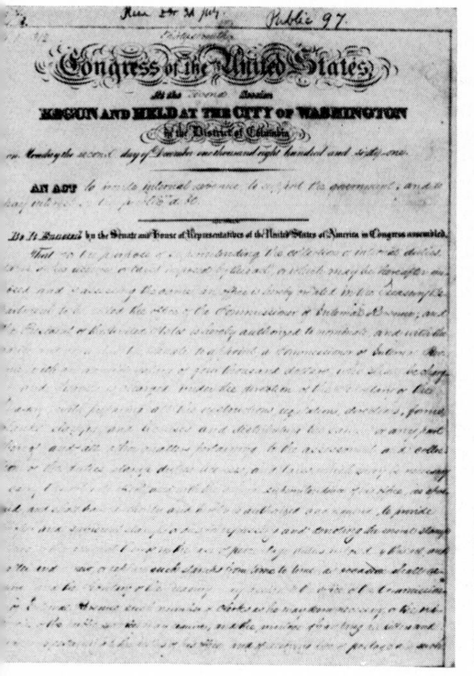

Congress of the United States

At the Second Session

BEGUN AND HELD AT THE CITY OF WASHINGTON

in the District of Columbia,

on Monday the second day of December one thousand eight hundred and sixty-one.

AN ACT to provide internal revenue to support the government, and to pay interest on the public debt.

Be It Enacted by the Senate and House of Representatives of the United States of America in Congress assembled,

General provisions.

COMMISSIONER ESTABLISHED. This was the Congressional bill which became the Revenue Act of 1862. It created the office of Commissioner of Internal Revenue and levied a range of taxes including the first individual income tax.

WITHHOLDING BEGAN EARLY. The withholding of taxes on wages and salaries was in effect early as shown by this 1864 receipt. This form was the equivalent of the present W-2.

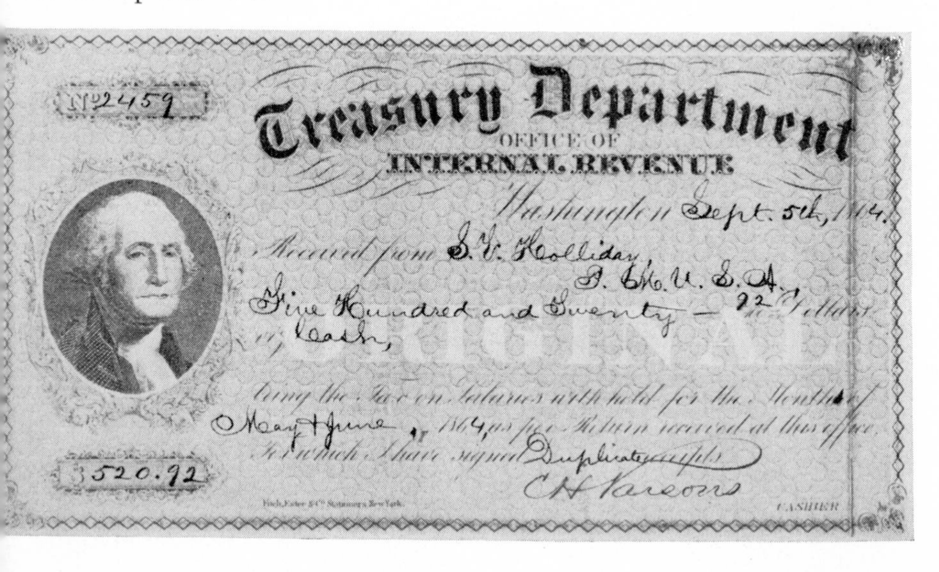

No 2459

Treasury Department

OFFICE OF

INTERNAL REVENUE

Washington Sept. 5th, 1864.

Received from S. V. Holliday

B. M. U. S. A.

Five Hundred and Twenty — 92/100 Dollars

in Cash,

being the Tax on Salaries withheld for the Months of

May & June, 1864, as per Return received at this office,

For which I have signed Duplicate receipts

$520.92

C H Parsons

CASHIER

MOONSHINE RAID. Internal Revenue agents, the "revenooers," put another illicit whisky still out of business. Evasion of alcohol taxes, a problem that goes as far back as George Washington's administration, is now largely eliminated except for some rural areas in the South.

BRANDY TESTING. An important function of Internal Revenue's National Laboratory in Washington is brandy and wine analysis. Established 75 years ago, the laboratory also analyzes moonshine and narcotics samples.

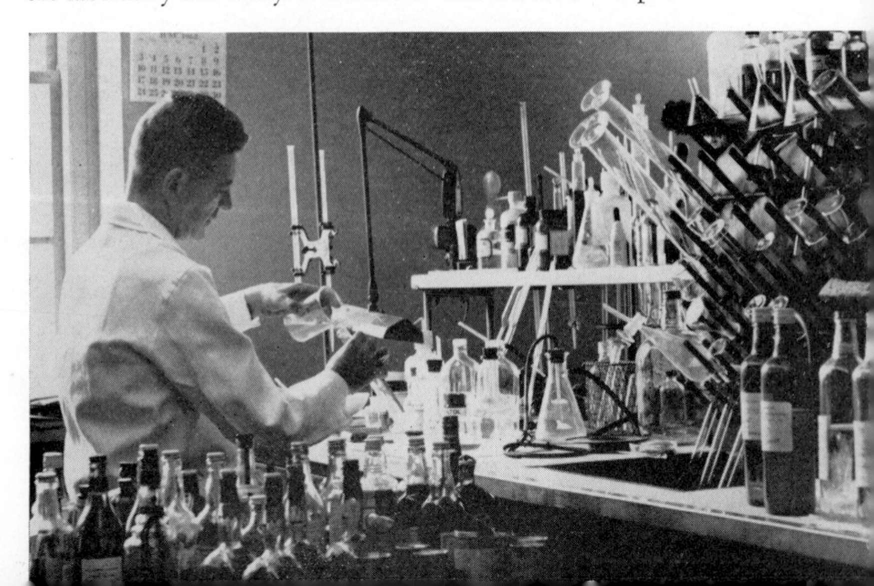

tilled spirits, carriages, refined sugar, snuff, snuff mills, property sold at auction, bonds, and slaves. A progressive tax on houses and lots also was imposed, based on their value.

Receipts from internal revenue were meager—only $208,943 in fiscal 1792—not one-tenth of the amount received from custom duties. The cost of collecting those taxes was about 20 percent of the revenue taken in.

Strong opposition to the excise taxes, particularly from the Antifederalist Party, at times tested the strength of the Government. In 1794 the tax on whisky ignited the Whisky Rebellion among a group of farmers in southwestern Pennsylvania who stood in armed defiance of the "obnoxious" levy until federal troups quieted the trouble. This was an historic demonstration of the Government's early determination to enforce its revenue laws.

Excise taxes were abolished; revenue offices eliminated.

When Thomas Jefferson took office as President, he abolished the Federalists' excise system and the offices then held by 400 revenue officials. The Federal Government relied on revenue from the tariff. It was not until the war with England in 1812 that the nation again needed funds from internal revenue.

War of 1812 revived internal taxation.

A special session of Congress in the summer of 1813 approved the tax recommendations of Treasury Secretary Albert A. Gallatin. Among the proposals was a direct tax, which under the Constitution had to be apportioned among the states according to population. The then 18 states were to pay their quotas into the federal treasury.

A new list of taxes was levied to help meet the costs of the war. Coincidentally, what is believed to have been the first sales tax in this country came with these levies. Gold and silverware, jewelry, and watches were among new additions to the tax roster.

Internal taxes were again abolished.

The nation recovered rapidly from the difficulties of the War of 1812, and despite recommendations by the Secretary of the Treasury in 1815 that a permanent internal revenue system be set up, Congress in 1817 abolished all internal revenue taxes. It was prompted to this action by the high customs receipts realized from

THE EVENING STAR.

WASHINGTON CITY:

THURSDAY................ JULY 3, 1862.

Reading matter on every page. See outside for interesting Telegraphic and other matter.

The President has approved and signed the following important bills:

The bill to aid in the construction of a railroad and telegraph line from the Missouri river to the Pacific ocean, and to secure the use of the same to the Government for postal, military, and other purposes.

The bill to provide internal revenue to defray the expenses of the Government and pay interest on the public debt.

The bill to prevent and punish the practice of polygamy in the Territories of the United States, and other places; and disapproving and annulling certain acts of the Legislative Assembly of the Territory of Utah.

The bill to prescibe an oath of office, and for other purposes.

FINANCIAL.—New York papers of last evening say: Stocks took a strong downward surge to-day. The continued silence of the Government in regard to affairs before Richmond produces an uncomfortable feeling, which is further increased by the call for three hundred thousand troops. The market would rally very quickly upon the slightest good news from Washington, and this may come at any moment. Prices seem to be controlled almost entirely by news from the seat of war.

FRONT PAGE NEWS. The signing by President Lincoln of the 1862 Revenue Act made front page news. Also signed that day were the authorization for a rail and telegraph line between the Missouri River and the Pacific Ocean and a bill to prevent and punish polygamy.

imported goods. The office of Commissioner of Revenue was abolished for the second time in less than a score of years. There was no need for internal revenue machinery again for more than forty years.

The Mexican War did not require tax financing, nor did the Indian campaigns carried on sporadically during the first half of the nineteenth century.

Civil War brought major tax changes.

With the Civil War, tremendous demands were made on the national treasury. In an emergency session, Congress on August 5,

1861, passed the first Civil War revenue measure which later proved to be inadequate.

By spring of 1862, revenue needs were mounting fast. Public debt was climbing at the rate of $2 million a day. A hesitant Treasury Secretary, Salmon P. Chase, and a slow-moving Congress were prodded by public opinion and newspaper editorials to enact more effective tax legislation.

Finally, on July 1, 1862, President Lincoln signed into law the most sweeping revenue-producing measure in the nation's history to that time. That act was the foundation for our present internal revenue system and marked the birth of the permanent Internal Revenue Service. The purposes and organization of the agency are basically the same today.

The office of Commissioner of Internal Revenue was created, and under direction of the Treasury Secretary, the Commissioner was charged with preparing all instructions and regulations needed to carry out the law.

The new law provided for progressive taxation, for levies on incomes and for tax withholding, which are all vital features of modern revenue statutes.

In addition to taxing incomes, the new law taxed estates, public utilities, occupations, liquors, beer, tobacco, banks, insurance companies, advertisements, slaughtered cattle, railroads, ferry boats, and other specified commodities. It provided stamp taxes on certain commercial papers, perfume, cosmetics, medicines and playing cards.

In the last year of the Civil War, fiscal 1866, internal revenue reached its peak with a total of more than $300 million. In July 1866 and March 1867, Congress progressively reduced or eliminated many taxes.

Collection of the various taxes, particularly those from the states, was carried on until 1868. Three years later Congress decided the money was no longer required and returned the funds on hand to the states.

In mid-1868, taxation of distilled beverages and tobacco became the major source of internal revenue. From that year to 1913 nearly 90 percent of all internal revenue collections came from taxes on those products.

First Income Taxpayers. This drawing shows taxpayers lining up at a collector's office during the Civil War. The first income tax law was passed in 1862.

FIFTH AUDITOR'S
APR 27 1872
OFFICE

United States Internal Revenue,

Assessor's Office, District of Columbia.

Washington, April 27th, 1872.

I hereby certify that Abraham Lincoln made two returns of income for the year ending Dec. 31, 1863, one for his tax on income outside of his salary. amounting to $7.75 being a tax of 1½ c on $1183; the second was for the tax as levied by the joint resolution of July 4. 1864, and known as the Special income tax, which embraced the above amount and his salary of $25.000 as President of the United States, amounting in the aggregate to $25.583 on which he paid tax of 5% amount of tax $1279 15/100. Both of these returns appear on Form 58 for Dec. 1864, and are the only returns he made to this office.

Walter S. Burr.
Assessor

LINCOLN'S TAX RETURNS. According to this report, President Lincoln filed two tax returns for 1863. One covered his salary as President and the other his outside income of $1,183.

In Executive Session, Senate of the United States,

July 12, 1862.

Resolved, *That the Senate advise and consent to the appointment of* George S. Boutwell, of Massachusetts, to be Commissioner of Internal Revenue, agreeably to the nomination.

Attest:

J. W. Forney
Secretary.

SENATE CONFIRMS. The appointment of Commissioner Boutwell by President Lincoln is officially confirmed in this Senate document. The office of Commissioner is still a Presidential appointment but the reorganization of Internal Revenue in 1952 removed all other offices from politics, placing them in the competitive Civil Service system.

New regulatory taxes were introduced.

Although financing of government business relied principally on tariffs in the latter part of the nineteenth century, some new taxes, intended more to regulate than to produce revenue, were introduced.

In 1866 Congress passed the oleomargarine tax, mainly to keep oleo from competing with butter. Instead of discouraging production, the oleomargarine output doubled in five years. Almost $1 million in taxes was collected the first year.

In 1899 a tax was levied on all opium manufactured in the United States for smoking purposes. This, too, was a regulatory rather than a revenue-producing measure.

The concept of using taxes to regulate rather than solely to raise revenue was tested and affirmed by the U.S. Supreme Court. The Court held that if the levy conformed to the requirements of an internal excise, it was a legitimate tax and the motives or intention of Congress was not involved.

After years of trying to curb international trade in opium and other narcotics through tax and import restrictions, Congress in 1914 passed the Harrison Act. This law gave the Commissioner of Internal Revenue responsibility for regulating the domestic manufacturing and use of these narcotics. Other regulatory levies of the same period were placed on manufacturers of phosphorus matches and the sale of cotton for future delivery.

Taxes would be used again in the future for regulatory purposes.

Early income tax was short-lived.

The nation's first income tax disappeared in 1872 with the elimination of the taxes referred to above. It had a short-lived revival from 1894 to 1895. In the latter year the United States Supreme Court first declared the law imposing taxes on income derived from real estate and from state and municipal bonds invalid, and on a rehearing decided that the whole income tax law was unconstitutional on the ground that it was a direct tax and was not apportioned among the states in conformity with the Constitution.[1]

---

[1] Pollock v. Farmers' Loan and Trust Company (157 US 429, 3AFTR 2557).

(24.)

UNITED STATES INTERNAL REVENUE.

INCOME TAX, 1871.

By the act of July 14, 1870, it is made the duty of every person of lawful age, the gross amount of whose income, gains, and profits during the year ending December 31, 1870, exceeded two thousand dollars, on or before the 1st day of March, 1871, to make a return of said gross amount to the assistant assessor of the district in which he resides.

Guardians, trustees, executors, and administrators, and persons acting in any other fiduciary capacity, or as resident agents for, or co-partners of, any non-resident alien deriving income from business carried on in the United States, or from rents of real estate situate therein, are required to make returns of the income belonging to minors, or other persons for whom they act, and the income tax will be assessed upon the amount of such income, after deducting such sums as are exempted by law; *provided* that the exemption of two thousand dollars shall not be allowed on account of any minor or other beneficiary of a trust except upon the statement of the guardian or trustee, made under oath, that the minor or beneficiary has no other income from which the said amount may be exempted and deducted.

"The assistant assessor shall require every such return to be verified by the oath of the party rendering it, and may increase the amount of any return, after notice to such party, if he has reason to believe that the same is understated. In case any person having a gross income as above, of two thousand dollars or more, shall neglect or refuse to make and render such return, or shall render a false or fraudulent return, the assessor or the assistant assessor shall make such return, according to the best information he can obtain by the examination of said person, or of his books or accounts, or by any other evidence, and shall add, as a penalty, to the amount of the tax due thereon, fifty per centum in all cases of willful neglect or refusal to make and render a return, and one hundred per centum in all cases of a false or fraudulent return having been rendered. * * * * * * * * * * * * *
But no penalty shall be assessed upon any person for such neglect or refusal, or for making or rendering a false or fraudulent return, except after reasonable notice of the time and place of hearing, to be regulated by the Commissioner of Internal Revenue, so as to give the person charged an opportunity to be heard."—[*Sec.* 11.]

"When the return of a person is thus increased, he may appeal from the decision of the assistant assessor to the assessor of the district; and the assessor's decision will be final, unless reversed by the Commissioner of Internal Revenue."—[*Sec.* 12.]

This appeal must be claimed of the assistant assessor within twenty-four hours after his decision is rendered, and a written statement of the grounds of appeal must be filed with the assessor within five days of the time it was claimed, unless special reasons (such as great distance from the assessor, lack of mail facilities, &c.) are shown why such statement could not have been filed in that time. Of the sufficiency of these reasons, the assessor, subject to an appeal to the Commissioner of Internal Revenue, is to be the judge; and when any such exist, the written statement must be filed at the earliest reasonable time.

It is required by law that all returns of income shall be made according to its value in legal tender currency.

When coupons of United States bonds, or gold received as interest on bonds, are sold within the year, the amount of legal tender currency received therefor should be returned as income under paragraph 10.

When any person has gold, or coupons payable in gold, on hand at the close of the year, its value should be returned at the value of gold at the close of the year. This value in New York was 110⅞.

The assessment list, when completed, will be returned to the collector, who will "give notice by advertisement in one newspaper published in each county in his collection district, if any there be, and if not, then in a newspaper printed in an adjoining county, and by notification, to be posted in at least four public places in each county in his collection district, that the said duties have become due and payable, and state the time and place within said county at which he or his deputy will attend to receive the same," and to any sum unpaid after the thirtieth day of April, and for ten days after demand, there will be an addition of five per cent. as a penalty for such neglect, and of interest at one per cent. per month.

EARLY REGULATIONS. Procedures for paying income taxes due in 1871 are outlined in this document from Internal Revenue.

OFFICE
U.O. JAN 3 1881 G.C.
S. K. of R.

$250 REWARD!

TREASURY DEPARTMENT,
Office of Internal Revenue,
Washington, Dec. 1, 1879.

With the approval of the Secretary of the Treasury, a Reward of

TWO HUNDRED and FIFTY DOLLARS

is offered for the re-arrest and confinement of Hutsell Amarine, charged with forcibly obstructing Deputy Collector W. R. Cooper in the performance of his official duty as an officer of Internal Revenue in the Second District of Tennessee, on August 9, 1878, said obstruction resulting in the death of John Cooper who was employed to aid and assist him, and said Hutsell Amarine having escaped from the Knoxville Jail on the night of November 8, 1879, while under confinement awaiting trial.

GREEN B. RAUM,
Commissioner.

Enforcement Hazards. Violations of the tax laws, particularly those on alcohol, often made the enforcement work of Revenue Agents a dangerous occupation. Twenty-six agents were killed and 57 wounded during the four-year span of 1876–1880.

Constitutional amendment authorized an income tax.

After an 18-year lapse the 16th Amendment to the Constitution became effective on February 25, 1913. It gave Congress the power to levy and collect taxes on incomes, from whatever source derived, without apportionment among the several states, and without regard to any census or enumeration. On October 3, 1913, Congress enacted the income tax law which imposed a tax on net income of both individuals and corporations.

Corporations were first taxed in 1909.

The proposal that Congress pass a 2 percent excise tax on corporations based on their net income was recommended by President Taft at the same time that he recommended that Congress propose an amendment to the Constitution giving the Government power to tax incomes without apportioning the burden among the states in line with population. One of the benefits of the proposed corporation tax, as many saw it, was that it postponed the enactment of the individual income tax.

Pressure, however, had been building up for a tax based on the ability to pay, as resentment against some of the ultra-wealthy was growing. The Greenback, Anti-Monopoly, and Populist parties were pushing for the income tax. Theodore Roosevelt dismayed many of his supporters by coming out strongly for the income tax in the latter part of his second term.

In August, 1909, the corporation excise tax became law. It was termed an excise on the privilege of doing business. It imposed a tax of 1 percent on net corporation income above $5,000. The Income Tax Act of 1913 repealed the corporation tax of 1909 and imposed a new tax on net income of corporations.

World War I brought new taxes.

The cost of World War I has been estimated at $35 billion. About one-third of it was paid in taxes.

Even before the United States was drawn into the war against Germany, a series of measures were being introduced to pay for heavy military appropriations and to make up for reduced customs receipts.

As early as 1913 Congress passed a revenue measure with many of the same excises on liquor and tobacco and other levies that had helped pay the bills for the brief Spanish-American War near the turn of the century.

The omnibus Revenue Act of 1916 was intended to raise funds to match rising expenditures. Besides boosting income tax rates, the act included a new estate tax, a tax on stock dividends, and a tax on munitions manufacturers' profits.

From 1917 to 1919, new tax laws were both revenue-producing and regulatory. The War Revenue Act of 1917 was a sweeping measure. It dealt with income, excess profits, beverages, tobacco and tobacco manufacturers, public utilities and insurance, excises, admissions and dues, stamp taxes and estate taxes. Internal revenue receipts for fiscal year 1918 amounted to $3.6 billion, compared with $809 million the year before.

In the spring of 1918, President Wilson called for a new measure to raise billions more for war. Of the pending military programs, President Wilson said, these "are not programs, indeed, but mere plans on paper, unless there is to be an unquestionable supply of money." However, it was not until February 1919 that the legislation was enacted. The law was retroactive and was called the Revenue Act of 1918. It marked the beginning of a new era of internal revenue taxation.

The new law codified all the existing tax laws. It provided amortization allowances to permit manufacturers who invested in special war equipment to write off the cost. The income tax provisions imposed a normal and surtax rate structure that went up to 77 percent. The law also included new excess profits and estate taxes. But it had a number of relief provisions. For example, it was the first U.S. tax to minimize double taxation of individuals and domestic corporations having foreign incomes. In computing income taxes, credits were permitted on levies paid other countries. Liberalized deductions were also allowed for depletion of natural resources.

The act also included a tax on anyone who employed child labor. This was an attempt to ban child labor by tax regulation, but this section of the law was declared unconstitutional in 1922.

The combined effects of the revenue legislation of the first

World War reached a high point in 1920. Total internal revenue collections hit about $5.5 billion that year.

Taxes were cut in the 1920's.

The early years of the twentieth century brought increasing growth, urbanization and industrialization. Society became more specialized and more interdependent. As the economy expanded and grew more complex, the government assumed more responsibilities for conservation, supervision, and regulation. This meant new and different taxes were to be collected.

On top of the pressures for government to assume a larger role, was the determination of the public and its leaders to hold costs down and balance the budget.

The need for economy in government spending was stressed during the Harding and Coolidge administrations. In the decade of the 1920's taxes were cut five times and receipts still were high. The dominant popular conviction was that government expenditures and debts were burdens on the people in good times and bad. The nation was anchored to that principle when the stock market plunged in 1929 and the Depression began.

New taxes were added during the depression.

In 1932, revenue collections totalled $1.5 billion, lower than at any time since 1917. Congress raised income taxes and reduced the exemption level; it more than doubled the rates for estate taxes. Gift taxes were re-enacted. The budget had to be balanced.

Democrats as well as Republicans were sure that the way to revive business confidence and bring recovery was to have a balanced budget each year. The theory that the Federal Government should play an active role in trying to stimulate the economy had attracted only minor attention before Franklin D. Roosevelt took office as President.

With increasing acceptance of the idea that government should lead the way to recovery even if it meant a deficit budget, came the massive legislative program during the New Deal's first decade.

Unemployment, particularly among the aged, was a central problem. More than 13 million workers were jobless in 1933.

The Federal Government had made numerous relief grants to states and had established a variety of agencies to provide employment and help for those needing it. But there was pressure for a more permanent kind of security. It led to enactment by Congress of the Social Security Act of 1935.

The new law provided several different benefits. Jobless workers received payments for a varying number of weeks depending on state laws. The act also provided old age and survivors' benefits for a large segment of the population. Both employers and employees paid originally one percent of the first $3,000 of salaries and wages to finance these benefits.

Public assistance programs were created for the aged, the needy, for children and the blind, for maternal and child welfare services, and for vocational rehabilitation.

Social Security taxes yielded a mere $250 million in 1937. The receipts were to grow to more than $12 billion in 1962 through extension of coverage and boosts in rates.

From 1922 to 1941 tax collections climbed from $1.6 billion to $7.4 billion. But this considerable growth was dwarfed in the next four years as war clouds rolled over most of the world. By 1945, the Internal Revenue Service would collect a staggering $45 billion in taxes.

World War II brought radical tax and economic changes.

War-time taxation, with its shift of emphasis from a narrow base income tax affecting 8 million taxpayers to a broad base ultimately affecting 60 million, brought the individual income tax to tens of millions of taxpayers for the first time.

Two comparisons reveal the radical changes wrought by the new tax laws:

—Taxpayers with income under $3,000 accounted for only 10 percent of revenue collections in 1939. By 1948, these taxpayers accounted for 50 percent of revenue collected.

—In 1939, 700,000 returns accounted for 90 percent of the total tax liability. By 1948, this number had climbed to 25 million returns.

Altogether about $153 billion in taxes was collected during World War II.

Fiscal as well as other policies were changed drastically by the war. During most of the 1930's, fiscal policy was directed at fighting deflation, creating employment, and reviving sluggish industry. During most of the war and immediately thereafter a major goal was to fight inflation.

Building and supplying a military structure for ourselves and our allies took all reins off spending. But as inflation increased, heavy taxes to support the war effort simultaneously helped to reduce purchasing power, which served as a check on rising prices.

Wartime taxation had still another purpose besides paying defense bills and curbing inflation. The excess profits tax on corporations was enacted with the basic purpose of recapturing for the Government profits arising from abnormal war-time conditions. It remained in effect from 1940 to 1946.

The Revenue Act of 1942 involved a variety of levies. Income tax rates were increased and individual exemptions lowered. A further tax on personal incomes was imposed by the Victory Tax. A corporation income and excess profits tax as well as a capital stock and declared-value excess profits levy also were imposed, making some corporations liable for taxes up to 80 percent of their net income.

The estate tax was made more restrictive and excise taxes were increased on tobacco, liquor, travel, and telephone service.

The Current Tax Payment Act of 1943 put wages and salaries on a withholding basis for tax collections beginning July 1, 1943. Partial forgiveness of the tax for 1942 was a feature of the act.

The Revenue Act of 1943 increased the rate of the excess profits tax on corporations to 95 percent and the specific exemption to $10,000. At the same time, it reduced the excess profits credit in certain brackets of invested capital, and repealed the earned income credit for individuals.

In his January 1944 budget message to Congress, Mr. Roosevelt recommended tax simplification. Ways and Means Committee Chairman Doughton promised simplification would be the Number One job of his committee.

The Individual Income Tax Act of 1944 was the result. It made personal exemptions uniform at $500 and replaced the Victory Tax with a new 3 percent normal tax on net income. The former normal tax was absorbed with a new surtax schedule with rates from 20 to 91 percent. The new law let small taxpayers file their withholding receipts as tax returns if they so chose, and it relieved millions of people from having to file declarations of estimated tax.

This act also provided for the standard deduction of 10 percent.

Tax cuts followed the end of World War II.

The first tax cut since Andrew Mellon was Secretary of the Treasury was recommended by Treasury Secretary Fred M. Vinson when World War II had ended. Congress upped the amount of reduction proposed, and President Truman signed a $9 billion relief bill, chopping both individual and corporate rates and taking 12 million persons off the tax rolls.

Congress passed another tax cut in the spring of 1948, this time of $4.8 billion and over the veto of President Truman. This law brought the individual exemption to the present $600. It also gave married couples the option of filing joint returns, a multi-billion dollar tax saving for married people over the years.

Korean conflict brought back an excess profits tax.

Again to limit the war profits of corporations and to raise revenue, an excess profits tax was enacted on January 3, 1951. It remained in force for the years 1950-1953, the period of Korean hostilities. No excess profits tax has been imposed since then.

The Social Security Act of 1950 extended coverage greatly, bringing in most of the self-employed. It also raised the tax and broadened the tax base.

An excise tax on wagers became law and was upheld by the Supreme Court in 1953. Under it certain types of professional gamblers are required to secure a federal license and pay a tax of 10 percent on their receipts.

The 1954 Code has been amended.

The 1954 Internal Revenue Code (see page 7) has been amended in some way every year since its adoption although there have been no important changes in rates for individuals or corporations. A new excise tax, the highway use tax on trucks and buses, was levied in 1956 as part of the huge federal highway construction program authorized by Congress that year. The rate of this use tax was doubled in 1961.

Several changes in the Code were made in 1962 affecting individuals and businesses. The revisions provide a 7 percent investment tax credit for corporations, create a new formula for taxing mutual savings banks and savings and loan associations, introduce new procedures for taxing dividends earned by domestic corporations abroad, allow self-employed persons certain exemptions on contributions to retirement funds, and tighten up rules on travel and entertainment expense deductions.

The Commissioner of Internal Revenue

Under the Act of July 1, 1862, the Commissioner of Internal Revenue was given the power to assess, levy, and collect taxes, and the right to enforce the law through seizure and prosecution.

The Act provided:

> . . . That, for the purpose of superintending the collection of internal duties, stamp duties, licenses, or taxes imposed by this Act, or which may be hereafter imposed, and of assessing the same, an office is hereby created in the Treasury Department to be called the office of the Commissioner of Internal Revenue; . . . Commissioner of Internal Revenue, . . . shall be charged, and hereby is charged, under the direction of the Secretary of the Treasury, with preparing all the instructions, regulations, directions, forms, blanks, stamps, and licenses, and distributing the same or any part thereof, and all other matters pertaining to the assessment and collection of the duties, stamp duties, licenses, and taxes, which may be necessary to carry this Act into effect, and with the general superintendence of his office, as aforesaid, and shall have authority, and hereby is authorized and required, to provide proper and sufficient stamps or dies for expressing and denoting the several stamp duties, or the amount thereof in the case of percentage duties, imposed by this Act, and to alter and renew or replace such stamps from time to time, as occasion shall require. . . .

First Commissioner was outstanding.

The first Commissioner of Internal Revenue, George S. Boutwell, took office on July 17, 1862 and served until March 4, 1863, when he became a Congressman. He was a Republican lawyer from Massachusetts who, at age 44, had already served in the

Massachusetts legislature, and been Governor of his state. Later he was to serve in both the House of Representatives and the Senate and as Secretary of the Treasury.

He attacked his job with vigor. First with one clerk then with many more, he decided what forms would be needed for records and returns and contracted for the printing of revenue stamps.

"The public anxiety in regard to the construction of the law," he reported, "induced a large amount of correspondence with persons in various parts of the country." Soon the letters reached a level of 800 a day. Before he had been in office five months, Commissioner Boutwell had made more than 100 decisions relating to principles of the new law and twice as many rulings.

The Commissioner also devised a system of bookkeeping so that his agency could furnish at any time a statement of the amount of revenue from every article taxed in every collection district.

One cardinal principle Mr. Boutwell applied was: "To levy a tax in those cases only which are clearly provided for by statute, and consequently, whenever a reasonable doubt exists, to rule against the Government and in favor of the individual."

A large field force was established.

In addition to the difficulties of interpreting a brand new tax law, Commissioner Boutwell struggled with the problem of getting a collecting force into action.

Under the law, the President was authorized to divide the country into collection districts, 185 in all. For each district, there was to be a collector, an assessor, and deputies and assistants. But President Lincoln was a hard-pressed man in those Civil War days. According to Mr. Boutwell, President Lincoln designated only two collectors whom he knew personally. Mr. Boutwell built the revenue force at a spectacular rate. By January, 1863, the number of employees had risen to 3,882.

The bulk of the operations of the agency was in the field, from handling appeals to punishing frauds. A key official of the system was the assessor. He kept his office open at all hours, heard appeals, issued summons to those who failed to make returns after being issued notices, examined taxable property, and inspected accounts.

Assessors were paid from three to five dollars a day, depending on their duties. Often the entire pay of an assessor was spent in setting up an office. But Congress soon approved Mr. Boutwell's request for more pay and expenses. Revenue collectors were paid a commission based on how much they collected. After receiving annual lists from the assessors, they notified taxpayers by newspapers and posters that their taxes were due. Delinquent taxpayers were notified by mail or in person.

Revenue inspectors—another kind of fiscal agent—also were appointed. They served on a fee basis, paid by the manufacturer whose property or goods were inspected. This fee system proved to be one of the weakest features of the internal revenue system.

Deputy Commissioner was appointed.

Soon after the first Commissioner was appointed, it became obvious that he would need the assistance of a qualified Deputy Commissioner. The position of Deputy Commissioner stems, then, from 1863. In recent years this position has become the top career assignment in the Internal Revenue Service. The Deputy Commissioner generally acts for the Commissioner in the latter's absence from his desk during travel, illness, or for other reasons.

Important organizational changes were made in 1872.

In 1865 Congress authorized the appointment of a special Revenue Commission to look into all phases of federal taxation. The Commission was to ". . . inquire and report . . . upon the subject of raising by taxation such revenue as may be necessary to supply the wants of government . . . to inquire into the manner and efficiency of the present and past methods of collecting the internal revenue . . ."

In the Commission's report, lack of authority within the agency and inadequate pay were cited. It also criticized the appointment of employees with little or no experience or appropriate qualifications who got jobs through the political patronage system.

An important organizational change came several years later. Then Commissioner John W. Douglass concluded that revenue collectors and assessors, both operating in the field, seemed too much like two sets of officials doing the same job.

He worked out a plan which had lasting administrative effect. Legislation in 1872 to implement the plan did away with assessors and their assistants. Some of the assessors' duties were transferred to the collectors of internal revenue. But the investigative, tax determining, and assessing functions were placed clearly with the Commissioner.

In 1874, Congress stopped the Treasury Department's practice of signing contracts with independent private collectors to bring in delinquent taxes. Some 50 percent of the proceeds used to go to the private collector, who often had the help of revenue service employees in obtaining the overdue revenue.

Growth of the Revenue Service is shown in comparative figures.

The Bureau of Internal Revenue, as it was called for many years, expanded as burdens were added to it through new tax laws.

Upon passage of the income tax law of 1913, a Personal Income Tax Division was established in the Bureau. A correspondence unit with 30 employees was created to answer a flood of questions about the law and its enforcement. With new responsibilities, the Bureau's staff was enlarged noticeably. At the end of fiscal year 1913, some 277 persons were employed in Washington and 3,723 in the field. At the end of fiscal year 1915, the Washington staff stood at 531, the field force at 4280.

The growth that accompanied the vastly increased work of the agency in later years is reflected in the following table.

Fiscal Year	*Internal Revenue Receipts (in millions)*	*Service Expenditures (in millions)*	*Service Employees (end of year)*
1863	39.1	?	about 4,000
1873	113.5	6.6	5,136
1883	144.6	5.1	4,341
1893	161.0	4.2	3,744
1903	230.7	4.8	3,960
1913	344.4	5.5	4,000
1923*	2,621.7	36.5	17,613
1933	1,619.8	30.0	11,524
1943	23,227.3	98.6	36,338
1953	69,686.5	268.6	53,463
1963 (est.)	105,119.0	490.0	59,000

* Excludes costs and employees involved in Prohibition and Narcotics enforcement.

The changes in tax administration that were introduced over the years will not be traced here. Most of them will be brought out in subsequent chapters that are devoted to the organization and operations of the Internal Revenue Service today.

The task of Commissioner has become onerous.

One hundred years after the creation of the office of Commissioner, the incumbent heads a $100 billion operation that employs 57,000 people and has offices scattered throughout the world. Even in this day of tremendously large organizations, few heads of industry have as staggering a task as the Commissioner of Internal Revenue.

The Commissioner's task goes far beyond matters of administration and management. He must have an intimate, current, and working knowledge of both fundamental and special aspects of tax law and tax administration.

Generally speaking, the Commissioner of Internal Revenue should be either a tax lawyer or an accountant. In either capacity he should have an extensive background to be able to step readily into the imposing demands of the office. Naturally, in this day of high specialization, few individuals possess in complete degree each and every quality that might contribute to the absolute ideal.

The United States has been fortunate in recent years in having available to head its tax collection agency men who are well qualified for the onerous task of the commissionership. The marked ability of top level assistants has naturally contributed measurably to their success in supervising the agency's operation.

A glimpse reveals the broad scope of Commissioner's job.

As a Presidential appointee, the Commissioner's primary responsibilities are: applying the President's policies to the administration of the Internal Revenue Service; bringing the general public's point of view to bear upon administrative decisions; providing leadership in relating administrative experience to the development of national tax policy; and seeing that all the internal revenue laws are effectively and faithfully executed.

The Commissioner must be constantly aware of important tax matters that are the immediate or pending concern of his regional, district, zone and area offices and service centers in this country, and of the strategically located overseas offices and their agents.

He must seek to maintain the efficiency and economy of the operation to keep error or dubious policy at a minimum, while keeping the cost of tax collection at about one-half cent per dollar collected. He must be able to absorb rapidly details concerning such matters as the budget on which the agency will run each year, and to analyze and explain that budget if occasion demands.

He must lead in discussions concerning forward movements, such as the automatic data processing program, and the location of new offices within the fifty states.

He must be able to select or approve competent key officials of the tax agency, and must be able properly to delegate authority, so as to expedite the administration of the tax laws and to assure the proper functioning, at all levels and in all phases, of the agency itself.

The Commissioner must be knowledgeably diplomatic in his relationship with Congress, with the tax representatives of other nations and, quite often, with various types of businessmen, within and without the United States.

Above all, perhaps, the Commissioner must see to it that the best possible human relations are maintained with the taxpayer. He does this in order that the taxpayer may be aware of his obligations and also of his rights, and that he may receive such assistance as should be provided him to prepare a proper income tax return. Incidentally, the Internal Revenue Service itself profits through the increased accuracy of returns that results from such public relations efforts.

Years ago, when taxes were simpler and less vital than they are today, the Commissioner was but rarely called upon to explain issues and elements of public concern. With the growth of instant communication media, he must now be prepared to explain all manner of technical details in a way that is readily understandable to the listener or the reader and that conveys succinctly the policy of the agency.

Apart from matters of policy and the extensive work of analysis and judgment, each Commissioner must face daily a tremendous barrage of correspondence as well as numerous telephone calls.

Scope of Commissioner's authority is vast.

Working through departmental assistant commissioners or directors, the Commissioner's authority touches matters as trivial as cigarette-smoking and as important to national interest as space exploration and highly significant defense activities. To these latter, indeed, go more than half of the revenue annually collected.

Commissioners have lasted a short and long time.

During the first century of operation, the Internal Revenue Service has been headed by a total of 45 Commissioners. Of these, a dozen served in an "acting" capacity. Their tenures of office were usually short-lived and ranged from as little as five days to perhaps a couple of months. Oddly enough, two served consecutively for ten days each.

During that same century, three Commissioners of the 45 actually served in total more than one-quarter of the 100-year period. One served slightly more than ten years, one eight, and another seven years.

The longest individual term of office occurred in comparatively modern times. Guy T. Helvering of Kansas served as Commissioner from June 1933 into October 1945—one-eighth of the revenue agency's history.

Chapter Three

ORGANIZATION OF THE INTERNAL REVENUE SERVICE —THE NATIONAL OFFICE

When the office of Commissioner of Internal Revenue was created in 1862, a governmental function of its importance was traditionally performed by a bureau. That Congress intended to establish a Bureau of Internal Revenue is clear from the language of the Act of March 3, 1863 in which provision was made for the President to appoint with Senate confirmation a Deputy Commissioner of Internal Revenue who was charged with certain duties "in the bureau of internal revenue."

The name "Bureau of Internal Revenue" was used until about 1953 when it was changed to Internal Revenue Service under the reorganization decreed by Congress in 1952.

Growth led to complex structure.

In 1863 a relatively simple organization was adequate to manage the functions of the Washington office with its less than 300 employees, and field offices with only 3,000 employees. The laws then were easily understood and enforced. As the financing of government operations shifted from the levying of import duties to internal taxation, the Bureau began to grow. Ratification of the 16th Amendment and the passage of the first modern income tax law in 1913 led to considerable expansion. Four years later, in 1917, the Internal Revenue was reorganized to meet the new demands of a systematic program, when both audit and accounting procedures were overhauled.

The enactment of the successive income tax laws, and the amendments of the Internal Revenue Code gave the work of the Revenue Service a highly complex, technical character. The complex structure of the Service that consequently evolved served through both World War I and II and the Korean conflict.

Briefly, this structure had three main characteristics: (1) management control was highly centralized in the national office in Washington, D. C.; (2) The Bureau and its field offices were set up on a "type of tax" basis (Income Tax Unit, Employment Tax Unit, etc.); (3) each group of the some 200 field offices—for example, 64 Collectors of Internal Revenue, 39 Internal Revenue Agents in Charge, 15 Supervisors of Alcohol and Tobacco Tax, etc.—reported directly to their Bureau headquarters office.

From 1913 to 1951, tax collections skyrocketed from $344 million to $50 billion. Rates increased on existing taxes, new taxes were added, and the force of employees required to keep up with the workload jumped from 4,000 to 58,000 in the same period. The organization staggered under this growth and it became increasingly apparent that unless a radical reorganization of both structure and work methods were undertaken, the Service would run the risk of breaking down. Something had to be done, especially to cope with the increasing tempo forecast for the 1960's.

Proposed reorganization met opposition.

Despite the conviction of most Treasury and Internal Revenue officials that a reorganization was absolutely necessary, some opposition was met. Some opponents pointed to the successful collection of vastly increased taxes during the war years as proof that no radical change was needed. Others were opposed because they foresaw the end of their tight little empires of personal centralized control over individual or vast nationwide segments of Service operations.

Another roadblock was the politically potent system of Presidential appointment of Collectors of Internal Revenue which dated back to 1862. Though the vast majority of the Collectors were honest, conscientious public servants, they could not, as political appointees, hold themselves completely aloof from the influence of those who arranged their appointment. Quite understandably, the political sponsors of the Collectors were, in many cases, also loathe to approve a change in the system that had given them substantial political patronage.

External, if not internal, opposition to reorganization began to crumble under the impact of preceding studies by private management consultants, the Hoover Commission, and Congressional committees. Finally it gave way completely under public pressure and indignation resulting from the removal of six Collectors of Internal Revenue under charges ranging from inefficiency and misconduct to accepting bribes and defrauding the Government.

Reorganization Plan No. 1 of 1952 became effective.

On March 15, 1952, Reorganization Plan No. 1 became effective. It brought about four basic changes.

1. *Functional organization.* The organization was changed from a "type of tax" structure to one with like functions grouped together under one responsible management official. For example, audit functions formerly assigned to an Income Tax Unit, Accounts and Collections Unit, Employment Tax Unit, and Excise Tax Unit were pulled together under a new Audit Division. Similarly, rulings and regulations functions (other than alcohol and tobacco tax) were reassigned to newly created divisions in the Office of the Assistant Commissioner (Technical). Administrative and budgetary responsibilities, likewise formerly fragmented among the various units, were assigned to an administrative organization. And all internal audit and security functions were placed under an Assistant Commissioner (Inspection).

2. *Integration of field programs.* Field programs, dispersed among various field offices, each independent of one another and reporting directly to one of several management officials in the headquarters office, were integrated under the line management control of District Directors of Internal Revenue.

3. *Regional management.* Regional offices were established to provide direct field supervision of a manageable number of dis-

trict offices. This spread reduced Washington's management responsibility to an intermediate field level and vastly reduced the unwieldy number of field officials reporting to the Washington headquarters.

4. *Strengthening of Civil Service career system.* In recognition of the sound principle that administering the nation's tax laws should be wholly freed of the possibility of improper political influence, the appointive position of Collector of Internal Revenue was abolished. The position of Commissioner of Internal Revenue, which is primarily a policy making one and necessarily must be responsive to Administration tax policy and philosophy, remained as the only non-Civil Service career appointment in the Service.

By the end of 1952, the basic changes provided for by Reorganization Plan No. 1 were installed.

Current organization has three operating levels.

The current organization, fundamentally unchanged from the 1952 reorganization, has a three-operating-levels structure. These are the National Office, Regional Offices, and District Offices. There are nine Regional Offices and 62 District Offices.

How these three levels of operations are organized and performed will be explained in some detail in the following sections and in Chapter Four.

The National Office, Washington, D. C.

From the earliest days, the headquarters of the Internal Revenue Service have been located in the national capital. The first Commissioner's office was in the Treasury Department; today the Internal Revenue Service is housed in its own building on Constitution Avenue between 10th and 12th Streets.

The National Office, under policy direction from the Treasury Department, has over-all responsibility for planning how the Service can carry out most effectively the tax laws enacted by Congress. It also recommends to the Treasury any changes in existing laws which it believes would improve their administration and suggests new laws believed to be desirable.

The National Office prescribes the nationwide programs, policies, and procedures to be followed by Internal Revenue employees in all offices throughout the country. It follows up systematically to be sure that the regional and district offices are getting the job done on schedule and at the lowest cost, and to see that these offices are otherwise performing in accordance with the authority delegated to them.

The principal offices which form the National Office are: The Office of the Commissioner; six Offices of Assistant Commissioners (for Administration, Compliance, Data Processing, Inspection, Planning and Research, and Technical); the Office of the Chief Counsel; and the Director of Practice.

The Office of the Commissioner.

The role of the Commissioner has been explained at page 35. To recapitulate briefly: In conformity with the policies and delegations of authority made by the Secretary of the Treasury, the Commissioner, assisted by a Deputy Commissioner, gives top executive leadership to the activities of the Service. This includes establishing the basic policies; approving all major program decisions; directing and coordinating the work of the executive management staff (Assistant Commissioners and Regional Commissioners); deciding how much money will be requested by the Service for running its operations (the annual budget request) and distributing the money made available by Congress to the various operating offices; consulting with the Treasury Department on tax legislation; [1] and approving significant general management decisions having broad impact, for example, major changes in organization structure.

The Commissioner's Office also includes a Foreign Tax Assistance Staff which advises and assists foreign governments (notably the South American nations under the Alliance for Progress program) in improving their tax administration systems.

Offices of Assistant Commissioners—common functions.

As indicated, there are six Assistant Commissioners to whom the Commissioner has delegated broad authority to help him man-

---

[1] The Treasury Department, and not the Internal Revenue Service, is responsible for legislative recommendations to the Congress.

age the National Office and field organizations. Within their respective areas each Assistant Commissioner is responsible for the timely and systematic development of budgetary recommendations, policy and program proposals, and the issuance of work schedules and procedural instructions to carry them out in all offices, after approval by the Commissioner. They then must watch the progress of approved programs to be sure that planned objectives are being met, and must act promptly to overcome any lags. Leadership in developing improved and more economical ways to get the job done is also a key responsibility.

Each Assistant Commissioner (whose immediate office is quite small) works through a staff of Division Directors, one for each of the program functions under his direction. The divisions vary in size depending on the breadth and complexity of their program assignments. The divisions are immediately responsible for developing program recommendations, preparing procedures, and following up on program execution in all offices—in short, for the day-to-day operations which are connected with program management.

Office of Assistant Commissioner (Administration).

The Assistant Commissioner (Administration) is responsible for the administrative operations of the Service. These are "support" programs—that is, they are not connected with the basic mission of the Service (administering the Internal Revenue laws), but rather serve an essential purpose in helping to get this job done.

Administration's programs include:

—budget and fiscal management of funds appropriate for running the Service;

—personnel management (recruitment, placement, wage classification, employee relations, etc.);

—training employees in technical, supervisory, and managerial skills;

—administering the program for teaching taxes in the nation's secondary school system;

—providing information to the public through the press, radio, television, and other informational, educational, and professional media to improve general knowledge and understanding of the federal tax laws and their administration. The primary purpose of the public information program is to encourage and facilitate maximum taxpayer voluntary compliance;

—meeting the logistic needs of the Service in areas such as paperwork, space, property, supplies, printing, emergency relocation planning and safety, and management improvement.

The foregoing functions are carried out by divisions for Fiscal Management, Personnel, Training, Public Information, and Facilities Management. The Assistant Commissioner and the divisions give functional supervision to counterpart Administration activities in field offices.

Office of Assistant Commissioner (Compliance).

The Assistant Commissioner (Compliance) is the principal assistant to the Commissioner on all matters pertaining to the compliance programs of the Service. These are carried out through divisions under his supervision with the following principal functions:

The Alcohol and Tobacco Tax Division administers the laws relating to the production, processing, distribution, and use of alcoholic beverages, industrial alcohol and related products; tobacco materials and products, cigarette papers and tubes; and alcoholic beverage advertising. It is responsible for the investigation, prevention and detection of willful and/or fraudulent violations of the Internal Revenue Liquor and Tobacco Laws, the Liquor Enforcement Act of 1936, the Federal Alcohol Administration Act, and the National and Federal Firearms Acts, and in this activity coordinates with federal agencies and state authorities having related functions.

The Division also conducts a laboratory program for applying chemical and physical analytical techniques to the problems of the division and other offices, drafts regulations implementing the law, and issues rulings and interpretations of the law and regulations.

The Division provides functional supervision to the Alcohol and Tobacco Tax programs carried out in the field by regional and branch offices under the line supervision of the Regional Commissioner and the Assistant Regional Commissioner (Alcohol and Tobacco Tax).

The *Appellate Division* is responsible for the operations which provide taxpayers with an avenue of appeal within the Service from tax determinations which have been made by District Directors. It is also responsible for deciding the disposition of these cases as well as those in which the District Director's determination has been taken to the Tax Court of the United States for review. Certain other operations, for example, review and recommendation on final closing agreements for past taxable years, are handled by the Division in the National Office.

Functional supervision is given to the field appellate program which is carried out in the regional and branch offices under the line supervision of the Regional Commissioner and the Assistant Regional Commissioner (Appellate).

The *Audit Division* supervises the program for selecting and examining (auditing) all types of federal tax returns (except alcohol, tobacco, and firearms taxes) and for examining claims and offers in compromise. It is also responsible for certain limited volume operations which it is administratively infeasible to decentralize.

The Division gives functional supervision to the audit program carried out in the field in regional offices under the line supervision of Regional Commissioners and Assistant Regional Commissioners (Audit), and in district and local offices under the line supervision of the District Director and the Chief, Audit Division.

The *Collection Division* is responsible for programs for collection of delinquent accounts, securing delinquent returns from taxpayers who have failed to file, and for providing assistance to taxpayers who need help in filing returns. It has a limited National Office operational responsibility for certain functions administratively infeasible to decentralize.

The Division gives functional supervision to collection activities carried out in the regional offices under the supervision of the Regional Commissioners and the Assistant Regional Commissioners (Collection) and in the district offices and local offices under the line supervision of the District Directors and the Chief, Collection Division.

The *Intelligence Division* is responsible for the program involving criminal violations of the tax statutes, including racketeer and wagering tax cases but excluding alcohol, tobacco and firearms tax cases.

The Division gives functional supervision to these programs carried out in regional offices under the line supervision of the Regional Commissioner and the Assistant Regional Commissioner (Intelligence), and in district offices and local offices under the line supervision of the District Director and the Chief, Intelligence Division.

The *Office of International Operations* is comparable to a district office in that it has responsibility for the total Service program for administering the internal revenue laws in all areas of the world outside the United States. These functions are carried out by divisions for audit, collection, and intelligence and by various posts and personnel stationed overseas.

Office of Assistant Commissioner (Data Processing).

The Assistant Commissioner (Data Processing) is responsible for implementation and operation of the Service's plan for converting as many of its operations as possible to automatic data processing procedures using high speed electronic data processing equipment. He is specifically responsible for all of the programs and procedures for receiving and processing tax returns, including statements of income paid and tax withheld, receipt and processing of tax payments, and revenue accounting, billing and refunding operations.

In addition, he is responsible for working with other Assistant Commissioners and their divisions in planning how operations in their areas now done by manual methods may be converted to data processing systems. He works with them to determine how the data processing system can best produce significant information from the processing of tax returns which will help improve their operations, facilitate voluntary compliance, and increase revenue collections.

The Assistant Commissioner also directs the Service's reports management program. This program is aimed at providing management, at minimum cost and with fewest reports, with all meaningful information it needs to appraise the status of Service operations in terms of accomplishment of stated objectives, fund utilization, and inter-relationships of programs.

The National Computer Center at Martinsburg, West Virginia, is under his line supervision. This Center is the heart of the data processing system. It maintains the master file of business and individual tax accounts against which all input data from the regional service centers are processed. The process produces data on magnetic tape which the regional service centers use to issue refund checks, bill, check on failure of taxpayers to file returns, detect fraudulent refund claims, classify returns for audit purposes, and for various other processing and enforcement activities of the Service.

The Assistant Commissioner (Data Processing) supervises the work of divisions for Systems, Operations, and Reports in the National Office and provides functional supervision to data processing functions in the regional and district offices and the regional service centers.

Office of Assistant Commissioner (Inspection).

The Assistant Commissioner (Inspection) is responsible for the internal audit and internal security programs of the Service. Internal audit involves an independent review and appraisal of Service operations in the National, regional, and district offices and service centers. It provides the officials in charge of each office with factual information on the condition of the office, its adherence to established procedure, and with other data to aid them in efficiently managing the functions under their supervision. Internal audit also involves the verification and analyses of financial transactions and a review and appraisal of the measures and controls established by management to protect revenue collections and administrative monies.

Internal security is aimed at assisting management to achieve and maintain the highest standards of honesty, integrity, and security among Service employees and to maintain public confidence in the integrity of the Service. This mainly involves (1) background investigations of applicants for employment, and investigation of complaints or allegations of misconduct or irregularities against employees; (2) background investigations of applicants

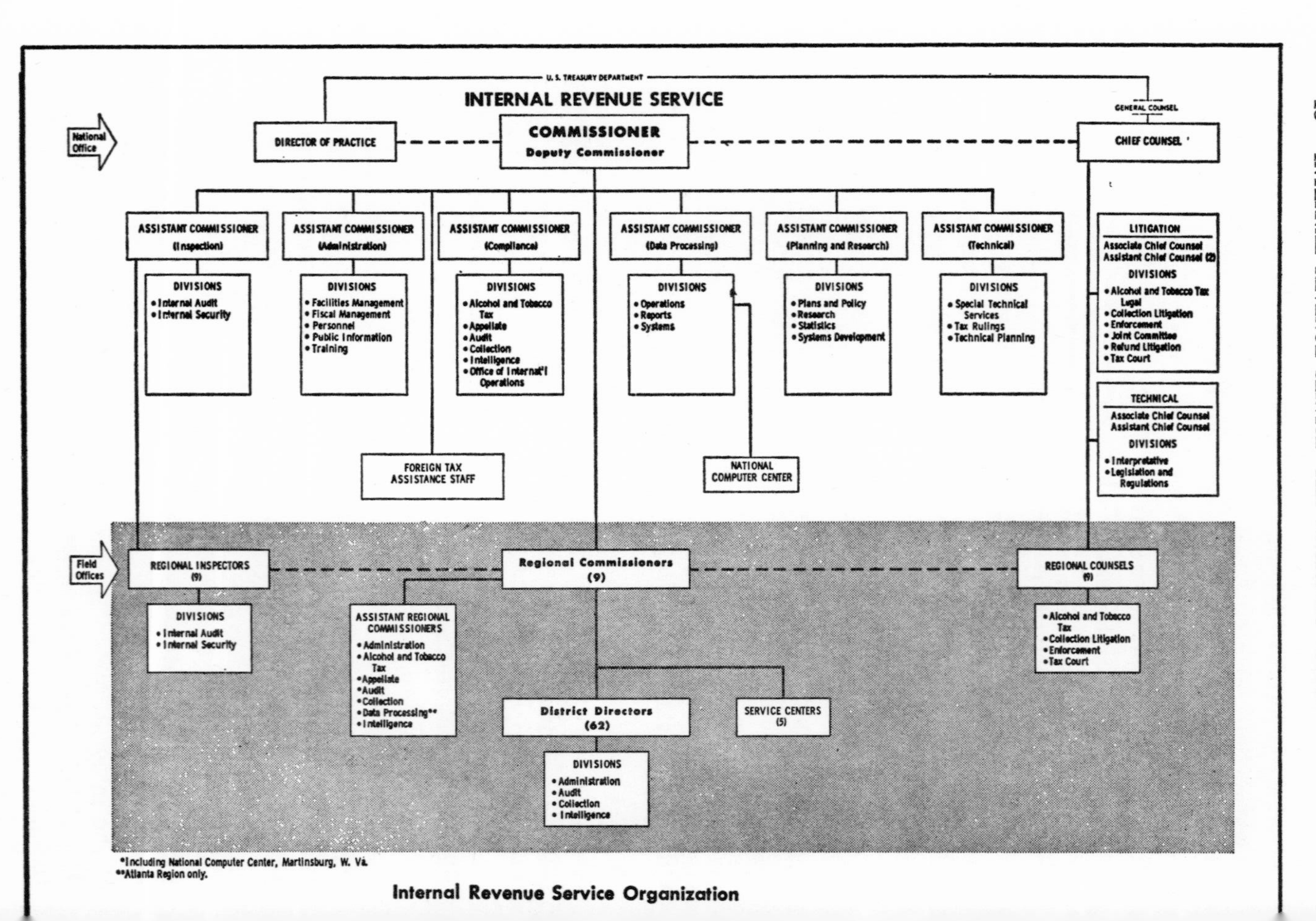

Internal Revenue Service Organization

for enrollment to practice before the Service and of any subsequent charges against enrolled practitioners; (3) investigations of non-Service persons when their actions may affect the integrity of the Service, including attempts to bribe or otherwise corrupt Service personnel.

Inspection's functions are carried out by the Internal Audit and Internal Security Divisions in the National Office and by Regional Inspectors located in each of the nine regions, who are under the line supervision of the Assistant Commissioner (Inspection).

Office of Assistant Commissioner (Planning and Research).

The primary responsibility of the Assistant Commissioner (Planning and Research) is to look beyond the day-to-day operations of the Service and to forecast and program its long-range plans and objectives. Such planning takes into account the changing national economy, emerging patterns of tax philosophy, population growth, and other factors affecting workload and tax administration.

This responsibility involves research into the federal tax system to develop new and better ways to improve the Service's operations and to reduce the compliance burden on the taxpayer; working with the states in negotiating agreements for the exchange of tax information; and integration of the plans of all Service activities into a long-range plan which charts the course of operations and manpower, budgetary, and other logistic requirements several years ahead.

The office also operates a system for identifying operational matters of such significance, particularly those which have an impact on taxpayers, that an official Service policy must be prescribed by the Commissioner within which Service action may be taken.

The general management responsibilities of the office include systems development studies and services to all other activities; preparation of statistics on the operations of the internal revenue laws to provide basic information for tax studies and legislation by Congress and administrative use within the Service and the Treasury Department; and general statistical services to other activities.

The office is also responsible for studying the over-all organizational structure of the Service and recommending improvements and for reviewing for the Commissioner organizational recommendations made by other Assistant Commissioners and Regional Commissioners. It is responsible for administering the Service system for documenting and communicating policies, programs, procedures and instructions to all operating offices and personnel.

The responsibilities of the Assistant Commissioner (Planning and Research) are carried out by divisions for Plans and Policy, Research, Statistics, and Systems Development. The office has no counterpart field organization although functional supervision in its general management areas is provided to the regional and district offices.

Office of Assistant Commissioner (Technical).

The primary responsibility of the Assistant Commissioner (Technical) is to provide basic principles and rules to help assure that the tax laws will be uniformly interpreted and applied by all Service personnel throughout the country. He has this responsibility in all tax areas except alcohol, tobacco, and certain firearms taxes which are administered under the supervision of the Assistant Commissioner (Compliance).

Technical coordinates the legislative recommendations of the Service to the Treasury Department and, upon enactment of tax laws by Congress, bears the brunt of preparing the regulations issued by the Secretary of the Treasury for their administration. Rulings and advisory statements on application of the law to particular cases are also prepared by Technical and issued to the public and Revenue officials, notably through the Internal Revenue Bulletin.

Technical also develops the technical content of tax return forms and instructions and spearheads Service efforts to simplify their wording and style and otherwise ease the compliance burden of the taxpayer. Tax guides to aid various categories of taxpayers, for example, *Your Federal Income Tax, Tax Guide for Small Business,* and the *Teaching Taxes* materials are also prepared in this office.

Various technical services (for example, engineering and valuation) are furnished to other National Office, regional, and district activities, and a technical liaison program is maintained to determine areas of tax abuse and inequity.

Technical also assists the Treasury Department in the negotiation of tax treaties and agreements with foreign governments and is responsible for rulings and regulations after they are approved.

The foregoing principal responsibilities are carried out by divisions for Special Technical Services, Tax Rulings, and Technical Planning. Technical has no counterpart organization in the regional or district offices.

Office of the Chief Counsel.

The Chief Counsel, an Assistant General Counsel of the Treasury Department, serves as a member of the Commissioner's executive staff (but not under his line supervision) and directs all Internal Revenue legal programs pertaining to the administration and enforcement of the internal revenue laws and related statutes. These programs fall into two broad categories: (1) litigation, and (2) technical.

The *litigation programs* involve the civil and criminal litigation activities of the Service, that is, preparing and presenting the Service's legal position in any tax matter or controversy where a legal opinion is necessary for disposition within the Service, or where the Service's position must be presented before the courts.

Civil tax cases (those not involving fraud or other criminal aspects) are disposed of in the Tax Court of the United States. The Chief Counsel has the sole responsibility for developing the Service's legal position and presenting the case in court. If the taxpayer appeals the decision of the Tax Court to the Court of Appeals, the Department of Justice then becomes responsible for presenting the Service position with advisory and supporting legal service from the Chief Counsel.

This relationship—the Department of Justice responsible for court presentation and the Chief Counsel for advisory support, recommendation, and assistance—applies as well to the initial presentation and appellate phases of all cases involving the prosecution of criminal tax cases. It applies also to other civil matters in the courts, such as taxpayers' suits for refunds of taxes and collection litigation matters involving, for example, suits for foreclosure of mortgages, federal tax liens, collection of taxes, and enforcement of summonses.

The office of Chief Counsel also reviews proposed refunds or credits exceeding $100,000, which are submitted to the Congressional Joint Committee on Internal Revenue Taxation.

The *technical programs* involve participation and assistance in the development and drafting of legislation; review as to legal form and substance of recommendations for new and amendatory legislation; and review as to form and legality interpretations of internal revenue statutes and regulations and other law and legal materials bearing upon the Service administration.

The National Office program operations are carried out under the Chief Counsel's direction by an Assistant to the Chief Counsel (who is responsible for general administrative and management matters), an Associate Chief Counsel (Litigation), and two Assistant Chief Counsel (Litigation) supervising divisions for Tax Court, Refund Litigation, Joint Committee, Collection Litigation, Enforcement, Alcohol and Tobacco Tax–Legal; and an Associate Chief Counsel (Technical) and Assistant Chief Counsel (Technical) supervising the Legislation and Regulations and Interpretative Divisions.

Field programs are carried out by the offices of Regional Counsel in each of the nine regions. The Regional Counsel are under the direct supervision of the Chief Counsel.

Director of Practice.

The Director of Practice, who is under the supervision of the Secretary of the Treasury, administers the law and regulations which require that those who wish to represent taxpayers in tax matters before the Service must establish their personal fitness and technical qualifications. The Director processes applications to practice (except those relating to customhouse brokers) and considers and acts upon charges that any enrolled person has violated any provisions of laws or regulations governing practice. The Director has no counterpart field organization, but some of his processing procedures are carried out for him in the offices of District Directors of Internal Revenue.

Chapter Four

ORGANIZATION OF THE INTERNAL REVENUE SERVICE —FIELD OPERATIONS

THE NINE REGIONAL OFFICES, supervised by Regional Commissioners of Internal Revenue, have administrative responsibility for five to as many as 11 districts, depending on the geography and density of population. Regions are named for the city in which they are located: Atlanta, Boston, New York, San Francisco, Omaha, Chicago, Dallas, Philadelphia, and Cincinnati.

The regional offices have both management and operational program responsibilities. Delegation of management responsibility to regional offices simply recognizes that the Service and its operations have grown too large and complex to function at peak efficiency under tightly controlled centralized management from the National Office.

There are 62 district offices supervised by District Directors of Internal Revenue. At least one district office is located in every state. To provide more readily accessible service to taxpayers and to speed district operations, each district has local offices placed generally in the areas of highest population and concentration of workload. There are about 950 such offices throughout the country.

A brief statement of the general functions of the regional office and the district office is given immediately below. An understanding of the organizational structure of the field operations and of the various functions performed in the regional and district offices can be obtained from the detailed explanation that follows.

What the regional office does, in brief.

Regional *management responsibility* includes: (1) carrying out National Office programs and procedures supplemented by locally developed methods to fit the needs of individual regions and districts; (2) evaluating the effectiveness of National Office policies, programs, and procedures, and suggesting how they may be improved; (3) directing and controlling, and giving broad supervision to, a manageable number of district offices, and in some regions a service center, including coordination and advisory supervision of their administrative, audit, collection, and intelligence functions.

Operating functions centralized in the regional office include the alcohol and tobacco tax laws, and appellate procedures. These are carried out in the regional office or in branch offices spotted throughout the region.

In addition, certain administrative functions which are not decentralized to the district offices are also a regional responsibility.

What the district office does, in brief.

The district office (and its local offices) is the point of contact for the average individual and business taxpayer. It is in the district office that the taxpayer files his return, pays his tax or gets his refund, and discusses and settles most of his tax problems. The district office is the source of advice and help to taxpayers puzzled by the complexity of the law. It is, in short, the point in the organization where the primary work of the Service is actually carried out.

The Regional Set-up

The present regional offices serve as an intermediate management level between the district offices and the National Office in Washington, giving direction and functional guidance to the dis-

Map of Internal Revenue Regions and Districts

LOCATION OF OFFICES FOR OTHER AREAS

Alaska................Anchorage District, San Francisco Region

Hawaii................Honolulu District, San Francisco Region

Puerto Rico.........Office of International Operations, National Office

- Regional Boundary
- District Boundary
- Commissioner of Internal Revenue
- Regional Commissioner and District Director
- District Director
- Service Center
- Computer Center

trict offices (and regional service centers) and carrying out programs to (1) provide taxpayers with an avenue of appeal from the determinations of district directors, (2) enforce the tax laws and related statutes concerning the supervision of the legal alcohol and tobacco industries, and the suppression of illegal activities in these areas, and (3) to carry out and implement the nationally prescribed administrative programs.

Need for regional structure was recognized early.

Although the present Regional Commissioner structure is a direct result of the 1952 Reorganization Plan, the concept has some precedent in earlier revenue acts. Alexander Hamilton, who first conceived such an administrative breakdown for field organization when he was Secretary of the Treasury, wisely remarked, "It is no ill recommendation of it that it has been tried with success."

The Revenue Act of 1791, passed during Mr. Hamilton's tenure and presumably with his advice and concurrence, specified that the Collector of Revenue "establish 14 Districts, one in each State, to be headed by Collectors, who shall subdivide such Districts into survey areas under inspectors of revenue." The legislation further provided that the Collector of Revenue place the District Collectors and Inspectors "under the management of supervisors of the revenue."

The Act did not prescribe a specific number for supervisors of revenue as it did for District Collectors, apparently because the position was to be administrative and coordinative in nature, and its value could best be determined by the Collector of Revenue. The fact that the post was mentioned in the legislation implies that it was considered to be of strategic importance.

The Revenue Act of 1813, passed when Albert Gallatin was Secretary of the Treasury, again emphasized the need for a principal assessor at a level between Washington and the Districts to coordinate the field activities.

Public administrators in those days questioned the extent of authority enjoyed by the Principal Assessor over the Districts as compared with that of his predecessor, the Supervisor of Revenue. However, in the language of the 1813 Act, "the Principal Assessor had the power to re-examine and equalize valuations determined by the District Collector," and "the power of review in such instances that he shall determine collection of taxes has varied from the law" or "where it has not been just and equitable."

Regardless of the extent of his power, the Principal Assessor was at an intermediary level of field administration between the Commissioner in Washington and the District Collector and as such bears historical relationship with the present Regional Commissioner.

Change in 1862. The 1862 Revenue Law provided for the appointment of the Commissioner and District Collectors by the President of the United States with the approval of the Senate, whereas under prior laws key personnel in the field were appointed by either the Secretary of the Treasury or his deputy in charge of the revenue organization.

Obviously, the new system of appointment precluded any strong administrative control from Washington over the field, except in cases of proven frauds or tax delinquencies on the part of District Collectors. In such an organization the District Collectors were virtually "commissioners in the field" with almost unlimited authority in the control of tax matters.

The weakness of the 1862 organization with its widespread variance in evaluation and enforcement of the revenue laws by the District Collectors led Congress to pass the 1868 Act to strengthen the administrative control that the Commissioner of Internal Revenue exercised over his field officers.

1868 Act. Under the 1868 Act the Commissioner was authorized to appoint 25 officers to be called "supervisors of internal revenue." Each Supervisor was appointed on the recommendation of the Commissioner. He was assigned to a permanent field station to report back to the Commissioner any discrepancies in district operations. The Supervisor had the power to transfer or suspend any officer or field employee of Internal Revenue for neglect of duty, abuse of power, or fraud. He made written reports on such matters directly to the Commissioner, who took such subsequent action as he deemed necessary.

Correction of weakness. From the 1868 Act down to the 1952 Reorganization Plan, no clear-cut effort was made to establish field administrative control to support the work of the Commissioner in Washington. However, each succeeding Commissioner was aware of the void in field adminstrative coordination and took whatever action was permitted under the revenue laws to correct it. Many distinguished, private, non-partisan study groups offered solutions geared to strengthening the Commissioner's control over district offices, but the political orientation involved in the appointment of key revenue personnel discouraged concrete action.

Nothing short of the sweeping reorganization of the Internal Revenue Service inaugurated in the 1952 Plan could have established the decentralized, career-oriented Service now in existence.

Office of Regional Commissioner.

The Regional Commissioner administers the nationally prescribed administration, appellate, audit, collection, data processing, and intelligence programs of the Service and establishes regional standards and programs to carry them out effectively within the region. He directs and coordinates the work of the regional office and district offices and is responsible for insuring uniformity of action among his districts. He suggests to the National Office ways in which the policies and programs could be revised to bring about improved operations or service to taxpayers.

The Regional Commissioner is also charged with appeals and alcohol and tobacco tax operations, which are not assigned to the districts. The regional service centers (of which there are now four in operation) are under his general direction.

The Regional Commissioners are directly responsible to the Commissioner in Washington.

Functionally, the Regional Commissioner is aided by six Assistant Regional Commissioners having charge of: (1) administration, (2) audit, (3) collection, (4) intelligence (taxpayer fraud), (5) appellate (taxpayer appeals), and (6) alcohol and tobacco (tax and regulatory control).

Two other key regional positions are: (1) the Regional Counsel, and (2) the Regional Inspector.

Assistant Regional Commissioners.

The six Assistant Regional Commissioners share the Regional Commissioner's management responsibilities. Each one is immediately responsible for managing the regional office programs in his area and for recommending to the Regional Commissioner ways in which they think National Office policies and programs could be improved. In addition, all except those in charge of the alcohol and tobacco tax and appellate programs (which are regional office operations) have responsibility for general direction, functional supervision, and evaluation of performance in their program areas in the district offices and regional service centers.

1. *Administration.*

The programs of the *Assistant Regional Commissioner (Administration)* cover personnel, training, budget and fiscal management, public information, property and records management, use of facilities, printing and reproduction, emergency relocation planning and reports management. He also coordinates organization planning and management programs.

2. *Audit.*

The job of the *Assistant Regional Commissioner (Audit)* is primarily one of management in assuring that the audit programs developed by the National Office are carried out in orderly and timely manner in the district offices. This involves developing a regional plan for implementing and coordinating the execution of the audit program in the district offices, for furnishing technical and management advice and assistance to district audit division officials and, of course, for evaluating district performance, identifying any weaknesses, and recommending ways to overcome them.

In addition, the regional audit division is responsible for maintaining the maximum degree of uniformity in the handling of cases and issues in the districts. For this and other management purposes, it operates a small centralized regional program for reviewing selected cases closed by the district offices. In the Cincinnati region the general review of district Audit Division cases has been centralized.

3. *Collection.*

The Assistant Regional Commissioner (Collection) has a similar managerial role with respect to the data processing (except where data processing areas have been set up) and collection programs of the Service which are all carried out in district offices and regional service centers. No collection work operations are performed in regional offices.

4. *Intelligence.*

The job of the *Assistant Regional Commissioner (Intelligence)* is primarily managerial in that he, like the Assistant Regional Commissioner (Audit), coordinates and evaluates the execution of the intelligence programs in the district offices and furnishes the District Director and intelligence officials with advice and assistance in getting the job done. Although the bulk of the day-to-day intelligence work is done in the district office, all district office reports containing recommendations for criminal prosecution and/or ad valorem penalties are reviewed by the regional office intelligence review and conference staff before action is taken.

5. *Appellate.*

The primary function of the *Assistant Regional Commissioner (Appellate)* is to provide taxpayers with an independent avenue of appeal within the Service from determinations of tax liability made by District Directors. This involves hearing and undertaking final settlement of appeals on income, profits, estate, gift and employment taxes, and excise taxes except those imposed on alcohol, wagering, narcotics, firearms, and tobacco.

Other responsibilities include hearing and, with concurrence of Regional Counsel, undertaking final settlement of certain cases docketed in the Tax Court; final review for the Commissioner of cases involving a refund or credit in excess of $100,000 requiring review by the Chief Counsel or the Joint Committee on Internal Revenue Taxation; and the hearing of administrative appeals involving offers in compromise.

Management of the regional appellate program is centralized in the regional office (no district office operations). The basic settlement work is performed in branch offices of the regional appellate division located in areas of highest workload concentration.

6. *Alcohol and Tobacco Tax.*

The Assistant Regional Commissioner (Alcohol and Tobacco

Tax) directs the execution of the region-wide alcohol and tobacco tax program which, as mentioned before, is a centralized regional operation. None of the work is done in the district offices. These programs fall into two categories—enforcement and permissive.

The *enforcement program* involves investigation, prevention, and detection of willful and/or fraudulent substantive violations of the internal revenue laws and other statutes relating to alcohol, alcoholic beverages and products, tobacco and tobacco products, and firearms, including the apprehension of violators and their prosecution. It also includes the enforcement of the laws and regulations for the control of the flow of raw materials intended for use in the illicit manufacture of distilled spirits, and the inspection of retail liquor dealer establishments for compliance with federal laws.

The *permissive program* covers the control and supervision of the legally qualified liquor and tobacco industries and permittees. This includes qualification of plants and premises and issuance of permits for the production, storage, disposition and use of alcoholic liquors and tobacco; also advice and guidance to the industry and examination and audit of reports on plant operations. Although program management is centralized in the regional office, most of the actual operations are carried out in Alcohol and Tobacco Tax branch offices in areas of highest enforcement workload or areas of industrial concentration.

Assistant Regional Commissioner (Data Processing).

The Assistant Regional Commissioner (Data Processing) serves as a point of liaison between the regional office and the office of the Assistant Commissioner (Data Processing) in implementing the automatic data processing programs in the individual regional installation. He is also functionally responsible for the district office for evolving regional service center programs involving accounting for the Internal Revenue and the receipt and integrated processing of tax returns and payments.

Office of Regional Counsel.

Nine Regional Counsels, one in each region, operate under the direct supervision of the Chief Counsel in the National Office and serve as the principal legal advisor to the Regional Commissioner. To a lesser degree they furnish legal counsel to the district offices.

The principal legal functions and services involve advice to the Assistant Regional Commissioner (Appellate) in connection with taxpayers' appeals; trial of cases before the Tax Court on field calendars and/or the settlement of such cases before or after session status; considering criminal cases (except alcohol and tobacco tax) and deciding whether prosecution should be recommended, and on request furnishing advice and assistance to U. S. Attorneys in criminal tax trial proceedings; and a wide variety of litigation matters generated by the collection of taxes, for example, liens, levies, foreclosures, offers in compromise, bankruptcy proceedings, etc.

In the area of alcohol and tobacco tax matters, the regional counsel gives advice on request to the Assistant Regional Commissioner (Alcohol and Tobacco Tax) on administration and enforcement of the laws and regulations pertaining to liquor, tobacco, and firearms.

Office of Regional Inspector.

The Regional Inspectors (one in each of the nine regions) are under the direct management supervision of the Assistant Commissioner (Inspection) and are not a part of the regional commissioner's office. They carry out the nationwide field office internal audit and internal security programs developed by that official in the National Office.

The *internal audit program* involves a periodic verification of financial transactions and analyses of operating practices and procedures in all regional and district offices (and their subordinate branch and local offices). The program is designed to help regional and district management (and their National Office counterparts) appraise the condition of the activities for which they are responsible and to serve as a basis for any necessary corrective action or changes in policies, practices, and procedures.

Internal security involves primarily the field investigation of the background of employee applicants; of any complaints or allegations of misconduct or irregularities against employees; background investigations of certain applicants for enrollment to practice before the Service and/or charges against tax practitioners; investigations of attempts to bribe or otherwise corrupt Service personnel; and miscellaneous other investigations such as alleged violation of Government employment policy and accidents involving Service personnel or property. As in internal audit, internal security investigations provide management with factual information on which decisions may be based.

Organization of the District Offices

The office of the District Director of Internal Revenue, as already indicated, is the basic working level of the Service. It is here that the bulk of the policies, programs, and procedures concerning administration, audit, collection, and intelligence are carried out.

District Office organization is by divisions.

The district office is organized into divisions for each of its functions and also has several offices where the taxpayer may transact business and get help with his problem.

The *Collection Division* is where the work of the district office begins. It receives and processes the tax return, deposits and accounts for remittances, determines tax refunds, credits, penalties, abatements or overassessments, and maintains prescribed accounting and ledger controls. The division is also responsible for securing returns from taxpayers who have failed to file, for collecting accounts from those who are behind in their payments, and for increasing voluntary compliance with the payment and filing provisions of the tax laws.

During the annual income tax filing period the division conducts an intensive program to keep taxpayers informed about tax filing (and payment) requirements and procedures and for assisting taxpayers in preparing and filing tax returns and claims for refund. This program continues on a modified scale throughout the year as the need diminishes.

The *Audit Division* examines tax returns (except alcohol, tobacco, and firearms) to determine the correct tax liability (including any penalties), considers claims, offers in compromise based on either doubt as to liability or inability to pay, and participates upon request with the Intelligence Division in cases involving tax evasion. As part of the tax determination process, the division holds informal conferences with taxpayers and their representatives aimed at reaching agreement on the correct tax liability.

The *Intelligence Division* is responsible for the investigation of alleged criminal violations of the tax statutes including racketeer and wagering tax cases, but excluding alcohol, tobacco, and firearms cases, and for recommendations as to their disposition. The division provides assistance to U. S. Attorneys and the Regional Counsel in the trial of cases.

The *Administration Division* provides internal management services including personnel, training, budget and fiscal, procurement and supply. It handles communications and other administrative services. It is also responsible for various programs aimed at improving the over-all efficiency of the district office. These programs include records management, incentive awards (including employee suggestions), and the coordination of a systematic effort to identify ways in which operations can be improved and to schedule plans for action.

Regional Service Centers

The evolving regional service center organization is the culmination of a series of changes in processing methods and procedures which were essential to enable the Service to keep up with the tremendous increase in workload over the past twenty years. There are now four operational service centers. Three were set up in the mid-1950's to take over under mechanized procedures a host of routine returns handling and processing operations which were bogging down the district offices during the income tax filing period.

These operations cover such things as verifying taxpayers' computations, listing and indexing returns filed, maintaining accounts and sending out notices and bills, matching statements of tax withheld and income paid, and mailing income tax forms to individual taxpayers. Most of these functions are in the nature of "service" operations to the district offices and many are performed in the name of the District Director.

New service centers are planned.

On January 1, 1962, a new type of service center commenced operation in Atlanta, Georgia. It, together with the National Computer center, is designed to take full advantage of the capacity of modern high speed electronic data processing methods for handling the Service's enormous volume of data and paperwork transactions, to facilitate and speed processing, and otherwise improve service to taxpayers, strengthen enforcement, and improve revenue-producing operations.

Significant phases of automatic data processing (ADP) when fully implemented will include systematic nationwide checks on failure of individuals or business entities to file returns; determining prior to refund whether a taxpayer is indebted for delinquent taxes for a prior year, for the same or a different tax, or whether he has already claimed and been paid a refund for the same period; and extensive matching of data reported on information documents with corresponding data reported on taxpayer returns. The first center's beginning operations involved processing business returns filed in the districts of the Atlanta Region. The centers will gradually expand to encompass all classes of tax as well as the other work operations performed in the centers which were set up in the mid 1950's.

There will be one regional service center for each of the nine regions. A key distinction between the existing service center operations and the automatic data processing system is that the ADP-oriented regional service center will be more a responsible operational entity than a "service" organization. It will have status comparable to that of a district office and many of the actions taken will be in the name of the Director, Regional Service Center.

Chapter Five

THE NEW DIRECTION IN TAX ADMINISTRATION

A SIGNIFICANT CHANGE in tax administration began in 1961 with the adoption of the "New Direction" program espoused by Commissioner Mortimer M. Caplin, who was appointed that year. Its main objectives are better service to taxpayers, more reasonable but vigorous enforcement, and curbing of abuses.

Commissioner Caplin pointed out that the program was not entirely new. Such a program had been proposed in part by various predecessors, Regional Commissioners, District Directors, and many officials and employees throughout the Service both in Washington and the field. But without a doubt the drive of the Commissioner and his conviction that the new direction program will strengthen public confidence in the fairness, impartiality, and integrity of the nation's tax system have stimulated the entire Internal Revenue Service to accomplish the objectives of the program.

In a message to members of the Service, Commissioner Caplin imparted these thoughts that reflect his philosophy in tax administration:

> We all should understand that the Service is not simply running a direct enforcement business aimed at making $2 billion in additional assessments, collecting another billion from delinquent accounts, and prosecuting a few hundred evaders. Rather, it is charged with adminis-

tering an enormous self-assessment tax system which raises over $90 billion from what people themselves put down on their tax returns and voluntarily pay, with another $2 or $3 billion coming from direct enforcement activities. In short, we cannot forget that 97 percent of our total revenue comes from self-assessment or voluntary compliance, with only 3 percent coming directly from enforcement.

Our chief mission is to encourage and achieve more effective voluntary compliance. Accordingly, we should concentrate our attention and efforts on getting the greatest possible number of taxpayers to voluntarily file returns, to report what they should report, and to pay their taxes in the amount they should pay. In turn, the activities of our professional people in Audit, Collection, and Intelligence should be aimed primarily at securing voluntary compliance—not primarily at quantitative goals in terms of cases and dollars.

In the light of these considerations, the new direction is really a shift in emphasis. *But it is a very important shift.*

It means that we will keep our eyes primarily on the maintenance and improvement of the $90 billion, the "voluntary compliance dollars" —rather than placing too much emphasis on the $3 billion, the "direct enforcement dollars."

It carries with it stressing qualitative elements, as opposed to quantitative ones. To illustrate, we prefer one competently made examination to two poor ones.

It frees us from many of the pressures for purely case and dollar production, permitting us to spend the time to get better coverage and improved enforcement.

It also permits us to eliminate many statistics that have occupied us in the past, such as work volume of cases and dollars in the financial plan.

It encourages us to apply professional standards to professional workers so that from now on, we will evaluate our professional people on a case by case basis; not on "how many" cases or dollars.

But, obviously, we are not going to remove over-all quantitative standards from every position in the Service. There is a large body of our work—just as elsewhere in government and in business—which is susceptible, and even necessarily subject, to reasonable quantitative standards of performance. Some production-type jobs exist in just about every one of our activities; for the most part, they are found in the service centers and in the mass operations of our district office collection divisions. Service center and collection operations, for example, are covered by the work planning and control system which we have adopted to plan our work intelligently and to cope with our ever-growing paperwork problems. Standards of performance established under this system will remain in effect although continuing attention will be given them to assure they are reasonable and fair.

Major activities of IRS have been changed by the program.

Implementation of the New Direction required changes and cooperation throughout the Service.

The audit program has been expanded to include many groups never examined before. It is believed that widespread and reasonable audits of this nature will (a) strengthen confidence that the tax laws are being applied across-the-board without favor and that all citizens are paying their fair share of taxes; and (b) encourage greater numbers of taxpayers to report income and deductions more accurately. A careful study is being made to plot the future audit classification program.

To extend the concept of "quality audits," a study, spearheaded by a group of top agents from different parts of the country, was completed to establish *Tax Audit Guidelines.* Naturally, this will not result in financial audits of the type made by Certified Public Accountants. Yet, for the first time, the Service has available carefully prepared guidelines, geared to different types of returns, to serve as guides to agents in making quality audits. They do not restrict the use of initiative, but form a base from which an examining officer can develop the examination more effectively and efficiently.

To permit agents sufficient scope to develop those cases which should be developed—including those with fraud aspects—Internal Revenue has taken a series of steps to eliminate the statistical approach in evaluating agent performance. New emphasis is being given to broader and more sophisticated evaluation standards, with greater reliance on the sound judgment of supervisors.

During his first year in Office, Commissioner Caplin personally visited more regions and more districts than any previous Commissioner. Managers at all levels were carefully instructed and meetings with Group Supervisors in various parts of the country were held to discuss the program changes and clarify their purposes.

New program has broad implications.

It is obvious that the various changes of the New Direction have broad implications of special interest to taxpayers, tax accountants, and tax lawyers.

The most important expectation is that the changes will bring better service to the public. As more resources are allocated to this end, there will be more and better trained revenue agents and a better informed public.

A public information program has been undertaken.

The Service has taken a new look at its responsibilities in the taxpayer assistance and education areas. Early in 1962 it began reorganizing and expanding the role of its public information program on a nationwide basis. The objective was to do a better job of keeping taxpayers adequately informed of their rights and duties, and to build a heightened respect for the self-assessment system generally. The self-assessment system vitally depends on (1) educating taxpayers to their responsibilities, and (2) assisting them when they have questions and problems.

The public information program calls for increased cooperation with newspapers, magazines, radio, television, public speakers, and other information and education media to inform taxpayers.

A "Teaching Taxes" program that provides student handbooks, teacher guides and other teaching aids to public and private high schools, colleges and adult educational groups, assists a large number of people to gain a better understanding of the tax system.

Meetings are held with industry representatives who have special tax problems in an attempt to iron out tax troubles that seem to recur. This is one way in which the Service has expanded its contact with the business community. Others are shown in Chapter Thirteen.

The Service is encouraging an exchange of information on tax problem areas with accountants, lawyers and other practitioners who advise and serve taxpayers.

A long stride is being taken to personalize and humanize correspondence and taxpayer contacts.

Officials of Internal Revenue are convinced that efficient, effective programs of taxpayer information and assistance—programs that demonstrate to the public that the Service is genuinely concerned with the rights and problems of taxpayers—will contribute as much as direct enforcement to assure honest self-assessment. The Service officials are likewise convinced that ineffective programs which drive taxpayers into the arms of the "fly-by-night tax experts" do more lasting harm than any amount of enforcement effort can overcome.

Forms and instructions are being improved.

A major effort is being made to simplify tax returns and instructions to the greatest extent possible under the complex tax laws. The overriding goal is to identify taxpayers with common tax situations and problems and to send them only the forms and instructions they need. In two major categories—the 18 million users of 1040A and the 8 million users of former 1040W—the Service has accomplished some simplification. For example, Form 1040W was replaced with a two-page Form 1040. In a third category—the 25 million users of the nonbusiness 1040—the Service recognized that there are probably 10 million taxpayers who could be sorted out and treated separately.

As a general rule, the Service tries to send each taxpayer the simplest form he can file. It is assisted in this effort by information furnished to it by the service centers. For example, in 1962 the service centers expected to be able to indicate the simplest form the taxpayer *could have filed.* However, changes in taxpayer reporting complicate the problem. To illustrate, every year the number of taxpayers who itemize deductions increases. The Forms Committee is grappling with this and other problems, including changes in the format of returns and the redesign of Form 1040.

The Service tries to remain alert to the effect on forms of proposed legislation and works closely with Congress in this area.

With automatic data processing on the horizon, the problem of simplifying forms and instructions and at the same time arranging the information on returns so that it can be extracted easily is formidable. The progress that has been made in this direction is explained in the next chapter.

Voluntary compliance is the keynote.

Roy Blough, an eminent tax authority, says in *The Federal Taxing Process:*

Complete and uniform administration of a tax system that rests on self-assessment by taxpayers is dependent in the first instance on law and report forms simple enough to be understood by taxpayers, and on taxpayers who both know their responsibilities and perform them. Perhaps the most important purpose of all tax administration activities is to bring about willing and intelligent compliance by taxpayers.

It is clear from the foregoing review of the "New Direction" that the Internal Revenue Service is exerting unprecedented efforts to encourage and achieve more effective voluntary compliance.

With the New Direction, many additional informative and educational documents are being issued for taxpayers. More are in the development process and will soon be available. In 1955, only three or four such pamphlets were issued. Since Commissioner Caplin took office, the number has grown to 59. Plain and understandable language is used to explain relatively complex tax laws. A vast variety of subjects are treated, ranging from the tax problems arising from real estate sales to the recent investment tax credit for new business equipment.

The program includes such well-known documents as the Government's "blue book" (*Your Federal Income Tax*), the *Tax Guide for Small Business*, the *Teaching Taxes* documents, and *Farmer's Tax Guide*. Documents are revised and improved annually, in time for the filing period, and in certain cases special editions are released because of new tax laws or other developments.

For example, when the new disaster "throw back" rule was passed by Congress, 1,500,000 copies of a revised "Hurricane Circular" were sent to the field offices to be on hand for public distribution when the President signed the bill in April 1962.

The Internal Revenue's alertness to the need for additional guidance material, is shown in a new booklet entitled, *The Tax Treatment of Condemnations of Private Property by Public Authority*, developed and issued in 1962. It stemmed from information from the Bureau of Public Roads pointing to the need for tax information on the tens of thousands of property condemnations throughout the country which will result from the Federal Highway Program.

Applying the New Direction to farmer taxpayers.

An excellent example of the new approach to obtain increased voluntary compliance is visible in the case of farmers.

A little more than two decades ago few farm families had sufficient income to be obliged to pay federal income tax. With improvement in their economic status, more farmers have become subject to income tax. However, the level of voluntary compliance has not kept pace with the improvement in farm income.

Although there has been a continual improvement in income tax reporting by farmers as a group in the last twenty years, the Federal Government still loses revenue through their failure to report fully. Accurate figures separating farm from business operations are not available, but some studies indicate that about $5 billion a year of farm income is not reported. This constitutes an estimated annual revenue loss of around $1 billion.[1]

A broad and comprehensive approach has been taken by the Internal Revenue Service to obtain increased voluntary compliance and better reporting of farm income. The steps in this program, indicated below, reflect an understanding of the causes for the laxity in reporting and a recognition of the need for more information to the farmer.

Steps in program for improving tax collections from farmers.

1. Wider and more sophisticated audits in the farm field, but not a "drive" against farmers.

2. Because a large portion of the under-reporting is due to a lack of understanding of the complex tax laws, a major educational and informational program to advise farmers of their rights and responsibilities under the income tax laws.

3. Broader distribution of the free 60-page *Farmer's Tax Guide.* This is written in plain language and gives farmers all the general rules necessary for them to file correct tax returns.

4. Expanded public information program on specialized farm tax subjects. A pattern of discussion programs at which farmers, farm agents, and Service personnel can go over practical tax questions that continually puzzle farmers has been developed.

---

[1] At a recent Congressional Committee hearing it was estimated that $12 billion in business and farm profits had not been reported.

5. Emphasis on good record-keeping practices by farmer tax-payers. The many small purchases a farmer makes during the year that are deductible are frequently forgotten by filing time unless they are properly recorded. Each item of income should be recorded as received.

6. Increased assistance in good record-keeping now provided by Internal Revenue, the U. S. Department of Agriculture, and various state departments of agriculture. Use of the assistance given by county banks, manufacturers of farm equipment, and other private organizations doing business with farmers is encouraged.

7. Revision of the *Farmer's Tax Guide* to place greater emphasis on the importance of good records.

8. Preparation of up-to-date material for national farm publications and the document system of the Department of Agriculture's extension service, on matters the Service wants to emphasize.

Internal Revenue officials help carry out this program by making themselves available for public speaking engagements to farm organizations and other important gatherings of farmers.

Chapter Six

THE GREATEST CHANGE IN A CENTURY OF TAX COLLECTION—AUTOMATIC DATA PROCESSING (ADP)

THE GREATEST CHANGE in tax administration since the institution of the income tax was undertaken in 1961 with the installation of a nationwide electronic computing system. Actual operation of automatic data processing—ADP for short—started on January 1, 1962 when the National Computer Center, a modernly handsome, low, sweeping masonry building situated near Martinsburg, West Virginia, was completed.

The National Computer Center is the heart of ADP. Here there will ultimately be maintained on magnetic tape a master file of taxpayers over the entire country. Data from tax returns and other related tax information, transcribed on tapes at a series of Regional Service Centers, will flow to the National Center.

The National Computer Center will process this data against the accounts in the master file, and in turn will produce "action" tapes for the issuance of bills, refund schedules, and other communications with taxpayers. It will provide a continuing check against tax delinquencies and evasions.

On January 1, 1962 the first Regional Service Center, at Atlanta, Georgia, also went into operation, processing data from business returns in seven southeastern states. Other service centers will be instituted and cut into the system over the next few years until, in 1965, the entire country will be covered by the ADP system of tax return processing.

So far as the taxpayer is concerned, ADP is a behind-the-scenes operation. Taxpayers will continue to file their returns with their District Directors and be serviced by them as in the past.

Latest mechanization answers a pressing need.

Automatic data processing had made considerable progress in the business world before the Federal Government began to apply this marvel of science to tax administration. Actually, the demands placed on the Internal Revenue Service by an ever-increasing workload made it imperative that electronic methods be adopted for processing tax returns.

In 1962 the Service handled 62 million individual income tax returns, 96 million tax returns of all types, and a total of 500 million information documents. By 1970, tax returns will increase to an estimated 111 million, and by 1980 are expected to reach a total of 135 million.

Taxpayers and government will benefit.

Improved enforcement of the tax laws which will result from the conversion to automatic data processing will increase tax revenues. This means added assurance that the honest taxpayer will pay only his fair share.

The master file provides proper application of taxpayer payments or credits with a minimum of erroneous billings. The taxpayer account number, which is part of the system, gives a double check in making entries to accounts.

The capacity and memory of the system will help taxpayers who forget prior year credits or who do not take full advantage of their rights under the laws, such as loss carryovers or extra allowances for age.

The master file will eliminate repetitive annual taxpayer contacts for explanations of items previously accepted.

For Internal Revenue, automatic data processing will facilitate and speed up processing and record-keeping, enabling it to handle the increasing volume of work. In addition, ADP will:

–Provide a better check on delinquent taxpayers.

–Facilitate mathematical verification of tax returns.

–Check for prior unpaid taxes before issuing refund checks.

–Detect duplicate refund claims.

–Improve ability to match information data from reports of wages, dividends, and interest paid with data from individual taxpayers of such income received.

–Enable Internal Revenue to determine a taxpayer's current tax status at any time.

–Enable the Service to do a better job of determining which returns should be selected for audit.

Search for labor-saving methods has been constant.

The volume of work entailed in effective tax administration leads to a search for labor-saving devices. It stimulated the invention some 300 years ago of the first calculating machine by Blaise Pascal, the son of a French tax collector. This original mechanism of simple wheel counters, designed to aid a hard-working tax-collecting father, was the forerunner of high speed electronic computers.

Internal Revenue Service used automation as various applicable processes were perfected. As early as 1950, it began to experiment with automatic punch card equipment. In 1955, the first service center for this type of operation opened in Kansas City, Missouri. Subsequently, two other service centers were opened in Lawrence, Massachusetts and Ogden, Utah. These three service centers processed the bulk of individual income tax returns. In 1961, magnetic tape systems were introduced into them. However, these centers are distinct from those being created as part of the new, integrated ADP system, and will remain so until they are ultimately converted to it.

Automation was applied in these original service centers to the processing of returns, billing, and addressing. Other operations, such as the association of returns for different years, returns filed in different places, returns relating to different taxes, and the comparison of information returns with tax returns were done by manual methods.

The electronic age offered far greater potentialities. In 1958, the Service began to apply the concept of recording data only once and using and reusing the data so recorded for all tax purposes. This is accomplished by a master file for each taxpayer, which brings data together in such a way that all parts can be compared and associated and exceptions identified.

How the master file functions.

The master file concept will be fully developed in the automatic data processing system. Actually, there will be two master files—an individual master file and a business master file.

The file will contain identifying information such as the taxpayer's name, address, and permanent number. It will also contain references to accounts of other taxpayers related to him in a tax sense. For example, accounts of a married couple filing separately will be cross-referenced to each other. Each member of a partnership will have his account cross-referred to the partnership file.

Details of income and deductions as reported on the taxpayer's returns or as changed by an audit adjustment will appear in the taxpayer's account. In the course of recording the data as to income and deductions, the tax return will be mathematically verified and the net amount due from the taxpayer or refundable to him will be determined.

The account will record estimated and withheld taxes paid by the taxpayer, bills sent to him, payments received from him, refunds made to him, and the balances due from him.

After an amount due or refundable in a particular return is determined, information will be obtained as to amounts due from the taxpayer for other returns and other taxes. Then a bill or refund consolidating all these amounts will be sent to the taxpayer.

If it develops that a particular taxpayer is filing more than one return to receive more than one refund, a device sometimes used to defraud the government, the erroneous filing will be detected immediately.

The account will contain information reported on Form W-2

(Withholding Tax Statement), 1099 (Information Returns), 1087 (Ownership Certificate—Dividends on Stock) and other informational returns by employers of the taxpayer and by other persons (including corporations and banks) from whom he receives dividends, interest, and other income. These data can then be compared with the data reported by the taxpayer.

In the same operation, returns actually received will be checked against the master file to detect cases of failure to file required returns. Automatic equipment will enable the Service to prepare letters to delinquent taxpayers and notices to revenue officers to follow up the delinquency more speedily, more accurately, and at lower cost than at present.

Study is being given to classification and selection of returns for audit examination by mechanical means, using not only information in the return itself, but also data in returns for other years and for other taxes.

Accounts are identified by number.

The Service will use numeric designations for identification and reference purposes. This use of a number in connection with the master file system is easily justified. Names and addresses are highly variable, due to mobility, marriage, and divorce. Also, there are alternate uses of given name and initials, various combinations in husband's and wife's name, and extensive duplications on a national basis of even unusual names.

The number assigned to each account will be permanent and not affected by mobility, marital change, or other conditions. Moreover, a numerical designation will reduce transcription costs and make it possible to refer to each taxpayer account in the same way each time the master file is posted.

In 1961, Congress passed legislation authorizing the adoption of a number identification system for tax administration purposes. After considerable study, the Service decided to use the Social Security number system for individuals, and the existing Employer Identification number system for all business entities.

The Service recognized that most individual taxpayers already had numbers as a result of employment at some time or other in a job covered by social security. For them, there was no problem. But it also knew that some millions of persons would have to be assigned numbers for tax account identification purposes.

It set out to accomplish this with a minimum of inconvenience to the taxpayers. An extensive information campaign was started to have all taxpayers having social security numbers enter them on returns filed in 1962, a year before their use generally was mandatory.

Those who do not indicate numbers on their returns will be forwarded applications in order that they might obtain numbers to meet the requirement on all returns filed in 1963. Thus, the number of taxpayers who have to initiate independent action to obtain numbers is reduced to a minimum.

It should be noted that assignment of this identification to persons not covered by social security will be for tax account purposes only. Should such a person later come under the Old Age and Survivors Insurance Contribution Act, this same number will be used for the social security account.

The law also requires payers of dividend and interest, who must report such payments to Internal Revenue, to obtain from each payee his social security number and to enter this number on the information return. This will facilitate cross-checking by computers to determine whether all such income is reported on tax returns. The payers are given until October 1, 1963 to obtain and initiate use of payee numbers on these documents.

Business taxpayers will use their regular Employer Identification Number on all tax documents they file.

A decentralized ADP system is planned.

Eventually the automatic data processing system will be a decentralized operation involving 62 district offices, 9 regional service centers, and one National Computer Center.

The National Computer Center. The master file will be established, maintained, and up-dated each week at the National Computer Center. The equipment there is large-scale, general-purpose, tape-oriented, digital data processors.

It has the capacity to read an estimated 42 billion data characters of input each year, to up-date 78 million master file accounts containing 45 billion data characters each *week*, and to write an estimated 140 billion data characters of output each year.

In addition to the capacity for file reference, the equipment at the computer center is capable of sorting the data records, both incoming and outgoing.

The computer center will receive data from service centers on tape. It will not receive documents or punched cards. It will send only tapes to the service centers, and there will be no communications with taxpayers by the computer center.

The National Computer Center is small in terms of personnel—about 70 in the next few years and no more than several hundred ultimately.

The regional service centers. As planned, the regional service centers will communicate back and forth with the district offices by paper, or perhaps by microfilm prepared directly from tape.

Tax returns will be processed initially by the district offices and shipped to the service centers. There, the data will be recorded on punch cards, verified, converted to tape, checked for arithmetical consistency, and forwarded to the National Computer Center.

Service centers will get back reels of magnetic tape from the National Computer Center. These reels will contain data for the preparation of correspondence with taxpayers, and the preparation of index registers for the use of district offices. The reels may be on paper or microfilm.

The service centers will be equipped with card punches, verifiers, sorters, interpreters, and electronic equipment that will convert data from cards to tape, and from tape to some other form of output such as a printed list or a microfilm. The service centers will be large employers with from 1400 to 1800 people.

Taxpayer contact is with the district.

Tax returns, the basic documents, will be filed by the taxpayer at his local office and the taxpayer will go or write there concerning his return. Likewise, any subsequent actions of audit review or conference will be between the taxpayer and his District Director. The new feature in the collection system is that the account records taken as data from basic documents will not be at the district office or at the regional service center. They will be brought together and maintained on magnetic tape at the National Computer Center.

Taxpayers have been informed of ADP.

As part of its New Direction program to foster willing and intelligent voluntary compliance, the Internal Revenue Service has kept the public informed of the conversion to automatic data processing. Articles in newspapers, magazines and other publications, have given the public highlights of the new system.

Before installing ADP, the Internal Revenue Service called a series of conferences with business and professional representatives to explain its plans for such a system. After satisfactory progress had been made, a nationwide conference was called on October 23, 1961 to discuss the effects of ADP on the federal tax system and on taxpayers, tax accountants, and lawyers. Internal Revenue wanted to be sure that businessmen understood the new system and had an opportunity to present their views on its procedural aspects. It also wanted to discuss ways in which large taxpayers who have their own computer systems could substitute magnetic tapes for some of the detailed documents required for tax purposes.

To make sure that all interested parties were heard from, Internal Revenue asked leading business and professional organizations to nominate panelists for the conference. There was active participation of a number of leading bankers, lawyers, accountants, and other business executives at the meeting. Some 600 other businessmen, practitioners, and specialists attended a follow-up seminar to get advance information on a matter that will affect their businesses vitally.

As part of this same program, Internal Revenue announced it would continue to give out as much information as it could to keep businessmen informed at every step. In addition to its own efforts to publicize the new system, Internal Revenue cooperated with various publishing firms who issued special reports to various groups based on the information released at the conference.

Many businessmen not in attendance thereby got much of the data discussed at the meeting.

Transition requires cooperation.

To permit Internal Revenue to operate efficiently and on a production-line basis, information must be reported on the returns in such a way that it can be extracted routinely. Consequently, the Service now insists that all required information be on the return itself. Formerly, it had been rather lenient about permitting information to be included on attachments to the return without being carried forward to the return.

Ingrained practices may be hard to change, the Service realizes, and it therefore plans to make a sustained effort to elicit broad cooperation before exercising its authority to reject incomplete returns as not properly filed. The cooperation of the taxpayers will be won, the Service feels, once they understand that great expense and time are involved if key punch operators and others must extract information from papers attached to returns.

ADP will affect Service personnel.

From the start there has been careful planning by the Internal Revenue Service for the adjustments in the personnel area that ADP will entail. The Civil Service Commission cooperated by permitting a flexibility in procedures to accomplish transfers, reassignments, details and temporary hiring while the change-over is in progress.

The Service is offering extensive training to affected employees to facilitate their re-deployment. This, plus natural attrition through retirements and voluntary separations, makes the change to ADP one of a minimum of hardship for employees whose jobs are absorbed.

Chapter Seven

ENFORCEMENT OF THE TAX LAWS—AUDITS AND APPEALS

A FIRM BUT FAIR ENFORCEMENT PROGRAM is essential to the preservation of our voluntary system of tax collection, first to deter the minority who would evade their fair share of the costs of government, and second, to give assurance to honest taxpayers that their neighbors are meeting their responsibilities.

Appearing before the Sub-Committee of the Committee on Appropriations, United States Senate, Commissioner Mortimer M. Caplin said:

> It (our tax system) is manned by decent, dedicated people, who . . . are seeking to administer the law vigorously, but in a reasonable manner with full regard to the rights and convenience of taxpayers; they are attempting to provide better services for taxpayers, while at the same time curtailing tax abuses which serve to undermine confidence in the soundness and integrity of our self-assessment system.

To the Audit personnel of the Service he has said:

> . . . Our attitude should be one of proper and reasonable appraisal of the merits of the issue. We must not allow our decisions to be unduly influenced by the potential tax adjustment involved; we should never adopt a superior attitude; nor should we take advantage of the taxpayer's technical ignorance. The examining officer should explain the pro-

posed adjustments to him in simple, non-technical language to enable him to understand the issue. If agreement is not reached, then the taxpayer should be given exact and full information as to his further rights of appeal. . . .

What is included in enforcement activities.

The Internal Revenue Service devotes a substantial amount of manpower to its enforcement activities. These activities include the mathematical verification of returns; auditing of returns and taking appropriate action thereon; securing delinquent returns and collecting delinquent taxes and penalties; and, where warranted, prosecuting taxpayers who ignore or seek to evade their just tax responsibilities.

Auditing of returns is of prime importance.

The greatest concentration of manpower, and the greatest revenue recovery from enforcement, occurs in the auditing of returns. For several years, with Congress providing additional manpower and funds, Internal Revenue has been stepping up its audit coverage.

As already noted (page 68), the tax administration is stressing broader coverage in the audit program, reaching all groups of taxpayers on at least a sampling basis. Also, improved quality and thoroughness of audits are being urged. To quote Commissioner Caplin again:

> We do not audit returns for the purpose of making additional assessments. We examine returns to see if the tax laws have been obeyed. And if the return is faulty, it is corrected. If too much has been paid, it is refunded. And if additional tax is due, it is assessed. But we don't stop there. We instruct and advise and assist the taxpayer to understand the laws and their application so that his compliance in the future years will be improved.
>
> We also know that if we didn't audit returns public confidence in our self-assessment system would deteriorate.

Since all returns cannot be audited, Internal Revenue has developed certain criteria by which it can identify those that warrant a "second look." The returns are classified by experienced examining officers in accordance with an over-all program designed both with a view of revenue potential and of broad-range coverage for deterrent value, and to identify areas of abuse.

Automatic data processing will provide still another tool for identifying returns for audit purposes.

How an audit is made.

The audit of a return follows a well-defined course. The taxpayer is contacted personally by an Internal Revenue agent, who arranges a mutually satisfactory date for an examination of his records. If the taxpayer is in business, the examination usually takes place at his business office where his records are located.

The production of proper records to support the return—brokers' statements, bank statements, checks, etc.—is essential. Usually paper work in good order speeds up the examination.

The taxpayer may be represented by a lawyer or an accountant. The agent is himself a skilled accountant and an expert in tax law. After examination, he may accept the return as filed, or may disagree with the taxpayer on some points, and find additional taxes due. He may even find that the taxpayer is entitled to a refund. In the great majority of cases, agreement is reached readily between the agent and the taxpayer and the matter is terminated.

If the taxpayer disagrees with the agent's finding, he can appeal his case all the way from first examination to and through the federal courts. (See page 91.)

To help assure the proper handling of audit cases by revenue agents, Internal Revenue reviews cases at the district and regional levels. This review includes cases where agreement has been reached with the taxpayer as well as those where it has not. Reviewers check for uniformity in interpreting tax laws and fairness in their application. A full discussion of the review procedure is given at pages 93 et seq.

In 1961, an experiment was begun in the Cincinnati Region to improve this review procedure. Review at the district level was eliminated with all cases sent right to the region after initial processing by the Audit Division. The new procedure is called centralized review. Results of this experiment are being closely watched for possible adoption in other regions.

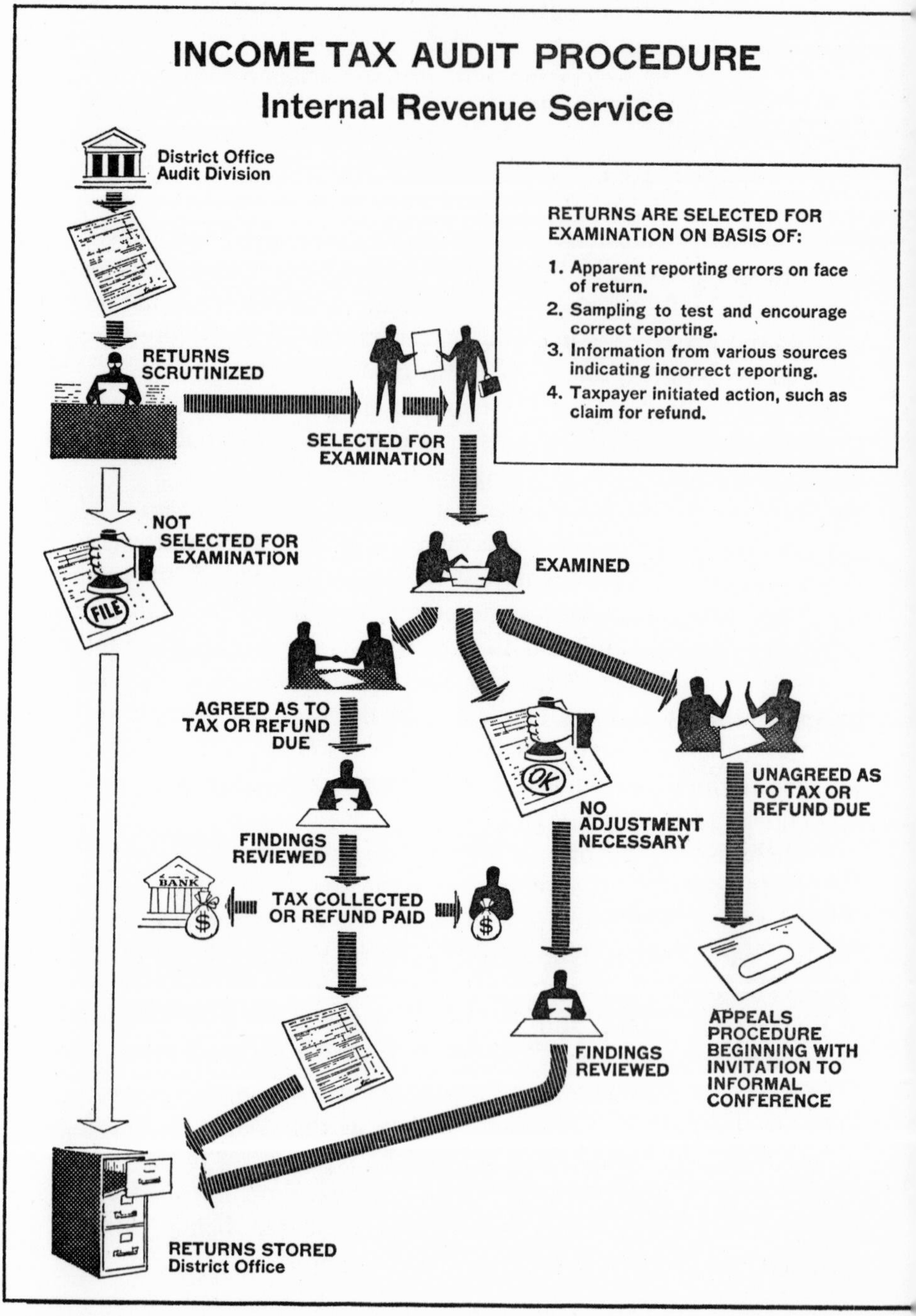

INCOME TAX AUDIT PROCEDURE

Internal Revenue Service

District Office
Audit Division

RETURNS SCRUTINIZED

RETURNS ARE SELECTED FOR EXAMINATION ON BASIS OF:

1. Apparent reporting errors on face of return.
2. Sampling to test and encourage correct reporting.
3. Information from various sources indicating incorrect reporting.
4. Taxpayer initiated action, such as claim for refund.

SELECTED FOR EXAMINATION

NOT SELECTED FOR EXAMINATION

FILE

EXAMINED

AGREED AS TO TAX OR REFUND DUE

OK

NO ADJUSTMENT NECESSARY

UNAGREED AS TO TAX OR REFUND DUE

FINDINGS REVIEWED

BANK

TAX COLLECTED OR REFUND PAID

FINDINGS REVIEWED

APPEALS PROCEDURE BEGINNING WITH INVITATION TO INFORMAL CONFERENCE

RETURNS STORED
District Office

How deficiencies arise.

Aside from purely mathematical errors, deficiencies in tax may arise from a taxpayer's misinterpretation or misunderstanding of the tax laws. When this misunderstanding is explained, agreement between the taxpayer and Internal Revenue is generally reached. Cases involving technical or legal issues may, of course, involve administrative appeals procedures, or ultimately litigation in the courts. Six percent interest on deficiencies established is assessed, and in appropriate cases, a 5 percent penalty for negligence may be imposed.

Under-reporting of federal taxes may result from failure to include all income, or overstatement of deductions, or both. Where underpayment of tax has undertones of fraud, the applicable penalties are severe. Civil fraud penalties of 50 percent of the underpayment may be assessed against the delinquent taxpayer. In flagrant cases of willful attempt to defraud the Government, criminal prosecution also is recommended.

The Internal Revenue Service has identified a number of areas in which abuses exist and to which particular attention is directed. These problem areas are discussed in Chapter Eight.

Enforcement covers the securing of delinquent returns.

A number of methods are used to identify delinquent returns. One is the compliance survey, whereby Internal Revenue officers visit taxpayers in person in selected areas to determine if all required returns have been filed. Also, lists of federal taxpayers may be checked against lists of state licenses or other lists the nature of which indicates possible liability for federal taxes. Other sources of information are also available. Willful failure to file returns constitutes a misdemeanor with criminal sanctions upon conviction.

Automatic data processing will permit large scale comparison of information documents received by Internal Revenue with the taxpayer master file. It will thus provide vastly improved facilities for detecting failures to file required returns.

Laws provide strong remedies against delinquent taxpayers.

Internal Revenue has broad powers under the law to collect delinquent taxes. Filing levies and liens, and seizure and sale of assets may be used. Such drastic measures are exercised only as a last resort. The taxpayer who cooperates is given every chance to put his tax house in order, consistent with the Service's obligation to protect the revenues.

What happens when fraud is detected.

Fraud comes to the attention of the Service not only through the auditing of tax returns, but through independent information from a large number of sources. A vigorous enforcement policy is directed against those few who would deliberately defraud the Government.

In cases of suspected fraud, the special agents of the Intelligence Division enter the picture, usually working closely with the revenue agents. (See page 189.) The special agents investigate suspected willful failure to file tax returns and willful attempts to evade income, wagering, and all other federal taxes (except those on alcohol, tobacco and narcotics) and related criminal offenses. These special agents are highly trained investigators, experts at locating hidden evidence and skilled in the methods of determining the true income of a person who attempts to conceal it.

Where flagrant and willful attempts at fraud are indicated, criminal prosecution may be recommended to the Department of Justice. The federal courts generally deal severely with such convicted offenders.

The Appellate Division in the Enforcement Program

Under the New Direction in tax administration, the Appellate Division is particularly concerned with the shift of emphasis to encourage more effective voluntary compliance. This concern arises from the fact that the Division almost exclusively deals with taxpayers who have differed with another section of the Service and who not infrequently believe that they have been the victim of an "error" made by Internal Revenue.

The Appellate Division supports the philosophy of the New Direction that calls for removal of the shroud of mystery that surrounds the Service, especially since too little attention was given in the past to the rather wide area of appeals open to the taxpayer.

The laws which produce tax revenue also provide a series of informal and formal appeals procedures for taxpayers within the Service itself. In addition, there is the Tax Court of the United States and the judicial processes of the federal courts.

Three principles guide the appellate program.

Three basic principles guide the appellate program of the Internal Revenue Service: (1) prompt hearing and decision; (2) high quality decision; and (3) satisfactory number of settlements. These three guiding principles are based on Internal Revenue's obligation to provide a genuinely effective system of administrative appeals for the benefit of taxpayers as well as for the benefit of the Government. The appellate program is both taxpayer-oriented and quality-conscious.

Each principle is of vital importance to the taxpayer and the government.

The need for a prompt hearing and a prompt decision in each case is not peculiar to the administrative appeal system of Internal Revenue. This is a vital element of any appeal system, judicial or otherwise. In truth, there is no real appeal unless it is available without unreasonable delay. The taxpayer has a right to know the final decision of the Service as to the amount of his tax liability and he has a right to know this within a period of time that is reasonable in the light of all the circumstances of the case.

Moreover, the taxpayer should know also, with all possible dispatch, whether his case can be disposed of with finality in non-docketed status (completed with the administrative appeals process) or whether he is going to be faced with the need for seeking judicial review in the Tax Court or in the federal courts. And if his case is before the Tax Court, this right to prompt administrative consideration persists. It is essential that both the taxpayer and the Government be saved the time and expense of trial, as well as the delay incident to trial, if an appropriate and fair settlement can be effected.

The need for the second basic element—a high quality decision in each appellate case—always has been regarded as the dominant performance factor in appellate work. Again, from the taxpayer's standpoint as well as from that of the Government, there is no real appeal unless the decision is a sound one, fair to both parties, and based upon a judicious application of Service policy and legal principles. The importance of this element is such that the quality of the decision is not to be impaired by paying undue regard to the need for dispatch in beginning or concluding consideration of the case; and neither is the quality of the decision to be sacrificed for the purpose of securing agreement.

The last of the three basic elements—the need for a satisfactory number of agreed settlements, fair both to the Government and the taxpayer—must be clearly understood. There is no formula that would indicate that for any given number of examinations, and appeals voiced, a certain number should result in agreement at the administrative level. The words in the principle are therefore used in a relative sense.

On the surface, this call for a satisfactory number of agreed settlements would appear to be much more government-oriented than taxpayer-oriented. A closer look at this need should put to rest any idea that the element is designed only to prove that Internal Revenue is capable of reaching the settlement stage without requiring taxpayers to enter into the formal judicial processes. It is much more important from the taxpayer's standpoint to put at rest the differences over his tax liability. In the quest for more effective voluntary compliance, gaining the taxpayer's genuine acceptance of the Appellate decision is a vital element. Thus, the need for prompt decision gives way to whatever extent is reasonable to the need for gaining the taxpayer's acceptance of the decision. With the taxpayer's genuine acceptance of the decision should flow the incentive to voluntarily comply.

An examination of the appellate procedure itself will illustrate how the law protects the taxpayer's rights.

Steps open to the taxpayer who disagrees with an agent's findings.

If the revenue agent's examination of a taxpayer's return results in a proposed adjustment involving additional liability, to which the taxpayer does not agree, he may request an "informal conference" with a reviewing officer. At this conference, the taxpayer, his representative, or both, along with the revenue agent appear before a conferee and present the facts and interpretations of the case for his impartial judgment. This reviewing officer has authority to decide in the taxpayer's favor, if he is convinced that the taxpayer is right.

When the informal conference still yields no agreement, the revenue agent then submits his official report to his superiors. At this stage the taxpayer receives his first formal statement of an intent to adjust his tax liability. This is a so-called "30-day letter." It states the position of the Internal Revenue Service, and informs the taxpayer of his right to appeal to the Appellate Division within 30 days. In this appeal, the taxpayer may have a tax advisor to present his case.

If the taxpayer is not upheld by the Appellate Division, he will be mailed a notice of deficiency, stating that at the end of 90 days the additional tax will be assessed. The taxpayer may decide to pay up and end the matter; or he can withhold payment and appeal to the United States Tax Court within the 90-day period; or he may pay up and file a claim for a refund of the tax. If that claim is disallowed, or no action is taken by the Service within six months, he may then file a suit for refund in a U. S. District Court or the U. S. Court of Claims.

If a claim for refund was the original subject of the informal conference, the taxpayer may secure the disallowance notice either by requesting that it be issued, or by failing to answer Internal Revenue's statement. At this point then, the taxpayer may bring his suit for refund in the District Court or Court of Claims.

Once the taxpayer has entered the judicial process, he is entitled to pursue the judicial appellate procedures through the Courts of Appeals even to the Supreme Court of the United States.

At all of these administrative and judicial appellate levels, every door is left open for the reaching of an agreement between the Government and the taxpayer.

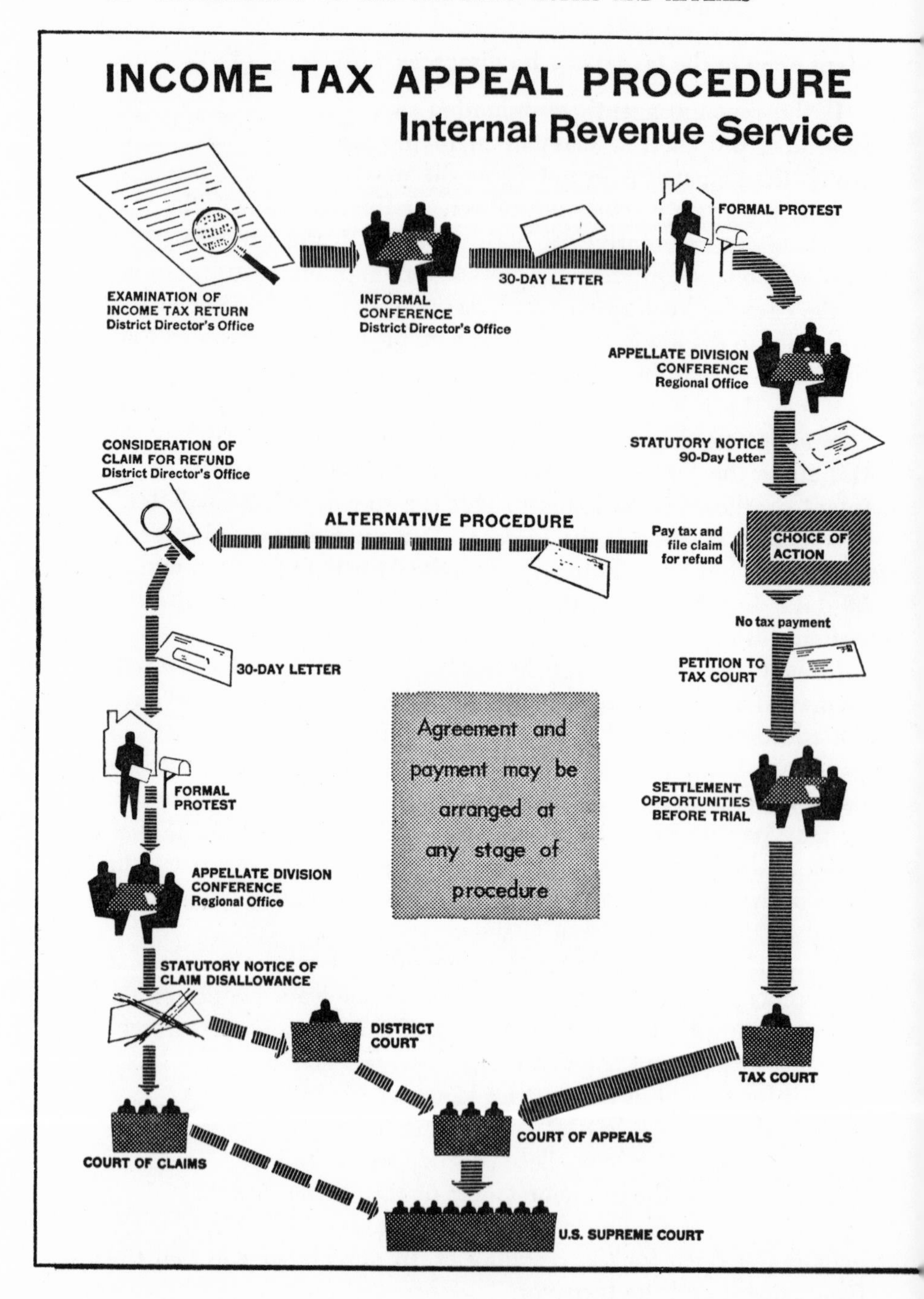
INCOME TAX APPEAL PROCEDURE
Internal Revenue Service
EXAMINATION OF
INCOME TAX RETURN
District Director's Office
INFORMAL
CONFERENCE
District Director's Office
30-DAY LETTER
FORMAL PROTEST
APPELLATE DIVISION
CONFERENCE
Regional Office
STATUTORY NOTICE
90-Day Letter
CHOICE OF
ACTION
Pay tax and
file claim
for refund
ALTERNATIVE PROCEDURE
CONSIDERATION OF
CLAIM FOR REFUND
District Director's Office
No tax payment
PETITION TO
TAX COURT
30-DAY LETTER
Agreement and
payment may be
arranged at
any stage of
procedure
FORMAL
PROTEST
SETTLEMENT
OPPORTUNITIES
BEFORE TRIAL
APPELLATE DIVISION
CONFERENCE
Regional Office
STATUTORY NOTICE OF
CLAIM DISALLOWANCE
DISTRICT
COURT
TAX COURT
COURT OF APPEALS
COURT OF CLAIMS
U.S. SUPREME COURT

Attaining Uniformity in Tax Determinations

The Internal Revenue Service constantly strives to attain uniformity in its examination of taxpayer returns and the treatment of tax issues by audit personnel. The review programs at the district, regional, and national levels, as well as other methods used to achieve the desired uniformity, are explained below.

District review staff works for uniformity.

In general, review programs are designed to measure the adequacy of the examination of returns by examining officers. The reviews show whether examinations are complete; whether the examiners' reports properly reflect their findings; and whether the findings are in accordance with established law, regulations, and procedures. The reviews ensure that quality audit programs are conducted and that taxpayers are being treated uniformly and equitably. At the same time, the review programs provide information as to types and degree of noncompliance.

In each District Office, a review staff, composed of men and women experienced in the various phases of tax enforcement, is responsible for reviewing examiners' reports to verify the determinations recommended by the examining officers. This review staff is also responsible for maintaining the quality of examinations and reports and for the technical accuracy of the determinations.

When a case reflects inadequate examination, failure to identify questionable items, or failure to utilize quality audit standards, or when a report contains significant discrepancies, it is brought to the attention of the group supervisor and examining officer, and appropriate corrections are made. If an item is of a minor nature, an informal advisory memorandum is prepared. The correction, advisory and inquiry letters are prepared by the district review staff to achieve greater correctness and uniformity of examination. Frequently, examples of common errors are distributed to help improve performance in the district.

Cases subject to the informal conference procedures are reviewed by the Conference coordinator before the report of examination is prepared. These cases are also reviewed by the district or region review staff to assure uniformity in the audit treatment of tax questions.

At the regional level audits are post-reviewed.

At the regional level, tests are made to determine the uniformity of examinations conducted at the district level. This is done by scientifically selecting a sample of audited cases after they have been closed out of the Audit Division in the District Office and post-reviewing them in the Office of Assistant Regional Commissioner (Audit). All errors disclosed in this post-review process are fed back to the various District Audit Divisions by means of exception letters. The cases are returned for corrective action, or advisory letters are prepared for training and future guidance of the technical personnel involved. These post-review letters are also utilized to promote uniformity among the various districts within the region. Data covering situations indicating common errors are distributed to examining officers in the region through a *Regional Post-Review Digest* or by circulating post-review memoranda.

National Office coordinates the review program.

The Audit Division in the National Office coordinates the post-review program of the regions through interregional studies of informal conference reports and of the exception and advisory letters issued by the nine Offices of the Assistant Regional Commissioner (Audit), and through its own special studies of troublesome issues.

In instances where issues have been improperly treated or procedures have not been followed, and the subject matter or issue is considered to be generally applicable to the majority of Internal Revenue technical personnel, a digest of the facts and circumstances is prepared. These digests are published in the *Audit Coordination Digest,* which is issued bi-monthly to Service personnel to alert them to areas in which errors are likely to be made. The digests cover a wide variety of subjects, including income tax, excise tax, estate and gift taxes, tax-exempt organizations, pension and profit sharing plans, and offers in compromise.

In addition, the Audit Division prepares and publishes semi-annually a national analysis of the informal conference reports. This analysis includes tabulations by region and district of the principal issues and those that fall into problem categories. A similar analysis is made, and published, of the exception and advisory material received from the regional offices.

The National Office Audit Division also has a program under which the Assistant Regional Commissioners (Audit) submit periodic reports, by principal issue, on the results of their post-review activity. These reports, known as *Patterns of Compliance Reports,* include the number of cases reviewed, significant errors and trends, together with proposals as to those areas needing improvement either through legislative or regulatory changes, improved audit instructions, or special training.

The reports are analyzed by audit personnel in the National Office and discussed by representatives from the Audit and Appellate Divisions, the Assistant Commissioner (Technical), and the Chief Counsel. The purpose of these discussions is to identify areas in which problems exist, recommend actions that would resolve the problems, and promote prompt corrective action.

Special projects help advance uniformity.

To further extend uniformity, the Service makes use of special projects. One such project, for example, was the development and publication of a Uniform Sales Tax Table for all districts in which state sales taxes are in effect. The tables are a guide to uniform treatment of deduction of sales taxes.

The special project technique has improved the method of selecting cases for post-review to give a more effective sampling of principal issues. It also results in national instructions for certain areas, such as depletion cases affected by a particular statute and changes in accounting methods.

Inquiries reveal where uniformity is needed.

When, during the course of an examination, either the District Director or the taxpayer has reason to believe that a lack of uniformity exists in the disposition of an issue, or if an issue is unique, novel, or complex, a request for technical advice may be directed to the National Office. The problems presented in these requests are excellent barometers for areas in which corrective action may be required.

The National Office also prepares replies to letters of complaint and inquiry from taxpayers, tax practitioners, members of Congress, and others, involving legal, factual, and administrative questions that arise in specific tax cases. These inquiries, like the technical advice requests, are constantly analyzed and studied for indications of general problem areas that need corrective action.

The Appellate Division refers copies of its decisions to the Audit Division initiating the action. These decisions are studied and the principles are applied in other cases to further assure uniformity in the treatment of taxpayers. In addition, mutual problems of local audit and appellate offices are discussed at periodic joint meetings to arrive at a mutually agreeable solution.

Chapter Eight

PROBLEM AREAS AND THE ENFORCEMENT PROGRAM

"FOR VOLUNTARY SELF-ASSESSMENT to be both meaningful and productive of revenues, citizens must not only have confidence in the fairness of the tax laws, but also in the uniform and vigorous enforcement of these laws." This statement by President Kennedy in his 1961 tax message has been a guidepost for the Internal Revenue Service in its program to control problem areas.

The Internal Revenue Service has expanded personnel, introduced good training programs and new techniques, and now has automatic data processing to enhance its enforcement capabilities.

A balanced fraud program and active participation in the administration's organized crime drive are important facets of an over-all effort to bring to the bar of justice those who have been guilty of willful evasion of their tax obligations. The broader goal, however, is to achieve maximum voluntary compliance by all taxpayers; to let the honest taxpayer know that his interest is being protected; and to deter others from attempting to use one type or another of tax evasion.

In 1962, the major problem areas that were absorbing much of Internal Revenue's attention, and raising civil as well as criminal issues, included: travel and entertainment expenses, hobby losses, dividend and interest payments, transactions between domestic companies and foreign affiliates, inventories, charitable contributions of works of art and other noncash items, charitable balls and theater parties, charitable foundations, and delays in paying over to the Government withheld taxes. Each of these areas is treated briefly below.

Travel and entertainment expenses stand high on the list.

During the past ten years, every Commissioner of Internal Revenue has championed an administrative program to check overstatement of travel and business expenses, but in some areas the T & E abuse still plagues the Service.

The principal problem in this area stems from the nature of the expenses, as they are normally of the type incurred by individuals in their personal lives. To determine whether an expenditure is a bona fide business expense or a personal expense is often difficult, time-consuming, and likely to cause poor taxpayer relations. Since each business may have its own idea of the best method to promote the growth of its company or product, it is difficult for Internal Revenue to set any definite guidelines in this area. Each decision must be based on the facts in each case. On the other hand, Internal Revenue expects that its increased emphasis on quality audits will assist in combatting improper and illegal deductions in this field, by encouraging a thorough analysis of the travel and entertainment expense account.

Internal Revenue is doing all in its power to eliminate these improper and illegal deductions. Taxpayers are being required to show that all T & E expenditures are ordinary and necessary business expenses which are directly related to the active conduct of a trade or business. Prosecution is being recommended in cases where fraudulent reporting of personal expenses as ordinary and necessary business expenses is found, or where there is fraudulent overstatement of alleged expenditures. The Revenue Act of 1962 contains provisions relating to abuses. See Chapter Nine.

Hobby losses are another problem area.

Another area calling for stricter enforcement involves so-called hobby losses. These are cases in which individuals, with income principally from other sources, engage in a venture for personal gratification with no expectation of profit; for example, farming, operation of kennels, etc. The question in each case is whether the enterprise is an avocation, a hobby, a legitimate business, or an opportunity to unfairly claim a tax deduction.

The problem of isolating enterprises carried on as hobbies is most difficult, particularly where they are efficient operations. One reason for the difficulty is that there are many legitimate trades or businesses of the same type as hobby enterprises. Also, for the first years of operation it is particularly difficult to isolate the hobby enterprise. Some enterprises will almost certainly lose money at the start whether conducted for business or for pleasure.

But enterprises that are "hobbies" must be isolated and denied the characterization of a legitimate trade or business. Otherwise the Government is subsidizing expensive activities carried on for pleasure. Internal Revenue is considering ways to correct this situation.

Dividend and interest income is not fully reported.

According to Treasury Department estimates, about $800 million in tax revenues was lost in 1959 due to the under-reporting of dividend and interest income by individuals on their income tax returns. Steps to close this gap through the withholding of dividends and interest payments at the source were considered but rejected in 1962 by Congress (see Chapter Ten).

Instead of withholding, a reporting provision was placed in the Revenue Act of 1962. This requires institutions paying $10 or more to any one individual to report the amount of such payment to Internal Revenue. With automatic data processing equipment now being installed, it will be possible to match this information with the income from dividends and interest reported by taxpayers.

Internal Revenue believes withholding to be a more efficient means to close the revenue gap caused by under-reporting of these payments. But the combination of automatic data processing and a greater awareness by taxpayers of their obligations to report dividend and interest income should increase compliance in this area.

Problems in the international field have mushroomed.

The recent activity of American business in foreign investment and commerce has created another problem area. While the majority of domestic corporations forming foreign affiliates do so for legitimate business reasons, a few look upon a foreign affiliate primarily as a means of shifting profits abroad that properly are taxable here. Internal Revenue is determined to, and will, curb improper practices in this area.

Among the many devices used are sham or paper corporations with no real business purpose or function, unrealistic sales or purchase prices in transactions between the domestic company and its foreign affiliates, and failure to properly allocate expenses to affiliates. Undetected, these schemes cause revenue losses for the United States. Furthermore, the unscrupulous saving of tax dollars by these companies creates competitive inequities.

To meet this growing threat to the tax system, Internal Revenue has developed a training course for enforcement personnel to broaden their knowledge of tax law and auditing techniques for foreign transactions. Particular emphasis is being placed on attempted tax-avoidance patterns that divert income abroad that should be taxed here.

One of Internal Revenue's biggest problems is to develop adequate information to deal with the situation. New rules and the additional reporting required by recent legislation should be of great assistance to the Service. In addition, the National Office is working very closely with its field offices on cases with international aspects.

Substantial improvement in enforcement procedures also is expected to result from data obtained in a controlled audit program. By early 1962, Internal Revenue already had received 1,170 reports concerning 6,000 foreign subsidiaries under this program. The current expansion of Internal Revenue operations abroad (see page 126) should also strengthen its audit and enforcement capabilities.

Understatement of inventories is sometimes hidden.

In his first tax message, President Kennedy directed the Internal Revenue Service to give increased attention to irregular reporting of inventories. The Service, therefore, revised individual, partnership and corporate returns to require taxpayers to answer a series of questions on inventory practices. These questions seek information on the method of inventory valuation, changes in inventory methods, cost and total market valuation, date when physical count was taken, and an explanation of how the inventory was counted. When taxpayers fail to furnish the required information, or there are indications of inconsistent inventory valuations or deviations from generally recognized inventory methods, such factors are important considerations in the selection of returns for examination.

In the past, revenue agents may not have placed proper emphasis on inventories, possibly assuming that all inventory errors are self-compensating. They also felt that a mere shifting of income from one year to another, when there is no change in the tax rates, would serve no purpose. However, some taxpayers have taken advantage of this attitude to hide consistent understatements of inventories.

In order to improve enforcement, the Service has developed inventory audit standards and procedures. These manuals guide agents in verifying inventories and furnish instructions on audit action required in cases involving inventory discrepancies.

Charitable contributions of art works involve valuation.

Charitable contributions of noncash items, especially art objects, have been increasing. The main problem here centers around highly inflated excessive valuations. When a contribution is made in property other than money, the deduction is determined by the fair market value of the property at the time of the contribution. Taxpayers are required to establish the fair market value. The Service, however, is not required to accept appraisals merely because they were prepared by "expert appraisers." Equal consideration must also be given to all other available evidence, such as donor's cost, date of acquisition, method of acquisition, and method of appraisal used by the appraiser.

Internal Revenue has come upon a number of cases in which it appeared that taxpayers and art experts conspired to arrange for the purchase, overappraisal, and donation of an article. The taxpayer pays one price for the article and claims a deduction far in excess of a fair and realistic value, even though the donation almost immediately follows the purchase. When evidence discloses indications of willful attempt to evade taxes through such an endeavor, prosecution is considered against the taxpayer and also the appraiser or any other person involved.

To curb this practice, Internal Revenue first issued a statement warning that the area is being watched and that the Service will prosecute vigorously where warranted. In addition, the Service alerted its examining officers to the situation and emphasized the Service's position and the examining officers' authority and responsibility in cases of this nature. Most important, Internal Revenue has made organizational changes and is getting valuable outside help to improve its means for making reliable and realistic appraisals.

Some tax-exempt organization practices are being scrutinized.

A report issued by Congressman Wright Patman in mid-1962 pointing to questionable practices by some tax-exempt foundations brought public attention to measures taken by Internal Revenue to curb these practices. Shortly after his appointment as Commissioner in 1961, Mortimer M. Caplin said greater consideration would be given to areas of apparent noncompliance such as the exempt organizations. Some months later, Internal Revenue announced that one of its objectives for fiscal 1962 was to achieve audit coverage for exempt organizations that was equal in quality to that achieved in income, excise and estate and gift taxes.

Measures implementing this objective were taken and Internal Revenue is moving ahead with a greatly expanded enforcement program for exempt organizations in the 1963 fiscal year. Also, more information will be required from exempt foundations and more of it will be made public.

The tax aspects of certain charitable balls, theater and other parties, as well as charitable foundations in general have been under examination. Organizations sponsoring these activities usually have received general rulings that they are exempt from income tax. However, because of some questionable practices, Internal Revenue has instituted a program for intensified investigation of a greater number of returns of exempt organizations. Special emphasis is placed on those conducting social affairs allegedly for charitable purposes.

Fund-raising activities sponsored by exempt organizations are theater parties, bingo games, white elephant sales, dances, dinners, and luncheons. If such activities do not become the primary function of the organization, its exempt status is not jeopardized. But if the fund-raising activities are regularly practiced in a commercial manner, it may result in a revocation of exempt status, or the income therefrom may constitute unrelated business income subject to tax.

Also involved is the individual's treatment of the contribution he makes to attend the social functions of exempt organizations. Many of the activities are conducted through contributions, generally greater than a reasonable charge for admission and other benefits to be received, and donors may deduct the true contributions for tax purposes. But when payment of an amount designated as a contribution entitles a person to admission to a charity ball or similar affair, only the amount in excess of the value of tickets or other benefits received can be deducted. Revenue agents have been instructed to scrutinize closely these deductions to be sure they do not include the value of goods or services received. In addition, taxpayers have been alerted to this restriction on charitable contributions in the instruction booklets distributed with recent tax forms.

The growth of family foundations has attracted public attention and may require additional study by the Service. Contributions up to the maximum amount deductible for tax purposes may be made by the donor, and ultimate distribution of income by the foundation may be delayed at the discretion of the donor-trustees. However, some organizations are accumulating funds in violation of the Internal Revenue Code. Others have engaged in ordinary business activity. When these practices are discovered, the tax exemption may be revoked and large deficiencies assessed. Here again, Internal Revenue is expanding the Service audit program to correct these practices.

Delay in paying over withheld U. S. taxes is a problem.

The taxes withheld by employers from wages of their employees are trust fund collections that belong to the United States Government. They are in no sense available for use by employers even for short periods. But there has been a tendency on the part of some employers to defer paying over these trust fund moneys to the Government. Therefore Internal Revenue Service streamlined procedures to trigger enforced collection action if timely deposits or prompt payments are not made. Notice of federal tax lien can now be filed or other enforced collection procedures can be initiated within a few days after receipt of a return without full payment. The new procedure has been noticeably effective.

Delinquency in remitting trust fund moneys has been a problem ever since withholding was introduced. To help solve it, a new law was enacted in 1958. It provides that an employer who collects and fails to pay over income, social security, and certain excise taxes, can be required, by notice, to deposit such collected taxes in a special trust fund account not later than the end of the second banking day after he is required to collect the taxes. With some exceptions, persons who fail to comply are guilty of a misdemeanor and upon conviction subject to a fine, imprisonment or both. The offense consists of failing to perform the required act regardless of whether the delay has been willful.

The criminal portions of the act have not been invoked often. But their mere existence has had a very significant deterrent effect. Actually, the Service in the first year had 11 convictions in the courts.

IRS is always on the alert to spot new trouble areas.

Personnel in the Internal Revenue Service are alert to new sources of information that may indicate possible violations of tax law. For example, in 1961 and 1962 the Service followed the investigations conducted by the Securities and Exchange Commission. Cases in which companies or their officers took unfair advantage of their inside positions to the detriment of investors, were studied to ascertain any tax implications.

Internal Revenue cooperates with other government agencies in exchanging such information as is permitted under existing laws. Investigations by other agencies frequently disclose items of tax significance, which are brought to the attention of the Service for its use in enforcing the tax laws. Thus, the Securities and Exchange Commission furnishes Internal Revenue with copies of all prospectuses and offering statements. These documents are forwarded to field offices for possible use in the tax enforcement program. Since this is a highly specialized area, the Service is preparing guidelines to help agents identify and analyze the tax problems arising in these transactions.

Studies and analyses of the problem of tax evasion are part of the everyday work of the staff in Washington and of personnel in the field. The National Office regularly conducts test programs designed to indicate areas where more vigorous enforcement activities are required. The Internal Revenue regions and districts in the field have been encouraged to initiate their own programs to identify local noncompliance patterns.

These test programs serve to stimulate thinking and generate interest among enforcement personnel in stamping out flagrant violation of the tax laws. They also provide a basis for modifying enforcement techniques and other administrative practices, or for recommending to the Treasury Department corrective legislation.

Chapter Nine

TRAVEL AND ENTERTAINMENT EXPENSES—A SPECIAL PROBLEM

For many years the deduction of travel and entertainment expenses has posed a special problem for Internal Revenue. Substantial tax loss was suffered by the Government, and heavier burdens inflicted on honest taxpayers, by those who misused or disguised personal expenses as business expenses.

Enactment of the Revenue Act of 1962 (PL 87-834) eliminated most of the problems resulting from too-casual use of the expense account. The new law disallows entertainment expenses when they are not incurred mainly in furtherance of the taxpayer's trade or business. The new law, in fact, crystallizes the rules for deducting travel and entertainment expenses.

It imposes strict requirements on proper record-keeping; it limits the deductible amount of business gifts; it disallows certain travel and entertainment expenses; and it defines proximity rules, to assure the close relationship of entertainment and travel to the predominant purpose of advancing the trade or business.

For ten years preceding the 1962 law there was an earnest effort by the Internal Revenue Service to correct excesses in this area. But the T & E problem, as it is called by Revenue people, remained serious because of the substantial amount of tax revenue involved. At the same time, history showed that the heart of the problem resists administrative solution and that legislation was necessary if the excesses were to be sharply curtailed.

Studies showed the extent of the problem.

Three studies compelled the Service to conclude that the T & E problem was more serious than had previously been documented. They were: (1) a 1960 three-month study made by the Internal Revenue Service; (2) a limited 1959 Audit Division study; and (3) a scientific sampling of 100,000 returns by the Statistics Division of the Service.

The 1960 three-month study. The findings of this study, based on a single three-month audit period, were impressive:

1. 48 percent of returns involving T & E items—or nearly one out of every two—required adjustment. Frequency of error in individual returns alone was even higher (58 percent).

2. A total of $28.3 million in claimed T & E deductions was disallowed (resulting in additional tax revenue of $11.1 million); and a total of $29.5 million was disclosed as unreported income in the form of compensation or dividends to related employees and stockholders (resulting in additional tax revenue of $8.3 million). In the aggregate, additional tax revenue of almost $20 million was assessed.

3. 63 percent of the adjusted T & E items was disallowed as constituting personal expense rather than bona fide ordinary and necessary business expense. In terms of dollar amount disallowed, 56 percent was disallowed as constituting personal expense.

4. 35 percent of the adjusted T & E items was disallowed for lack of substantiation. In terms of dollar amount disallowed, 41 percent was disallowed for lack of substantiation.

The 1960 study documents the frequent blending of personal and business expenses in the T & E account. As previously noted, 63 percent of all T & E items disallowed were disallowed solely on the ground of being personal rather than ordinary and necessary business expense. More specifically, the rate of disallowance as personal, by class of expense in returns covered by the 1960 study, was as follows:

Item	*Percent personal of total T & E deductions disallowed*	*Percent personal of total T & E dollars disallowed*
Club dues	92	91
Apartments—suites	90	93
Yachts or boat	89	89
Ranch or farm	85	75
Fishing camp	85	65
Resort property	82	75
Similar facilities	85	93
Automobiles	83	83
Airplanes	75	64
Other transportation	59	53
Conventions	71	61
Hunting lodges	69	33
Theater tickets, etc.	70	62
Meals	64	61
Lodging	62	63
Entertainment, food and beverages	50	46
Gifts	33	26
All other	51	43

But even the above statistics do not state the full limit of the problem. If evidence to substantiate the apparent fact of a business expenditure existed, essentially personal expenses were often found to be allowed as tax deductions.

The scope of the problem can be sensed in these questions: When a taxpayer makes a trip partially for business purposes and partially for pleasure, how does the taxpayer calculate accurately the portion of the trip expense allocable to business? When a taxpayer purchases a yacht or other pleasure-type facility which he uses both for business and personal pleasure, what fair formula can the taxpayer support for separating business from personal expense?

The limited 1959 Audit Division Study. This study was limited to 174 employer returns filed for 1958. Of the 174 employers studied, 15 percent did not use acceptable business practices in requiring accounting by employees. Approximately 1,100 employee returns related to the 174 employer returns were then examined to determine the accuracy of individuals in checking the Form 1040 expense account question boxes. Over 40 had not checked the blocks correctly. Of the 1,100 returns, 339 were completely audited and disclosed that 45 percent had not properly reported income received from employers.

Scientific sampling of 100,000 returns. The Statistics Division examined 100,000 returns filed for 1958. This study, together with the limited Audit Division study, indicated that 10 percent of all individual taxpayers—that is, 6 million taxpayers—receive expense account allowances or reimbursements, or otherwise charge expenses to their employers. (The 1959 study also indicated that 10 percent of all individuals are concerned with expense account issues.)

Ten years of administrative effort didn't solve the problem.

The general T & E problem first manifested itself significantly during World War II and the period following. Prior consideration related primarily to the question of travel expenses and per diem allowances.

In February 1952, Commissioner John B. Dunlap expressed concern over some lavish travel and entertainment items claimed as tax deductions, and announced that revenue agents were being instructed to examine carefully items on returns involving T & E expenses, executive expense allowances, business gifts, and similar items. Top administrative officials at that time believed that corrective legislation was necessary.

At the start of the Eisenhower administration, T. Coleman Andrews, Commissioner Dunlap's successor, although expressing substantial concern over T & E, believed that pending legislative proposals were not necessary and stated that the problem could be remedied by administrative action. In 1954, he emphasized the Service's awareness of the T & E problem and outlined guides to be used by revenue agents in determining the allowability of T & E deductions. The ruling constituted the first official recognition of the Cohan doctrine, but emphasized the need of secondary evidence at least to substantiate a claimed deduction.[1]

[1] If a taxpayer had some evidence, but not enough to make a mathematically exact determination, an approximate amount was usually allowed. This approximation principle is often referred to as the *Cohan rule of approximation*, from the name of the case which required approximation in the absence of records from which an exact amount of traveling and entertainment expenses could be determined. The "Cohan rule" was terminated by the Revenue Act of 1962.

In the period 1955-1958, Commissioner Russell C. Harrington attempted to improve on the administrative solution by emphasizing the need for record substantiation by employees on expense account or allowance arrangements.

In December, 1959, after a series of conferences with representatives of business and his Advisory Group, Commissioner Dana Latham launched his comprehensive T & E enforcement program by outlining tentative policy suggestions. His program, as announced in final form, again did not represent a change in the basic rules governing T & E deductions, but did constitute an important administrative step.

It consisted of adding to the income tax return (1) an expense account schedule for certain officers, partners, and highly-paid employees, and (2) a questionnaire concerning hunting lodges, yachts, apartments, conventions, and similar items. Although the primary purpose of the schedule was to aid in administrative identification of T & E items, the program had the practical effect of requiring a change in taxpayer record-keeping systems. Commissioner Latham also defined in greater detail the type of information required to be furnished by an employee to his employer in "accounting" for T & E expenses.

When Commissioner Caplin initiated the New Direction for the Service in 1961, he also tackled the T & E problem. Taxpayers were required to show that all such expenditures were directly and proximately related to their business and to present at least secondary evidence before applying the Cohan rule. Prosecution was also recommended in cases where fraudulent reporting was found. This included the reporting of personal expenses as ordinary and necessary business expenses or the over-statement of alleged expenditures.

In effect, during the last decade all Commissioners of Internal Revenue have carried out serious administrative programs attempting to solve the T & E problem, but it still continued unsolved. The T & E inquiries absorbed a disproportionate amount of the resources of the Service.

Examples highlight the problem.

Excerpts from two recent revenue agents' reports highlight the continuing problem under previous laws:

The president and one vice-president (of the taxpayer corporation) are father and son. . . . The father and son own memberships in the .... Club, ... Club, and various supper clubs . . . The corporation pays all dues and entertainment expenses. . . . It is, however, believed that the entertainment involves friends, and that the officers are in turn entertained by the same people. Each member of the club is supposed to give a party once each year for the others.

It has proven impossible to prove such entertainment and parties as personal expense because the officers can always point to some of the parties who were supposedly instrumental in their having obtained some (business). . . .

One thing is ever present with this taxpayer. A trip to Las Vegas, Nevada, . . . or some other place has always been opportune to attend some New Year's Day bowl game or other affair, yet the trip was to see some concern about selling. . . .

The second excerpt:

The president of the corporation is a gun collector and hunting enthusiast. Each year he goes on a hunting trip to Wyoming in the company plane or car (with four hunting companions). . . .

The four hunting companions were from . . . firms (which) may be instrumental in the award of contracts . . . and are hunting enthusiasts themselves as well as friends of the president. . . .

It has further come to the attention of the examiner that officers' salaries are held to a minimum . . . , but the expenses of the above nature are paid in behalf of the officer. It should be added that all events of the trip and associations of the companions are carefully documented and reported to the firm to avoid possible trouble in connection with the deduction.

Under the present law there has been found no basis for disallowance of the expense.

Legislative changes were proposed in recent years.

Two legislative proposals to correct the T & E situation were submitted over the years (82nd Congress and 86th Congress), but both were defeated, primarily by opposition voicing the opinion that T & E expenses could be cured administratively.

82nd Congress—King bill. In 1951 a subcommittee of the Ways and Means Committee under the chairmanship of Congressman Cecil B. King was appointed to examine administration of the internal revenue laws. Extensive hearings were held, and Congressman King then introduced a bill which in part would have disallowed any deduction for business expense unless "substantiated in accordance with regulations prescribed by the Secretary." This would have eliminated the Cohan rule.

On May 16, 1952, Congressman King declared:

> . . . One of the most flagrant sources of inequity and of corruption has been found in the inadequacies of existing record-keeping requirements and enforcement of these requirements. While the subcommittee will not sanction unreasonable requirements of record-keeping, particularly in the case of millions of small taxpayers, it has become clear from the investigations that under present law exorbitant unsubstantiated deductions have frequently been claimed for such items of business expense as entertainment and promotion. Without the power to enforce adequate record-keeping, Internal Revenue has been required to allow such deductions on an estimated basis.

86th Congress—Clark proposals. In the 86th Congress, after full consultation with experienced members of the tax bar and officials of the Service and the Treasury Department, Senator Clark introduced proposals for corrective legislation.

In 1959, he first proposed an amendment to the Tax Rate Extension Act of 1959, which in effect would have classified T & E expense according to types of activity most apt to constitute personal pleasure rather than business, or types of activity constituting an inseparable combination of both. Under this proposal, deductions would have been fully disallowed for: entertainment at places of public amusement; maintenance of yachts and lodges; gifts; dues to country clubs; and travel costs to conventions outside the United States. On the other hand, expenses for business meals would have been allowed if they otherwise met the "ordinary and necessary" test. This amendment was defeated in the Senate Finance Committee.

Treasury proposals led to legislative changes in 1962.

In April, 1961, Secretary of the Treasury, C. Douglas Dillon, submitted a comprehensive report to Congress on the extent of the T & E problem under existing law. The report was divided into four principal parts: (1) statistics disclosed by the 1960 three-month study made by the Internal Revenue Service (see page 107); (2) conclusions of the Service based on the 1960 study and other studies; (3) analysis of certain court decisions and administrative cases indicating the extent of unwarranted T & E expense allowances under present law; and (4) a compilation of newspaper and periodical publicity given to the T & E problem.

Based on the unsolved substantial scope of the T & E problem notwithstanding nearly a decade of administrative effort, Secretary of the Treasury Dillon proposed to Congress that a T & E provision be introduced as part of several legislative proposals included in the President's tax message of April 20, 1961.

Revenue Act of 1962—The rules are tightened.

Taxpayers who, after December 31, 1962, present claims for entertainment, travel, or gift expense deductions, will find one fundamental change in the new law which will vitally affect favorable consideration—the burden of proof now rests with the taxpayer. If any deduction is claimed, it will have to be backed up by accurate records.

The four specific changes in the Revenue Act of 1962 are:

1. New rules apply for travel expense—and they will be examined more critically. Expense for traveling, including meals and lodging away from home, must be substantiated, as to: (1) amount of expense, (2) time and place of travel, and (3) business purpose of travel. Expenses will be deductible only to the extent that cost and purpose can be substantiated.

2. Tighter application and stricter rules on deductions for entertainment expenses and luxury facilities. Expenses must be directly related to the active conduct of a trade or business, or in the case of such activities directly before or after a substantial and bona fide business discussion, including meetings at conventions, they must be associated with the active conduct of the trade or business.

Entertainment at country clubs, on yachts, or other such facilities owned by the taxpayer are not deductible unless the facility is used more than 50 percent for the furtherance of his business or trade.

3. A deduction ceiling is set on gifts—total business gifts to any individual, during the tax year, will not be allowed to the extent that the total exceeds $25. A gift to the wife or child of an individual is considered as a gift to the individual. A husband and

wife are treated as one taxpayer for the $25 test. A partnership is also limited to the $25 per year deduction.

(Exceptions: Items costing the donor not more than $4, on which his name is clearly and permanently imprinted, and which is one of a number of identical items distributed by him; signs, display racks, and other promotional material used on the business premises of the recipient; and items of obvious personal property, costing the donor not more than $100, if awarded to an employee because of length of service or for a safety achievement—shall not be included in determining the $25 limitation.)

4. Substantiation is the key—the Cohan rule is abolished. In addition to evidence that the amount was actually spent, a taxpayer now must also have other records and supporting evidence that will substantiate the fact that the amounts spent were in fact spent in the manner required.

New substantiation requirements for any deduction claimed with respect to travel, entertainment, or gift expenses mean simply adequate records.

(a) Clear, contemporaneously-kept diary, account book, or similar record containing the necessary information will do.

(b) With respect to cost of items—in addition to (a) above, there will be required cancelled checks, paid bills, receipts, stubs, or other corroborating evidence in many instances.

Commissioner Caplin believes this new law will eliminate most of the abuses in the T & E area. Regulations prepared by Internal Revenue to spell out the precise enforcement program indicated by the new statute will comprise a vigorous but fair program, he states. Legitimate business expense deductions will not be affected, but expense account living as a way of life should become extinct.

As President Kennedy stated when he signed the Revenue Act of 1962: "This is an important bill—one possessing many desirable features which will stimulate the economy and provide a greater measure of fairness in our tax system. . . . It includes several provisions designed to reduce tax avoidance on incomes earned by American companies and individuals at home and abroad. . . . It makes the distribution of tax burdens fairer and increases our total tax revenues from those sources. . . ."

Chapter Ten

COLLECTING TAXES THROUGH WITHHOLDING

WITHHOLDING TAX on salaries and wages today accounts for approximately two-thirds of all the individual income tax collected. Wage withholding, together with periodic payment by the taxpayer of estimated tax on other forms of income, results in current payment of the individual income tax during the year the income is obtained. This frees the great majority of taxpayers from a large tax liability at the end of the year and facilitates compliance with their tax obligations.

In this chapter, the development of the U. S. withholding tax system, which also applies to other taxes besides wages and salaries, is traced. Its history, dating back 100 years, shows a successful utilization of the principle of tapping revenue at the source during many of the critical periods of the nation's history.

Withholding began in 1862.

Early in the Civil War, the Revenue Act of July 1, 1862 introduced a withholding system for the first time in our history. The British had applied the principle of tapping revenue at the source as early as 1803.

Applying the withholding system for the first time, the bill required that the 3 percent tax on salaries received by all persons in the civil, military, and naval services of the United States (including Senators, Representatives, and delegates in Congress) after August 1, 1862, was to be withheld by all paymasters and other government disbursing officers at the time of paying the salaries.

The disbursing officer was also required to "make a certificate stating the name of the officer or person from whom such deduction was made, and the amount thereof, which shall be transmitted to the office of the Commissioner of Internal Revenue, and entered as part of the internal duties."

The withholding system was also applied to the tax on interest and dividends paid by all railroads, banks, trust companies, and fire, marine, life, inland, stock, and mutual insurance companies. These companies were required to withhold the tax of 3 percent on all money paid out as interest and dividends, and pay it to the Government. A $500 penalty was provided for failure to render the return and pay taxes withheld when due.

The Act of June 30, 1864, enacted because of the increased necessity for war revenue, increased the 3 percent tax on income up to $5000, and on interest and dividends paid by banks, railroads, insurance companies, etc., to 5 percent. Deduction of tax at the source was also extended to include a 5 percent tax on the interest and dividends of any canal, turnpike, canal navigation, or "slack-water" company.[1] Paymasters were required to withhold 5 percent on salaries of government employees over $600.

The withholding of tax on salaries of government employees and on interest and dividends continued until the end of 1871. The Revenue Act of 1864 expired by limitation in 1872. This brief and very limited application of the stoppage-at-source tax principle is of great significance in the development of the present withholding tax system.

The Revenue Act of July 1, 1862 has been called "the basis of the present internal revenue system, both as regards objects taxed and organizations for collecting the taxes."[2]

---

[1] Company engaged in "slack-water" navigation would dam or impede a stream by erection of dams or locks to produce stretches of deeper water for navigation.

[2] Service Monograph of the U. S. Government, No. 25, Institute for Government Research of The Brookings Institute, p. 7.

(2.)

RETURN ***by Railroad Corporations of the amount of interest paid on bonds, or other evidences of indebtedness, and dividends to stockholders, with the amount of tax withheld.***

(SECTION 81.)

Account of Interest paid on bonds, or other evidences of indebtedness, and dividends paid to stockholders, together with the amount of tax thereon, withheld and received from the persons to whom said interest and dividends were paid, pursuant to the provisions of the 81st section of an act entitled "An act to provide internal revenue to support the Government and to pay interest on the public debt," approved July 1, 1862, by the [illegible] Railroad Corporation, from the 1st day of January to the 30 day of June 1864, both days inclusive.

		AMOUNT.	RATE OF TAX.	AMOUNT OF TAX.
Amended Return	Interest on Bonds and other evidences of Indebtedness	16835	5 per cent.	841 75
	Dividends to Stockholders	[illegible]	3 " "	505 05
	TOTAL			$336 70

(Signed.) Stephen T. Olney Treasurer

I, Stephen T. Olney, do swear that the above statement contains, to the best of my knowledge and belief, a true and faithful account of the taxes withheld and received according to the provisions of the act aforementioned.

(Signed.) Stephen T. Olney

Sworn and subscribed before me, this 4th day of January, 1865.

Thomas [illegible]

DIVIDENDS WITHHELD. This 1864 corporate return shows the tax withheld on dividend payments to stockholders.

Withholding was again used in 1894.

The Act of 1894, based almost entirely on Civil War legislation with a few important exceptions, also contained provisions for withholding. Again, the tax was collected at the source on certain corporation dividends and on the salaries of government employees.

The 1913 income tax law extended withholding.

The 1913 Income Tax Law, enacted October 3, 1913, saw the most extensive application in this country of the collection-at-source method. The principle of stoppage at source, used so successfully in England, was applied wherever possible, to secure maximum revenue and to prevent evasion.

The normal tax on individuals was to be collected at the source as far as possible. A corporation, employer, or other "source of income" was required to deduct the tax and pay it to the Government, provided the income was regular, definite, and amounted to $3,000 or more. Interest, rent, salary or any other form of fixed annual income was covered by withholding.

In the case of interest, mortgages, or deeds of trust of domestic corporations, and the interest and dividends of foreign corporations, the tax was to be deducted on any amount, even if the income was less than $3,000. Certain exceptions were made to avoid double taxation. Recipients of such incomes were permitted to deduct the amount of tax withheld from the total tax due on their net incomes as shown on their tax returns.

The House Ways and Means Committee Report on the 1913 Act makes the following interesting comments:

> Probably two-thirds of the income tax proposed as to individuals would be deducted and withheld at the source of the income and paid in full to the Government. This method of collection saves the taxpayer annoyance and at the same time practically doubles the amount of revenue the Government would otherwise receive.
>
> This method of collecting as much of the tax as possible at the source rather than by personal return precludes strictly accurate graduation of the rates, for the reason that in cases where a person's income is derived from a number of different sources and persons required to withhold and pay tax upon the same would not know what the aggregate

amount of the taxpayer's income would be, and hence would not know which rate should apply to the income upon which the tax is to be withheld.

An able parliamentary commission in England recently made an exhaustive investigation and report on the question whether England should abandon collection at the source in order to adopt an accurate graduation of rates, and the commission unanimously reported against the proposal.

This proposal, therefore, embodies the best judgment and the longest experience of the oldest income-tax country.

The normal tax to be collected by withholding was 1 percent of taxable net income. Collection of the tax at the source began on November 1, 1913, only 28 days after enactment of the law, presenting many problems to the Bureau of Internal Revenue and the public. Necessary regulations, rulings, and forms had to be hurriedly issued to implement the new law.

Revenue Act of 1917 virtually abandoned withholding.

The Revenue Act of 1917 repealed most of the provisions requiring withholding of tax at the source, except for nonresident aliens and income from tax-free covenant bonds. It substituted "information at the source." Information was required from corporations, employers, and other persons making payments of any fixed or determinable gains, profits, and income of $800 or more.

At the time, only about 10 percent of total receipts from the personal income tax were derived from collection at the source; in 1916 less than 5 percent was so derived. Congress believed that changing to the "information at source" method would enable the Government to locate more effectively individuals subject to income tax, and would simplify administration in view of the enormous increase in the number of income-tax payers through the lowering of the exemption.

Eventually the tax system was to make good use of both "collection at source" and "information at source" methods, and utilize many features of each.

Enactment of employment taxes brought widespread withholding.

Enactment of the Social Security Act in 1935 saw a new application of tax withholding. Beginning in 1937, funds for payments of benefits were derived from taxes levied on employer and employee. The Social Security taxes on employees (under Chapter 21 of the Code—Federal Insurance Contributions Act) are collected by employers by deducting the tax from the wages paid. It insured the collection of the employee's tax by making the employer liable for it.

The Railroad Retirement Tax Act of 1937, which placed a tax on the compensation of railroad employees, similarly required that the employer withhold the tax. This tax on employees is now covered in Chapter 22 of the Code—Railroad Retirement Tax Act.

These Acts are noteworthy. They provided for "collection at source" by millions of employers, the first use of the withholding method on a large scale since the Revenue Act of 1917 virtually abandoned the withholding system.

Revenue Bill of 1942 introduced withholding of Victory tax.

The present withholding system developed actually during World War II. The war effort required unprecedented additional revenue, and Congress again returned to withholding. The Revenue Bill of 1942 enacted October 21, 1942, imposed a Victory tax of 5 percent upon "Victory tax net income" in excess of $624 for each taxable year. The Victory tax was subject to withholding at the source by the employer on wages and salaries.

Exceptions were made for agricultural labor, military personnel, domestic labor, and other cases where it was believed that withholding of small amounts would be too burdensome. The original House bill provided for withholding on dividends and bond interest, as well as wages. But the Senate limited withholding to salaries and wages, and the bill passed with this change.

As the forerunner of the Current Tax Payment Act of 1943, the 1942 Act is of importance. The Ways and Means Committee Report points out the need for collection at source, and its advantages to the taxpayer in permitting him to spread his payments evenly throughout the year. It states: "Under this system many recipients of income who would not otherwise pay income tax, either by reason of neglect to file return or not being employed in the year following the year when income is derived, or for other reasons, will be brought under the income tax. Greater equity and fairness is gained for the great body of income-tax payers by more uniform application of the law, and the administrative problem of collection will be made easier."

Definitions were provided for the terms "wages," "withholding agents," "employee," etc.; rules for computation of withholding deductions by employers were devised; and duties of employers were prescribed. Much of the 1943 Act can be traced directly to these provisions, developed to implement the 1942 Victory tax withholding.

Current Tax Payment Act of 1943 is basically in effect today.

Enactment of the Current Tax Payment Act of 1943 on June 9, 1943, was a great step toward achieving our self-assessment system. The "pay-as-you-go" plan it introduced has remained substantially unchanged to the present time. The Act contributed greatly to the successful administration of the income tax system during World War II, by putting an estimated 50,000,000 taxpayers on a withholding basis beginning July 1, 1943.

Wage payments in certain types of occupations, including members of the military forces, agricultural laborers, domestic servants, and casual laborers were excepted from the withholding requirement. In general, withholding tax at the rate of 20 percent was applied to income in excess of the withholding exemption of $624 annually for single persons, and $1,248 for married persons or heads of families, with an additional $312 for each dependent.

The 20 percent rate was approximately equivalent to the combined net normal tax, surtax, and Victory tax applicable to the first $2,000 of taxable income. It was designed to result in the collection of the full liability at the source. Through withholding, some 70 percent of the taxpayers became substantially current in their income tax liabilities.

Since collection at source through withholding would only approximate the actual income tax liability of each taxpayer, he was still required to file a final return for the year and determine the actual tax liability.

Current tax payment for non-withheld income was obtained by requiring taxpayers to make quarterly payments of estimated tax, with reconciliation on March 15 of the next year.

Many of the basic provisions of the Current Tax Payment Act of 1943, such as the requirement of withholding, the percentage method for computing the amount to be withheld, and the wage bracket withholding tables, modified by later Acts, are contained in the present Code.

Individual Income Tax Act of 1944 brought more withholding, easier returns.

The Individual Income Tax Act of 1944, enacted May 29, 1944, modified the withholding requirement. Approximately the full income tax liability on wages and salaries up to $5,000 was withheld by providing graduated withholding through the second surtax bracket. New simplified withholding tables with wage brackets substantially narrower than those in the tables under prior law further increased the accuracy of withholding.

Nearly 30 million taxpayers with incomes under $5,000, and whose income not subject to withholding did not exceed $100, were permitted to file their withholding receipts as optional tax returns. The Collector of Internal Revenue determined the tax. This greatly simplified filing for these taxpayers.

Revenue Act of 1951 allows additional voluntary withholding.

The Revenue Act of 1951 added a provision for additional withholding of tax upon agreement by employer and employee in cases where the required amount withheld failed to equal the final tax liability. Employees voluntarily agree with their employers for the withholding of amounts over and above that withheld through the regular operation of the system.

How tax withholding works under present law.

Generally, all employment is subject to the withholding system, with the exception of (1) agricultural labor, (2) domestic and certain nonbusiness services, (3) services performed by a minister, (4) services by a member of the armed forces in combat, and certain other services.

The employer is required to withhold the specified tax from each payment of salaries or wages to an employee. He may determine the amount to be withheld by either of two methods: the percentage method or the wage-bracket method. Both allow for the employee's exemptions and assume a 10 percent standard deduction.

The employee files with his employer a statement of the exemptions claimed by him, on Form W-4, Employee's Withholding Exemption Certificate. The amount withheld under present law is 18 percent of the employee's wage for the pay period, reduced by the value of his exemptions for the pay period. The wage-bracket tables are based on this rate, and the Code includes separate tables for weekly, biweekly, semimonthly, monthly, and daily or miscellaneous pay periods. Employees may enter into an agreement with their employers to have additional amounts withheld, if they desire.

The withholding tax is merely a tentative tax collection. Reconciliation with the correct tax liability for the entire year is made when the final return is filed on April 15 of the following year. The employer must give each employee by January 31 of the next year, or within 30 days after termination of employment, a Withholding Tax Statement, Form W-2. This shows total wages paid during the year, amount of federal income tax withheld, and Federal Insurance Contributions Act (F.I.C.A.) employee tax withheld.

The employee attaches a copy of the Form W-2 to his income tax return for the year, as substantiation for the amount of wage income reported and the amount of income tax withheld. The employer makes quarterly returns on Form 941, Employer's Quarterly Federal Tax Return, reporting the income tax withheld and also the employer and employee taxes (for Social Security) under the Federal Insurance Contributions Act.

The Social Security tax rate (F.I.C.A.) on wages paid during 1963 is 3⅝ percent for employees, which employers withhold on the first $4,800 of taxable wages paid each employee during the calendar year. Social Security Employee Tax Tables, showing the amount of F.I.C.A. tax to be deducted from wages, have been developed by the Internal Revenue Service for the convenience of employers. They are contained in *Employer's Tax Guide,* I.R.S. Pub. No. 15.

Withholding of tax continues on nonresident aliens, foreign corporations, and on tax-free covenant bonds.

Collection of income tax at source on wage and non-wage income of aliens goes back to the World War I period, long antedating the wage withholding system.

Withholding of tax is required by the person paying income such as rent, wages, dividends, interest, and other fixed or determinable income from sources within the United States to nonresident aliens, nonresident partnerships, and to nonresident foreign corporations. Withholding of tax from nonresident aliens is generally at the 30 percent rate, but this rate has been modified by treaties with some foreign countries. Special withholding provisions also apply to certain foreign students and exchange visitors.

In the case of interest on tax-free covenant bonds issued before January 1, 1934, withholding and payment must be made by the person paying the income. Withholding of tax applies to tax-free covenant bonds issued before January 1, 1934, by a domestic corporation or a resident foreign corporation, whether the payee is a resident or nonresident. The rate, with certain exceptions, is 2 percent.

Opposition to withholding from interest and dividends is strong.

Successful experience with wage withholding since 1943 suggests that the withholding technique could be applied with equal success to other forms of income, such as interest and dividends. Revenue collections would become more current if the tax were withheld at the time of payment, and the gap between income reportable and income reported would be greatly reduced.

Tax legislation considered by the 87th Congress, contained a provision that a payer of dividends, interest, and patronage dividends (of marketing or producer cooperatives) be required to withhold tax at a rate of 20 percent. The recipient of the interest or dividend payment would claim credit for the tax withheld by the payer when he files his income tax return.

The bill also contained provisions for reducing over-withholding, including exemption certificates and quarterly refunds for certain individuals and taxpayers, and offsets for governmental units and tax-exempt organizations. Under the offset provisions, those entitled to offset could take credit for amounts withheld from them against any liabilities that they might have as withholding agents of income and social security taxes.

The House Ways and Means Committee Report on the bill stated that while $15 billion in dividends and interest were reported by individuals in 1959, another $3.7 billion should have been reported but was not. The Treasury Department estimated that this under-reporting resulted in a revenue loss of about $800 million in taxes for that year. It also estimated that withholding would result in the collection of most of this lost revenue.

As was the case when income tax withholding from wages was before Congress in 1943, the opposition was vociferous in maintaining that such withholding is unnecessary and would create costly and burdensome paperwork as well as inconvenience to taxpayers. The administration's answer to these and other arguments was that application of withholding to interest, dividends, and patronage dividends was warranted on the basis of justice and efficiency.

Despite President Kennedy's comment in his tax message to Congress in 1961 that underreporting of interest and dividends "is patently unfair to those who must, as a result, bear a larger share of the tax burden," dividend-and-interest withholding was dropped from the bill by the Senate Finance Committee. A more stringent information return procedure was substituted.

Under the new law, any institution (bank, corporation, savings and loan association, etc.) paying $10 or more to any one individual is required to report this amount to Internal Revenue. The amount so paid is to be reported along with the name, address and Social Security number of the recipient. With the matching capabilities of automatic data processing equipment, these reports on dividend and interest payments can be compared with the amount of income reported from these sources by the taxpayer on his return.

Chapter Eleven

TWO FIELDS OF UNIQUE TAX ACTIVITIES

THE ACTIVITIES of two separate departments of the Internal Revenue Service are reviewed in this chapter: The Office of International Activities, which handles the administration of United States tax laws overseas, and the Alcohol and Tobacco Tax Division, which supervises the liquor and tobacco industries in connection with the collection of federal taxes imposed in this area.

The Office of International Operations (OIO).

To collect federal taxes due from individuals and corporations in foreign lands that owe allegiance to the United States, the Internal Revenue Service relies upon the activities of the Office of International Operations.

OIO activities have been expanded to meet the need.

A worldwide survey made by the Internal Revenue Service brought to light extensive noncompliance with tax laws among Americans who had gone abroad in great numbers after World War II to work, live, and do business. Following this survey, late in 1954, the Office of International Operations received permission and approval from the Treasury Department to develop and administer a program aimed at more effective enforcement of the federal tax laws. Much of 1955 was given over to completing this program and getting it actively under way. By the middle of 1956 it was operating quite smoothly, and presently Internal Revenue representatives are situated in Paris, Ottawa, London, Manila, Sao Paulo and Mexico City. An office is also maintained in Puerto Rico.

How OIO operates.

The new program systematized and coordinated the filing of income tax returns by nonresident Americans. It provided for the more than half a million Americans resident in foreign countries not only advice and assistance, but offices through which to maintain their proper tax contacts. Now, all returns filed by United States citizens abroad are processed at a central point.

The Service does not maintain large staffs of agents to carry on its collection work in the many countries in which it operates. It does, however, assign roving representatives who travel to all points in which records indicate Americans are in need of tax reminders or assistance.

Prompted by the success of its taxpayer education and assistance program in the 50 states, the Internal Revenue Service in the last few years has tried to bring as many elements as possible of this same service to taxpayers overseas. It has done this through press, TV, radio, motion pictures, various publications that reach the affected taxpayers, and by talks before civic organizations, which Americans tend to form wherever large groups of them reside in foreign lands.

In Washington, the Office of International Operations is headed by a director, who reports to the Assistant Commissioner (Compliance). In its own small and specialized way, the division maintains planning, research and review functions, and has an active audit department.

In addition to having a basic staff in key foreign areas, the Office of International Operations frequently uses agents on loan from district offices in the United States. They are chosen for special qualifications and unusual bilingual ability to properly carry on the work of giving information and collecting taxes in foreign countries.

The Office of International Operations also works closely with the Department of State, and with many business firms and organizations having overseas branches.

What the roving agents have found.

The agents of OIO, over the years, have ranged far afield. They have collected sizable amounts of taxes from points deep in the heart of Africa, Australia, and other distant lands. They have found Americans who have lived most of their adult lives in totally unexpected places. They have even found a hamburger stand in South Africa, along with many other businesses generally thought of as confined within U. S. borders.

They have found, too, Americans who left the country before the income tax became law in 1913, but who have retained their citizenship. Many of these nonresidents have been fully cooperative in paying taxes for the intervening decades.

Naturally, most of the Americans with whom OIO agents have made contact are in Europe. But a surprisingly large number have been located in out-of-the-way places where they have amassed fortunes. Many, indeed, have been grateful to see a fellow American after long years of no such contact, even when he turned out to be a tax collector.

The agents have frequently found an honest lack of understanding among citizens in foreign areas concerning their tax obligations to their native land. A typical report filed by one such roving agent pointed out that he and a companion had, in less than four months, collected more than one-half million dollars in taxes. This had been done with the full cooperation of the taxpayers involved, once their tax status had been explained to them. Agents have found that, in general, overseas taxpayers are as willing to comply voluntarily in filing proper and accurate returns as are resident taxpayers of the United States.

A correct impression is needed of American taxpayers abroad.

In the international phase of Internal Revenue activity, the public generally thinks only of Hollywood stars who have taken up residence in other countries to lessen their tax payments to the United States. While the number of such nonresidents has grown in recent years, the actual total is quite insignificant when compared with the thousands with whom International Operations has its major concern and contact.

More remains to be done.

Internal Revenue has made giant strides toward its goal of full revenue realization in the administration of U. S. tax laws overseas, but there are still some obstacles in its path. Actually, the United States is the only nation that has undertaken tax collection on a major international basis. In carrying on its activities, the Office of International Operations must be careful to avoid foreign complications either of law or of operation, and quite possibly of a diplomatic character. Significantly, the interest of other countries in both internal and external phases of this country's revenue collections is constantly increasing. More is told of this aspect of international operations in Chapter Twenty-one.

The Alcohol and Tobacco Tax Division (A&TT)

Liquor and tobacco taxes are among the earliest imposed under the internal revenue system. The first resort to internal taxes was the enactment on March 3, 1791, of taxes on distilled spirits. About the same time a tax was enacted on snuff and snuff mills. The Government's headaches from liquor taxes began early. In 1794, President George Washington had to call out the militia to put down the "whisky insurrection" in Western Pennsylvania. The farmers who produced whisky from the surplus grain rebelled at paying excises on their product. The law was repealed in 1802 abolishing all internal taxes. However, because of the effects of the War of 1812, Congress re-enacted similar laws for the period of 1813 to 1818. From 1818 until 1862 there were no internal taxes of any character.

The Act of July 1, 1862, the basis for the present internal revenue system, included taxes on liquors and tobacco. For this period through 1913, nearly 90 percent of the internal revenue came from taxes on distilled spirits, tobacco and fermented liquor.

In 1913, with the enactment of income, corporate, and more recent excise taxes, collections from liquor and tobacco taxes, while progressively increasing in dollar return in revenue, became a relatively smaller portion of the over-all tax receipts.

The enactment of the National Prohibition Act changed the Internal Revenue's responsibility regarding the production and distribution of liquors from the revenue aspect to one of police duty in the enforcement of the penal and regulatory provision of the new law. Prohibition was repealed in December 1933, and in 1934, the Alcohol Tax Unit of the Internal Revenue Service was created.

Alcohol Tax Unit became the Alcohol and Tobacco Tax Division.

The Alcohol Tax Unit was established on May 10, 1934 and made a part of the then Bureau of Internal Revenue. On June 30, 1940, the Unit took on the responsibilities of the Federal Alcohol Administration Act. On August 29, 1941, the Unit was required to administer the Federal and National Firearms Acts. All tobacco tax functions were transferred from the Bureau's Excise Unit to the Alcohol Unit on November 13, 1951, at which time the Unit's designation was changed to Alcohol and Tobacco Tax Division (A&TT).

A&TT functions through four branches.

The program areas of A&TT are:

1. *The permissive branch*
   Engaged principally in the supervision of the legitimate liquor industry.
2. *The basic permit and trade practices branch*
   Charged with the enforcement of the Federal Alcohol Administration Act and regulations relating to labeling, advertising, and unfair trade practices with respect to distilled spirits, wines and malt beverages.
3. *The tobacco branch*
   Responsible for supervision of the tobacco industry for the protection of the revenue imposed on tobacco products.
4. *The enforcement branch*
   Responsible for (1) investigating, detecting and preventing

willful and fraudulent violations of internal revenue laws relating to distilled spirits, wines, fermented malt liquors and tobacco; (2) enforcing the Federal and National Firearms Acts; the Liquor Enforcement Act of 1936; certain sections of the Federal Alcohol Administration Act; and related statutes.

The permissive branch.

The federal tax on the production and sale of alcohol, whisky, brandy, rum, vodka, gin, and liqueurs produced $2.4 billions of revenue for fiscal year 1962. These products may be produced only at plants qualified, registered, and operated under federal law and regulations.

The federal tax collection on wine and cordials for fiscal year 1962 was $100 million. With the exception of a tax-free allowance applying to 200 gallons per year made by the "head of a family," provided he registers his intent with the Internal Revenue Service, the nation's wine production and sale is closely watched and supervised by this branch.

Beer, a federal tax producer in the sum of $818 million in fiscal 1962, is also controlled.

To accomplish its task the permissive branch employs and carefully deploys storekeeper-gaugers and inspectors. These men, in person, "on the scene," carefully watch and see to it that the revenue is protected and the laws and regulations are rigidly observed.

Storekeeper-gaugers are assigned to premises established for the businesses of distilling and warehousing of spirits for beverage and industrial uses. At these premises they provide day-to-day supervision over operations concerned with production, packaging, warehousing, bottling, and denaturation.

Inspectors are responsible for examinations and audits at various establishments to determine whether operations are being properly conducted. They also see whether the premises and equipment meet the standards established by law and regulations. Inspectors check the effectiveness of on-premises supervision and review the proprietor's records (and those of the storekeepergauger) to see that the records adequately and accurately reflect the operations.

The basic permit and trade practice branch.

An important feature of the Federal Alcohol Administration Act is the protection it gives consumers of alcoholic beverages through the prohibition of false and misleading labeling and advertising.

The law requires that all members of the alcoholic beverage industry, except brewers and retail dealers, obtain basic permits. Permits serve as an effective regulatory and enforcement instrument in that they may be denied, suspended, or revoked for law violations.

The tobacco branch.

In fiscal 1962 the Federal Government collected $2 billion from this industry.

Inspectors periodically inspect tobacco producers and examine books and procedures to assure proper and complete compliance. Although violations in this area occur but rarely, this branch constantly polices the industry and applies controlling checks and balances.

The enforcement branch.

Among the most active members of government dealing with law violation are the Investigators and Special Investigators of the enforcement branch, Alcohol and Tobacco Tax Division.

These men are responsible for the investigation, prevention, and detection of violations of revenue laws relating to the manufacture, sale, and transportation of liquors.

The investigators are the successors to those who enforced the first excise law—the "revenooers." Except for short periods in revenue history, they have been tracking down illicit stills since 1791.

Today, using the latest police techniques with such modern equipment as two-way car radios and "walkie-talkies," the investigators destroy illicit plants, and arrest and prosecute the violators.

In recent years well-financed, well-organized, illegal, big-scale operations have been taking the place of the traditional small, family-type still. Since these large plants have great revenue-defrauding potential, the enforcement emphasis has been increased. Major violation cases are investigated by Special Investigators, a highly trained group.

Enforcement of firearms acts.

The National Firearms Act became law on June 26, 1934. Its purpose was to help prevent criminals from acquiring and using machine guns, silencers, sawed-off shotguns, and other weapons.

On June 30, 1938, the Federal Firearms Act was made law. This law was designed to regulate interstate traffic in firearms and ammunition, and punish the criminals who use them.

Investigators and special investigators of the enforcement branch, Alcohol and Tobacco Tax Division have, as a part of their duties, the investigation and detection of violations of these acts.

Laboratories are maintained to aid enforcement.

Modern chemical laboratories are maintained in the National Office and in each of the nine Internal Revenue regions under Alcohol and Tobacco Tax supervision. The laboratories make physical and chemical examinations of materials and samples submitted. In the enforcement field, most of the samples are illicit spirits or narcotics. In the field of legal operations the samples include thousands of industrial products produced from or with alcohol beverage products, and miscellaneous items such as soap, motor fuels, lubricants and other materials subject to excise taxes.

Chapter Twelve

THE COST OF COLLECTING TAXES

As TOTAL TAXES collected go up, the cost per dollar of intake goes down. Thus, the lowest cost ratios have been achieved during war years when revenue collections were at a peak.

The normal factors that affect the cost-collection ratio are the extent of voluntary compliance, the nature of the tax law, tax rates, non-revenue producing activities, salary levels, business conditions, and organization methods and procedures. These factors are discussed below.

A view is also presented of the relationship of costs to direct enforcement—that is, the investigative and enforcement activities that bring in the taxes not voluntarily paid. It is of special interest in the light of the recently authorized increase in Internal Revenue Service enforcement personnel.

Present low collection cost dates back to World War II.

At the end of the Civil War, collection costs were under $3 per $100 of taxes collected. In 1872, they were up to $5.30 per $100 and did not get back to the post-Civil War level until 1890. They went under $2 per $100 for the first time during the Spanish-American War, and reached a low level of 33 cents per $100 in 1918.

Costs rose again in the next two decades. They went over the dollar mark in 1922 and stayed there until 1941. With World War

II, the ratio returned to a range of 30-50 cents per $100, and has remained there ever since. In fiscal 1962, the cost was 45 cents per $100 collected, or less than half a cent for each $1 spent.

It is interesting to note that the English currently spend more than two and a half times what we do, or $1.15 per $100 of collections.

Voluntary compliance is the key factor in low-cost ratio.

The most important influence upon a favorable ratio is voluntary compliance. Down through the years, Internal Revenue officials have given full credit for the successful administration of the tax system to the compliance of the American taxpayer.

Sixty years ago Commissioner Wilson reported: "For the successful and economical manner in which the internal revenue laws have been administered, much credit is due the millions of taxpayers throughout the country for the generous, patriotic and prompt manner in which the taxes have been paid." In 1919, Commissioner Roper voiced the same sentiment when he reported, "The cost of collection has been so low that the result must be recognized as preeminently an accomplishment of the people." A similar tribute was expressed by Commissioner Caplin.

From an administrative viewpoint, tax dollars raised through direct enforcement activities are much more expensive to collect than those which flow in through voluntary compliance. Yet while enforcement is expensive, it is an integral part of the self-assessment system. The awareness that the few taxpayers who try to avoid the full payment of their taxes will be penalized through enforcement procedures bolsters the faith of the vast majority of taxpayers in the fair and just administration of the tax system.

As noted in the chapter on New Direction, the present administration is more concerned with achieving maximum voluntary compliance than with swelling the dollar volume collected through enforcement or audit activities. An example of how this concern is manifested occurred recently in the case of insurance company returns. For some years, additional assessments were made because a common practice in the insurance industry ran counter to federal tax laws. The administration officials explained to the insurance company executives what was required, and they made the necessary changes in their practice. As a result, voluntary compliance has been improved and a sizable expenditure of tax dollars for enforcement has been eliminated.

Nature of the tax laws and rates affects costs.

Some taxes are more difficult and more costly to administer than others. In the excise tax era, that is, before the income tax began to yield the bulk of the revenue, costs were directly tied to the organization needed to meet the problems of enforcement in the alcohol and tobacco tax field. Of the two, alcohol presented the greater difficulties. Men had to be assigned to primary manufacturing operations, distilling and bottling plants, and to warehouses to keep track of the alcohol produced. Control of the illegal operators, the moonshiners and bootleggers, presented especially difficult and costly problems.

In the income tax era, the character of tax administration changed drastically. From a policing operation, the administrative problems became those of developing an organization and procedures to handle enormous volumes of returns. To gain voluntary compliance with the income tax laws, public understanding of the laws and their provisions was necessary. The first all-out information campaign on a national scale was carried out in 1917. A carefully planned audit system was required in the new tax era. Also, drastic shifts in office procedures and methods were required.

With all of the increase in administrative work, the cost ratio declined because of the steadily widening tax base. The first widening occurred with the imposition of the tax on corporation income in 1909. That tax brought in $21 million the first year and required just $25,000 in collection costs—a collection rate of slightly over 10 cents per $100. Further widening of the base occurred with the passage of the Income Tax of 1913 and with the changes in income taxation made during World War I and World War II (see Chapter Two). The steady increase in the number of income tax returns filed is shown in Table 1, page 281.

Although the policing function of the Service declined in relative importance during the transition to the present tax system, it still plays an important role.

Tax rates are obviously important, for collection costs are generally the same whether the tax is at a 5, 10, or 20 percent rate. However, a higher tax rate does not always produce higher revenue.

Non-revenue producing activities are a ratio cost factor.

Non-revenue producing activities assigned to Internal Revenue by Congress have a bearing upon collection costs. In 1923, for example, nearly $9 million was spent on the regulatory function of enforcing Prohibition and the narcotic laws. This $9 million produced no direct revenue and comprised 20 percent of the year's total administration costs.

Salary levels affect costs.

Salaries have always been the major cost item in tax enforcement. In fiscal 1962, over 80 percent of the cost of collecting taxes went to pay the salaries of the men and women working for the Service. The remaining 20 percent went for printing tax forms and booklets, office rental, equipment and furniture, travel expenses, and the like.

With salaries taking the major bite of the cost dollar, stability of personnel must be maintained. In the Service, as in industry, labor turnover is costly. Before the Internal Revenue developed its present Blue Ribbon program (see page 201), with effective procedures for recruiting, training, and promoting employees, personnel turnover was a pressing problem. Employees were constantly being lost to industry, sometimes faster than they could be hired and trained.

In 1927, the Joint Committee on Internal Revenue Taxation reported that between 1919 and 1927 the cost of the constant shift in personnel was over $13 million. The report added, "This is insignificant in comparison with the actual cost resulting from loss of ability, experience, and judgment." Current efforts to maintain a top-notch, stable work force have produced good results. The loss of top personnel to high-paying industry jobs has been cut, and good efficiency levels have been maintained.

Business conditions affect collection costs.

Since the cost ratio declines as revenue increases and rises as it falls, business conditions influence the collection-cost ratio. A good business year will produce more revenue from a given tax structure than a bad one because there is more taxable income. In recession years, the cost of collection ratio suffers.

Organization, methods, and procedures are reflected in costs.

The decentralization of the Service in 1952 helped reduce costs. So, too, has modern office equipment, and the mechanical handling of returns. Commenting on the shift now under way to automatic data processing, Commissioner Caplin said, "The amazingly efficient computer of today stands in marked contrast to the methods of the early-day tax employee who, equipped with three-legged stool and green eye-shade, laboriously made his pen and ink entries in the ledgers."

Enforcement personnel pays for itself in collections.

The revenue dollars collected through direct enforcement are usually considered by Congress when additional enforcement personnel is sought by a tax Commissioner.

In 1948, Commissioner Nunan pointed out in testimony before the House Appropriations Committee, that taxes which would not have been paid but for the investigative and enforcement activities of the Service were being collected at the rate of $20 for each $1 spent. With Congress in a cost-cutting mood at that time, and making every effort to bring government spending back to prewar levels, the Revenue Service cited this 20 to 1 ratio to justify personnel increases.

The use of the 20 to 1 ratio, however, has had unfortunate consequences for Internal Revenue and taxpayers. The present Commissioner and his staff are attempting to remedy this. Among the unfortunate consequences was the practice by some revenue officials of rating agent performance by the volume of additional assessments produced, the so-called "quota system." With such a system in vogue, agents often took pride in how many dollars they were able to squeeze out of the returns they audited. They

COMPUTER CENTER. Here is some of the electronic equipment installed as part of Internal Revenue's conversion to Automatic Data Processing. It is located in the National Computer Center in Martinsburg, West Virginia. All returns will be processed here by 1965.

COMPUTER INSTALLATION. As seen from visitors' observation booth.

ROUTING RETURNS. This is the first step in the processing of tax returns. Returns are opened, scanned and directed to other departments for further handling. Most of this work is done by temporary employees hired for peak filing months.

RETURNS PILE UP. These returns are bundled into 100 unit lots for filing and processing operations. The electronic memory system of giant computers will reduce the need to dig out a specific return from this mass of paper.

sometimes called for additional assessments without regard to whether the changes in the returns were warranted.

As a result of such practices, some taxpayers, for their own protection, overstated deductions and expenses, or deliberately made errors on their returns. They expected that if a revenue agent made an additional assessment, they would only be paying the amount of tax that was rightfully due. Of course, if such a taxpayer's return was not audited, he got by with an underpayment.

The 20 to 1 ratio has been dropped.

The unfortunate consequences of the 20 to 1 ratio were soon recognized. In 1951, Assistant to the Commissioner T. C. Atkeson told the House Appropriations Committee that "we should get away from the 20 to 1 ratio for several reasons. The big reason is that we are in the business of correcting incorrectly filed tax returns, whether they are in favor of the Government or in favor of the taxpayer." But reliance on the ratio was not so easily eliminated.

In the spring of 1962, the House Appropriations Committee was concerned that the Government might not get its money's worth if more personnel were added for enforcement purposes. The Committee's report stated, "In past years the Committee has been informed that the Service would collect $20 for every $1 spent on additional personnel. That ratio has now been reduced to 6 to 1—and even that figure is not supported by the justifications."

Commissioner Caplin's comment on this report, in testimony before the Senate Subcommittee of the Committee on Appropriations, was that the 20 to 1 ratio had probably been derived by dividing the amount of additional revenue by the agents' salaries only, whereas the 6 to 1 ratio takes into account all costs, including clerks, equipment, training provision of processing additional assessments, settling appeals, handling additional fraud investigations, etc. In Commissioner Caplin's opinion, there has probably been relatively little fluctuation between comparable ratios over the last ten years. He emphasized, too, that what the Service is striving to attain is not a paper record showing more dollars collected through direct assessment, but the really valuable asset of voluntary compliance.

More enforcement personnel authorized for 1963.

Evidently Congress felt that more enforcement personnel were needed. In 1962 a law was enacted permitting an increase of 2,790 in Internal Revenue personnel for fiscal 1963. The additional manpower will be used for more audits, more mathematical checks, more tax fraud investigations, and more checks on non-filers.

Chapter Thirteen

COOPERATION WITH THE BUSINESS COMMUNITY—NEW DEPRECIATION GUIDELINES

THE COMMENT is sometimes heard that the Federal Government is not responsive to the needs and aspirations of business. Conversely, it is said that the business community is not sufficiently appreciative of what the Federal Government does in its behalf. Both of these opinions are largely distorted. Actually, there is a strong mutuality of interest between business and Government which forms the basis for broad cooperative efforts. This is especially true in the area of taxes.

The welfare of the business community is of deep concern to the Internal Revenue Service, according to Commissioner Caplin. Well it might be. Corporate income tax alone amounted to over $21 billion in fiscal 1962. Furthermore, a Commissioner these days is well aware of many of the problems faced by managers of private business and industry, for the Internal Revenue Service is itself big business. It is the largest tax administering agency in the world, responsible for roughly $100 billion in revenue.

Some of the services provided by the Internal Revenue Service to the business world, and its contacts with business and industry, are described in this chapter. An objective analysis will show that much of the work is designed to help business function more efficiently and competitively.

Advance tax rulings help business decision-making.

Taxpayers and Internal Revenue personnel may request a ruling as to the application of tax laws to specific situations. Some two-thirds of the 30,000 to 40,000 rulings issued each year are made at the request of business organizations. This vital service helps businessmen to plan transactions and project tax liability. Many of the rulings take 30 to 60 days to prepare, and highly complex cases may take even longer. Most businessmen agree that in this area the Internal Revenue Service is extremely attentive to the needs of the business community.

The people in the Service who prepare the rulings deal every day with matters involving both small and large amounts of money. The cases range from whether a particular item of jewelry sold in a small variety store is subject to federal excise tax to the tax affect of an extremely complicated reorganization of the domestic and foreign operations of a large business concern, and similar involved transactions. Typical of the complicated transactions on which the Service has ruled was the divestiture of the Dupont-owned General Motors stock, ordered by the Supreme Court. In this instance, Dupont asked Internal Revenue to provide an advance ruling on the tax consequences of the company's plans for distributing the stock.

The Internal Revenue Service recognizes that it is imperative to provide advance tax rulings in this age of complex business arrangements and high taxes. Business simply cannot afford to consummate many proposed transactions without some assurance of what the Government's position will be as to the tax consequences.

Internal Revenue intends to expand and improve this service as a necessary function of the self-assessment tax system. In line with this intention it has begun republishing certain procedures to give taxpayers clear, ready references to major rulings areas.

The procedure for obtaining rulings, the historical development of the existing liberal policy, the limitations that still exist, and other related information on advance rulings will be found in Chapter Fourteen.

Advisory Group acts as a sounding board.

The Commissioner of Internal Revenue has an Advisory Group consisting of twelve distinguished lawyers, accountants, and other executives who serve one-year terms. They are selected on the basis of prominence in the tax field, geographical considerations, and diversified interest. In 1962, the group included the former Internal Revenue Commissioner in the Eisenhower administration, Dana Latham, now a prominent Los Angeles lawyer. This group is one of Internal Revenue's most valuable sounding boards.

Every three months the Commissioner's Advisory Group assembles in Washington for a three-day session with top Internal Revenue officials and gives them the benefit of its thinking on tax administration. The Group has made outstanding contributions to the handling of current problems and to the shape of future programs to improve tax administration.

Ideas are exchanged with industry and business groups.

Many meetings and consultations with business groups are held and the expansion of such contacts throughout every level of the Service is being encouraged. The purpose of such contact is the exchange of ideas with business groups, a practice that has proved beneficial to the Government as well as to business.

In this type of meeting, Internal Revenue provides the business community with advance knowledge of major changes being made in the operations of the Internal Revenue Service. For example, when automatic data processing was projected, a series of conferences was called to explain the contemplated change (see page 81).

Following the conferences on automatic data processing, a meeting was held with representatives of a number of business and professional groups to discuss how dividend and interest payments will be affected by the taxpayer account-numbering system. In this instance, Internal Revenue Service conferred with these businessmen to get the benefit of their experience and advice before drawing up a first draft of proposed regulations in this area. The all-day session made it possible to draw up regulations with reasonable assurance that obvious stumbling blocks would be avoided. It saved both the business community and the Service much time and effort.

Industry-wide conferences are held when necessary.

On broad issues that have an industry-wide impact, Internal Revenue cooperates with the trade associations for the industries concerned. For example, the hotel industry recently was disturbed by a rumor that the Service was conducting a "drive" against conventions at resort hotels. Officials conferred on this problem with members of the American Hotel Association and the Florida Congressional delegation and asked the Association to submit a brief. On the basis of this conference and the brief, the Service made a special survey of audits of convention expenses and assured itself that there was no evidence of arbitrary disallowances because of a convention's site. Internal Revenue issued a statement to this effect. In the fall of 1961 Commissioner Caplin addressed the annual meeting of the American Hotel Association to restate Internal Revenue's position that legitimate business convention expenses will not be disallowed merely because a convention is held at a resort area.

Contact is maintained with professional organizations.

Top Internal Revenue officials in Washington and in the field maintain good working relationships and a high degree of cooperation with organized bar, business, and accounting societies, such as the American Bar Association, the Tax Executives Institute, the American Institute of Certified Public Accountants, National Association of Public Accountants, the Federal Tax Forum, and other groups.

Through these relationships the Service is able to reach 70,000 tax accountants and 8,000 tax lawyers, and through them many business organizations. These contacts include not only speaking engagements, but liaison with their committees in discussing common problems.

Internal Revenue frequently invites these professional associations to confer with Service officials in Washington or to submit written positions on technical issues in which they have an interest.

A number of discussions have been conducted with them on the subject of the responsibility of the tax advisor. Such matters as how to raise the level of tax practice, what constitutes decent standards of practice, and what good practitioners will and will not do have been discussed. There is tremendous interest in this subject, and a high degree of enthusiasm shown by practitioners to raise standards.

On the related subject of strengthening the integrity of relationships at three levels—the tax accountant and the tax attorney, the taxpayer, and the Internal Revenue Service employee—Internal Revenue officials also conferred with prominent attorneys and accountants. Again the officials were encouraged by the interest and cooperative attitude of leaders in the legal and accounting professions.

Business community is consulted on revision of forms.

Another regular point of contact with the business community is in the area of revision of tax forms. The forms committee of the Service meets annually with members of national business, law, and accounting groups to review proposed changes in the principal tax forms and to receive suggestions from them on ways to improve the forms. This cooperation goes on during the year. If a problem arises on a particular form, Internal Revenue calls on them for advice. On some occasions these groups take the initiative and make suggestions with respect to certain forms.

Sometimes a suggestion is made to Internal Revenue in a rather informal way. Early in 1961, when Commissioner Caplin was on the West Coast to address a business group, he was handed a note that read, "Your slip is showing." Naturally, he took the bait and asked for an explanation. It developed that the blue corporate income tax form was a quarter of an inch narrower than the letter-sized attachments that accompany it. Many secretaries were up in arms because of the quarter inch of white paper peeking out the side of the blue form. Tax officials looked into this matter with the Government Printing Office and, after appropriate debate, got them to add a quarter of an inch to the corporate form.

On this incident, Commissioner Caplin's comment was, "I hope that we have now satisfied these aesthetic objections adequately and that our slip will not be caught showing at the end of this tax year. I'm sure you will agree that making secretaries happy constitutes an invaluable service to the business world."

Special brochures assist business and other taxpayers.

A significant number of special brochures are published each year by Internal Revenue to assist business and other taxpayers. The "best seller" of the program is *Your Federal Income Tax.* The *Tax Guide for Small Business* is another very useful and popular publication of the Service. From this Guide, Internal Revenue has made excerpts on specific subjects and has published them as individual documents covering *Manufacturers' Excise Tax, Business Expenses, Depreciation, Amortization, Depletion,* and other subjects.

Among the publications there are also a *Tax Calendar and Check List,* which has proved particularly valuable to business groups, *Farmer's Tax Guide, Tax Guide for U. S. Citizens Abroad,* and such special publications as *How the Federal Income Tax Applies to Hurricanes, Floods, Tornadoes, Other Disasters, and Thefts.*

A special feature of this publication effort has been the development of what is called the *Mr. Businessman's Kit.* This kit contains instructions, illustrations and pertinent tax forms and is of special value to the small businessman. Revenue officers in some of Internal Revenue's districts personally deliver the kits to business taxpayers, and the reaction among businessmen has been uniformly excellent. Furthermore, it has led to better taxpayer compliance in these areas. The program benefits businessmen by giving them clear and timely instructions that keep them out of tax difficulties. It benefits the Service by eliminating at the source many problems that would otherwise have to be handled by enforcement officers.

Taxpayer assistance reaches into business community.

Internal Revenue's services in the field of taxpayer assistance and advice on preparation of income tax returns are well known. Among the millions of taxpayers who benefit by this service, a large percentage is business groups.

Annually the Service holds Taxpayer Assistance Institutes that are widely attended by business firms with large numbers of employees. These three-day sessions are held primarily for the instruction and training of selected qualified employees of business and government, who in turn will assist their fellow employees in the preparation of their returns. In this way, employees are able to obtain valuable tax assistance in their own organizations without losing time away from their work to seek aid elsewhere.

Internal Revenue has also taken other steps through educational and public information programs to promote better understanding of tax requirements. Typical of these programs was the effort to get payers of dividends and interest to remind recipients of such income to report it on their tax returns. Internal Revenue asked the cooperation of a number of major organizations in the field, such as the New York and American stock exchanges, the National Association of Securities Dealers, and the Investment Company Institute. Their response was excellent.

Cooperation with industry helps achieve New Direction goals.

The practices described above, which bring the Internal Revenue Service into contact with the business community, help to carry out the primary goal of the present tax administration, namely, better service to taxpayers.

Similarly, to implement the second goal—a vigorous but more reasonable enforcement of the tax laws—several new ideas have been introduced that are of service to business taxpayers. These are explained in the following paragraphs.

Audit problems of particular industries are identified.

The Internal Revenue Service is attempting to identify audit problems common to particular industries and is trying to resolve them before they become troublesome.

The Audit Division has initiated a plan to isolate and classify points of continuing issue between the Service and various industry, trade, and professional groups and do something to reduce their effect. It has been found that many taxpayers with complex tax problems belong to some identifiable group. A good way to resolve some of these problems, therefore, has been to work through these groups. By concentrating on the main points of tax dispute or difficulty, Internal Revenue hopes to provide guidance to these various groups and assist them in their tax planning to avoid expensive pitfalls and unnecessary litigation.

One aspect of this program has been to write audit technique guidelines for specialized industries. This approach was expected to give agents the proper knowledge and directions to conduct examinations effectively in the light of conditions peculiar to the industry. Eventually, Internal Revenue expects to have such guidelines for every major industry in the country.

To carry this idea further, in 1961, Internal Revenue began a series of meetings with industry groups to thrash out disputes before returns must be filed rather than wait for Internal Revenue people to attempt to resolve differences of interpretation of requirements in the audit process.

To get this innovation started, pilot projects were undertaken with representatives of several industries in areas in which there were new laws and some misunderstanding of their meaning. For each meeting, the agenda contained all the problem items that Internal Revenue and industry representatives could identify. The discussions helped these industries to avoid erroneous reporting, which, of course, resulted in saving time and trouble for everyone involved.

Handled as they are on the basis of a mutual consideration of common problems rather than an adversary confrontation, the meetings were well received by industry. The National Council of Salesmen's Organizations Inc. presented its Distinguished Public Service Award to Commissioner Caplin in appreciation of his leadership in setting up the meetings and for his firm but fair policy in administering the tax laws for all citizens.[1]

Experience with these pre-filing discussion meetings in 1961

---

[1] Award presented November 26, 1962.

and early 1962 encouraged Internal Revenue to extend the program to many other segments of the business world.

Quality Audit Standards program will aid business.

As part of its service to taxpayers and primarily to business, Internal Revenue has developed a Quality Audit Standards program, to guide its agents in making proper examinations of income tax returns. These examinations obviously do not require the detailed audit of a Certified Public Accountant, but will serve as a suggested guideline where closer tax examination seems warranted. These standards outline audit procedures for various enterprises of taxpayers, such as individuals, partnerships, fiduciaries and corporations, and will vary with industries.

New depreciation policy will benefit entire business community.

In 1961, tax engineers and other experts of Internal Revenue began a broad depreciation study, with particular reference to the estimated useful lives of different assets. At President Kennedy's request, Internal Revenue gave early study to the standards for estimated useful lives for textile machinery and equipment and found that the technology of the industry had progressed so rapidly in the last few years that a downward revision was in order. Accordingly, the estimated lives of textile machinery and equipment were reduced from 25 years or longer to periods of from 12 to 15 years. The reduction was expected to help the industry by enabling it to modernize, meet foreign competition, and provide jobs.

On July 12, 1962, the Treasury Department made public the new "Depreciation Guidelines and Rules" (Revenue Procedure 62-21), embodying a basic reform in the standards and procedures to be used in determining depreciation for tax purposes. Estimated useful lives for property used throughout business and industry were shortened, resulting in lower taxes throughout the business community. A new concept for gauging depreciation ceilings by arithmetical standards rather than by revenue agent opinion was introduced. Less friction between taxpayers and the Internal Revenue Service over depreciation deductions should result.

President Kennedy has hailed the new depreciation reform as a stimulant for business. He said, "By encouraging American business to replace its machinery more rapidly, we hope to make American products more cost-competitive, to step up our rate of recovery and growth, and to provide expanded job opportunities for all American workers."

A closer view of the new liberal and simplified system under which businessmen can now report the declining value of their property follows.

The New Depreciation Guidelines

For the past two decades American industry has been handicapped by the outmoded guides and procedures set forth in Bulletin F for determining the taxable lives of depreciable property. During the same two decades, most of the major industrialized nations have provided their business communities with a special incentive.

A basic reform in the treatment of depreciation was imperative. The needs were: (1) greater freedom for businessmen in determining for themselves the rate at which they would write off their equipment for tax purposes; (2) simplification of administrative procedures; (3) an objective approach to determining standards for depreciation; and (4) recognition, in a realistic manner, of the rapid pace of technological change inducing early obsolescence, and the rising costs of capital goods.

Under the new Revenue Procedure 62-21, depreciation practices are now realistic and flexible. They reflect the fast-moving pace of economic and technological change.

Not only will business benefit as American firms discard obsolete equipment and machinery under the encouragement of faster write-off, but all segments of the national economy will benefit. American products will be more competitive in the market places of the world.

Guideline lives are based on broad asset classes.

The current shorter guideline lives apply to about 75 broad classes of assets. A single industry guideline class will, in most cases, cover all of the production machinery and equipment for a business. Certain assets, in general use by all industries, such as automobiles and trucks, and office equipment, machines, and furniture, are covered by guideline classes which cut across industry lines. Three or four of the new guidelines, at most, will encompass all depreciable assets in most businesses.

This broad class approach will make it easier to achieve a reasonable over-all result in measuring depreciation than was possible under the former item-by-item guide in Bulletin F.

New Guideline lives shorter than in Bulletin F.

The new Guideline lives in Revenue Procedure 62-21 are generally about one-third shorter than the 19-year average in the superseded Bulletin F. A few examples illustrate the changes.

Under the old Bulletin F procedure, the soap industry had to depreciate the "life" of 201 separate individual items. These ranged from 6 years for fat acid pumps to 30 years for lathes used in making barrels. Under the new Guideline, all soap manufacturers are covered by the chemical industry's broad 11-year guideline. Every tax write-off related to producing soap may now be taken over 11 years. Similarly, the ice cream industry is now covered in the guideline class for food products, which is set at 12 years. Under Bulletin F there were 111 separate item lives ranging from 4 years for ice cream cans to 25 years for cast iron flavoring bottles.

For service industries, the new guideline is 10 years. The hotel industry comes within this broad class. Whereas Bulletin F called for 18 separate specified lives for equipment used in hotels, ranging from 6 years for blankets and spreads to 20 years for fire alarm and prevention equipment, now all hotel equipment has a 10-year write-off.

The new guidelines provide 40 percent or more reduction of lives for the following industries: aerospace, apparel, chemicals, fabricated metal products, lumber and wood products, nonferrous metals, professional and scientific instruments, railroad equipment, stone and clay products, ship and boat building, and textile products.

According to a Treasury Department survey conducted in 1959, the average life of production machinery and equipment reported was 15.2 years. The effect of the new Guidelines will be to reduce the average depreciable life for those assets to approximately 12 years. Some taxpayers who have justified shorter lives than the new Guidelines, will continue to use those shorter lives.

Change to new lives will not be questioned for three years.

Depreciation claimed by a taxpayer will not be disturbed if there is an over-all consistency between the depreciation schedule he uses and his actual practice in retiring and replacing his machinery and equipment.

Business has the right to begin to use the Guidelines immediately and to remain unquestioned by the Internal Revenue Service for a transitional period of three years. At the end of the three-year period, use of the Guidelines will continue to be accepted, unless there are clear indications that replacement practices do not conform to depreciation claimed, or are not showing a trend in that direction.

Reserve ratio test will cut down disputes.

A reserve ratio test is used under the new Revenue Procedure to show whether the taxpayer is in fact replacing his depreciated assets at the same rate as the useful life he is using. By applying the test, the taxpayer may justify a shorter life, or the Service may impose a longer life. An "Adjustment Table" puts limits on the correction upward or downward. The test, being based on objective standards, cuts down disputes between taxpayer and Revenue agents over depreciation deductions.

Upward adjustment will replace former "penalty rates."

"Penalty rates," used in the past to correct a too rapid rate of depreciation claimed by the taxpayer, will no longer be imposed. Instead, lives will be lengthened to correspond to the actual replacement practice justified for that guideline class, or lengthened in accordance with the Adjustment Table for class lives, whichever is shorter.

Any necessary lengthening of depreciable lives will be put into effect no earlier than the first year in which the reserve ratio test is not met, and the life cannot be justified. Lives will not be lengthened for any earlier taxable years.

Chapter Fourteen

ISSUING RULINGS AND DETERMINATION LETTERS TO TAXPAYERS

ANY TAXPAYER contemplating an investment or a transaction that would seriously affect his tax liability should take the time to look at the tax consequences before he commits himself. In the ordinary transaction, a lawyer, accountant or tax practitioner can usually tell his client what the transaction will cost in taxes. But if the transaction is unusual, complicated or uncertain in its tax implications, the tax expert himself may not be sure of the position the Internal Revenue Service will take and may recommend that an advance ruling be obtained.

The way in which the Internal Revenue Service cooperates with the business community through issuing rulings in advance of consummating the transaction has already been mentioned (page 142). Here a closer look is taken at this unique service to show how it functions. Incidentally, the U. S. Government is the only government in the world that issues tax rulings in advance of the consummation of a transaction.

What is a ruling? What is a determination letter?

A *ruling* is a statement in writing to a taxpayer from the National Office which interprets and applies the law and regulations to a specific set of facts, and states a conclusion as to the tax consequences of that particular transaction.

A *determination letter* is a written statement issued by a District Director of Internal Revenue to a taxpayer which applies the law, regulations, and published rulings to a particular set of facts. It generally has the effect of a ruling. Determination letters are issued only when it is possible to answer the taxpayer's questions on the basis of clearly established rules as set forth either by the statute or regulations, or in rulings, opinions or court decisions published in the Internal Revenue Bulletin. Requests involving any new or unusual questions must be referred to the National Office. Also certain matters are excluded from the District Director's jurisdiction.

A letter or memorandum which merely recites or paraphrases the Code or regulations or calls attention to a well-established interpretation of the law and does not present a definite conclusion based on a particular set of facts is an "information letter." It does not have the force or effect of a ruling. Generally speaking, before any information received from the Service, even though in writing, will have the effect of a ruling, it must be in response to a specific written request from a taxpayer and be based on facts presented in the request.

Letter rulings are distinguished from published rulings.

Rulings are issued to taxpayers by letter and are therefore commonly called "letter rulings." These letter rulings apply only to the specific taxpayer requesting the ruling and those taxpayers whose tax liability is directly involved in the ruling, for example, the shareholders when the ruling relates to a reorganization of the corporation.

Letter rulings are directed to a specific taxpayer, are issued as rapidly as possible, and are issued on the basis of the facts presented by that taxpayer with his problem primarily in mind. However, when a ruling has wide application or value as a precedent, it is published in the weekly Internal Revenue Bulletin, after a review by the top officials of the Service who consider its value as a precedent, its application as a general rule, etc. It is then known as a "revenue ruling."

Can a taxpayer rely on rulings given to others?

In general, any taxpayer can rely on a published or revenue ruling if his circumstances are essentially the same as those in the revenue ruling. This is not true of letter rulings. With some 30,000 to 40,000 ruling letters being issued each year, the writer and reviewer has time to consider the question presented but only from the facts presented in the request.

He has little time to consider the effect of slight variations of one or more of the facts. Therefore, a taxpayer should not rely on someone else's letter ruling even though the circumstances may appear similar. A change in the facts can affect the basis of the ruling because the law often pivots on a date, an amount, type of taxpayer, and so on. Likewise, a letter ruling issued with respect to one transaction may not be good to the same taxpayer for a subsequent transaction even on what might appear to be identical facts.

To adopt the policy of having every ruling apply generally would require each one to receive the type of review and consideration which is now reserved only for published or revenue rulings. This procedure would slow the issuance of rulings down to a trickle and taxpayers needing quick decisions would not be able to get them.

No rulings are issued where two exceptions apply.

In the following two areas, the National Office will not issue a ruling nor will a District Director issue a determination letter:

1. Where the ruling or determination request is primarily one of *fact;* for example: (a) the market value of property; (b) whether compensation is reasonable in amount; (c) whether a transfer is one in contemplation of death; (d) whether retention of earnings or profits by a corporation is for the purpose of avoiding surtax on its stockholders.

2. An obvious tax avoidance scheme.

In addition to these two general limitations, there are several others spelled out in the *regulations* which apply to the National Office, the District Directors, or both. These limitations are largely of an administrative nature. They do not change the policy of the Service to answer inquiries of individuals and organizations as to their tax status and tax effects of their acts or transactions.

Some situations "must" be ruled upon.

There are some provisions in the tax law that require the taxpayer to seek a ruling and the Commissioner to issue the ruling. For example, the Code requires the Commissioner to rule on changes in accounting methods or accounting periods and certain corporate reorganizations. Only a very few areas such as these are found in the Code. Other than these, taxpayers are not required to seek a ruling nor is the Service required to rule. The privilege of refusing to rule is exercised by the Service when it feels it needs time to explore the question or when the question appears to be susceptible to abuses.

Present liberal policy is based on fifty years' experience.

The rulings, policies and procedures of the Service have a history of fifty years, commencing with the Revenue Act of 1909 which imposed a 1 percent excise tax on corporations. This legislation, which was in effect through 1912, resulted in a flood of questions from all over the country. The adoption of the Income Tax Amendment to the Constitution and the enactment of the Revenue Act of 1913 unloosed another barrage of inquiries. A policy was adopted to answer all questions which appeared to be legitimate and proper.

This early policy was not limited to completed transactions but covered prospective transactions and hypothetical questions as well. The object was to be as helpful as possible to taxpayers in preparing their returns. Rulings on numerous hypothetical cases were published in the form of primers for the guidance of the public. Commissioner Roper stated at that time (1913-1914) that the agency's job was too big to be carried out without the cooperation of the taxpayers. Cooperation could best be secured by giving taxpayers all the assistance possible in resolving their tax problems.

As early as 1914 attempts were made to get away from answering hypothetical questions, but the practice of answering all questions continued until the sheer volume made a change in policy necessary. The complexity of the succeeding revenue acts brought so many requests for rulings from taxpayers, lawyers, and accountants that the work of answering the inquiries interfered with the ordinary duties of Internal Revenue. It was found, too, that in some instances, after giving advice upon which the taxpayers had relied, the Service reversed its position when the filed returns were examined. In those early days, rulings were merely advisory and the Commissioner did not feel bound by a ruling if it later turned out to be wrong, even though the taxpayer had relied upon it in carrying out a transaction and in filing a return.

1919 to 1935 policy. The problem became especially acute after the enactment in February 1919 of the Revenue Act of 1918. This imposed an excess profits tax as well as an income tax and was extremely complex even by today's standards. As a result, the Commissioner gave notice that rulings would be issued only in connection with completed transactions and not with respect to transactions merely proposed or planned. The Commissioner also required, for the first time, that all facts relevant to the case, including contracts and other documents, must be submitted together with the names of all the interested parties.

The policy of issuing rulings only with respect to completed transactions continued from 1919 to 1935. It was changed then to permit issuance of rulings on proposed transactions in those few instances where the statute required such a determination by the Commissioner.

Closing agreements introduced. By 1938 taxpayers and tax practitioners were becoming increasingly concerned about their inability to obtain reliable advice from the Service on the tax effects of proposed transactions. The Service and the Treasury Department recognized this as a genuine problem.

At about this time the Committee on Ways and Means of the House of Representatives recommended certain legislation which resulted in laws granting the Commissioner specific authority to enter into closing agreements on prospective transactions. The closing agreement, binding on all parties, provided for the first time a means of settling in advance the tax consequences of a proposed transaction. It gave taxpayers some assurance of certainty before entering into an important business venture.

Under the closing agreement procedure, the ruling was incorporated into a formal legal document. It was a legal agreement between the taxpayer and the Commissioner, and required the approval of the Secretary of the Treasury (or an Assistant Secretary) before it was binding. With such a cumbersome and time-consuming procedure, not many rulings could be issued.

Present procedure less cumbersome. Beginning with World War II, a vast amount of new tax legislation was put on the books and another great increase occurred in requests for rulings. Some simpler and quicker method was needed than the closing agreement procedure. It was found in the expedient of treating all requests for rulings as involving potential closing agreements. So in 1940, the Service began to issue rulings on proposed transactions without going through the formal and formidable closing agreement procedure.

After the war, at least one serious proposal was made to revert to the old procedure of limiting rulings to completed transactions. By that time, however, the liberalized program had become too deeply entrenched to be curtailed.

The present tax administration regards the existing pattern of furnishing advance rulings to individual taxpayers as beneficial to both the taxpayer and the Government. The Service expects to continue to provide rulings on contemplated actions whenever it is appropriate and consonant with the public interest and sound administration of the tax laws. Through this policy the Internal Revenue Service aims to foster confidence in the tax system and its administration.

Requests for a ruling or letter should conform to requirements.

The Service does not issue rulings or determination letters upon oral request. The procedures and requirements for asking for a ruling or determination letter are covered in full detail in Internal Revenue Bulletin 1962-47 dated November 19, 1962. The text of this Bulletin, consisting of Revenue Procedures 62-28 through 32, consolidates and brings up-to-date all the previous issuances on rulings requirements and procedures.

Requests with respect to matters on which a ruling is desired from the National Office should be addressed to the Commissioner of Internal Revenue, Washington 25, D. C. Requests with respect to matters on which a determination letter from a District Director is desired should be addressed to the office of the District Director in which the tax return is filed.

Each request for a ruling or determination letter must include a complete statement of facts regarding the transaction, including (but not necessarily limited to) the names, addresses and taxpayer identification numbers of all interested parties, the district office where each files or will file his return, together with a copy of each contract or other document necessary to present such facts. (Exhibits and documents are retained in the Service files, hence original documents should not be furnished.)

Except with respect to employment taxes (F.I.C.A., F.U.T.A., and withholding tax) and excise taxes, District Directors may not issue determination letters until after the transaction has been consummated. Thus, generally speaking, taxpayers should address all requests relating to prospective transactions to the Commissioner in Washington. If the transaction has been consummated, and the taxpayer is inquiring so he will know how to report the transaction on his tax return, the District Director will probably be able to issue a determination letter. If the District Director cannot answer the inquiry he will send it to the Commissioner. There may be instances where the National Office will refer a request to a District Director if he can act on the matter.

When documents and exhibits are submitted they must be accompanied by an analysis of their bearing on the question, specifying the pertinent provisions. If the subject matter is a corporate reorganization, distribution or similar related transaction, the corporate balance sheet nearest to the date of the transaction must also be submitted (the most recent balance sheet if the transaction is prospective).

The request must also set forth a full and precise statement of the business reasons for the transaction. If the taxpayer is contending for a particular determination, he must include an explanation of the ground for such contention together with a memorandum of relevant authorities. If it is a proposed transaction, the taxpayer must state his views as to the tax results and furnish a statement of relevant authorities to support his views, even though he is urging no particular determination.

A taxpayer may ask in his letter for a conference in Washington and it will be granted to him. At the conference he can confer with the government expert on the matter, present his views, and receive a sympathetic hearing. While the Rulings Division people are expected to discuss the issues in depth, they are not required to indicate the course of the final decision at a conference. The purpose of the conference is to afford the taxpayer an opportunity to have a free and open discussion of vital issues. For this reason it is usually not scheduled until the Service has had an opportunity to thoroughly study the issues. The taxpayer is usually entitled to only one conference. However, there are circumstances which will entitle the taxpayer to a second conference, in which case the Service will advise him of that right.

Does the Commissioner ever revoke a ruling?

Revocations seldom occur under present policy. However, the Commissioner is not bound by his own rulings and a ruling can be revoked if it appears to be wrong. In these cases the revocation or modification applies to all open years, unless the Commissioner exercises certain discretionary powers that he has and limits the retroactive effect of the revocation or modification. The Commissioner will usually exercise this authority, and not apply the revocation or modification retroactively if (1) there has been no misstatement or omission of material facts; (2) the facts subsequently developed are not materially different from the facts presented; (3) there has been no change in applicable law; (4) the ruling originally issued was with respect to a proposed transaction; (5) the taxpayer directly involved in the ruling acted in good faith in reliance on the ruling and its retroactive revocation would be to his detriment.

This generally can also be said with regard to determination letters issued by District Directors. However, a District Director cannot limit retroactive effect of a revocation or modification, but he may refer it to the Commissioner if he believes the circumstances warrant limiting the effect of the revocation.

Chapter Fifteen

THE LEGAL ADVISORS IN THE INTERNAL REVENUE SERVICE

TAXATION essentially is law. Before a tax can be levied, Congress must enact a taxing statute. Thereafter, in the assessment and collection of taxes under the statute, its terms and provisions must be carefully interpreted and properly enforced so that the intent of Congress will be fulfilled. Thus, it was early recognized that the Commissioner needed a lawyer. The activities revealed in today's complex organization of the legal branch of the Service all have to do with interpreting and enforcing the law.

First legal officer was a Solicitor of Internal Revenue.

The first legal officer for internal revenue, provided by Congress in 1866, just four years after the first Commissioner of Internal Revenue was appointed, was a Solicitor of Internal Revenue. It is an interesting sidelight that Congressional recognition of the need for a Solicitor followed the publication of a report in 1865 of a special commission investigating the administration of the internal revenue laws. The report had referred to the British practice of attaching to its revenue boards a "law officer of great ability and large salary."

The first incumbent was Walter H. Smith, a lawyer from Ohio, but there is no record that the American official got a "large salary."

First transfer was to Justice Department.

In 1870 the Department of Justice was established as an executive department of the Federal Government and the law officers associated with other departments, including the Solicitor of Internal Revenue, were transferred to the Justice Department. The purpose was to promote general consistency and harmony in the legal decisions and practices of the several solicitors. Although the Solicitor of Internal Revenue continued to serve as chief legal advisor to the Commissioner of Internal Revenue, by statute he performed his duties under supervision and control of the Attorney General.

Next transfer was to Treasury Department.

In 1926 Congress directed the creation, in the Treasury, of the Office of General Counsel for Internal Revenue. He was appointed by the President with confirmation of the Senate.

In 1934 Congress created the basic legal organization of the Treasury that exists today—the Office of General Counsel of the Treasury. In addition, the Office of Assistant General Counsel for Internal Revenue was conceived, the Assistant General Counsel to be appointed by the President and confirmed by the Senate.

The first Assistant General Counsel for Internal Revenue was Robert H. Jackson, later Justice of the U. S. Supreme Court.

Chief Counsel is top legal officer today.

Beginning in 1934, then, the law officer for Internal Revenue held office as Assistant General Counsel of the Treasury with authority to serve as chief law officer on matters of internal revenue. He began to operate under the title of Chief Counsel and his office became commonly known as the Office of Chief Counsel.

In general, the authority of the Chief Counsel and his essential relationship to the Treasury and to the Commissioner of Internal Revenue have remained unaltered since 1934. He has served and continues to serve as counsel and legal advisor to the Commissioner of Internal Revenue in all matters pertaining to the administration and enforcement of internal revenue laws. He is responsible directly to the General Counsel of the Treasury for the establishment and maintenance of appropriate standards of professional competence of his legal staff. The Chief Counsel serves as a member of the Commissioner's executive staff.

Under Reorganization Plan No. 1 of 1952, the Office of the Assistant General Counsel for Internal Revenue, the Presidential appointive office, was abolished. In its place, a new office of Assistant General Counsel with appointment under the classified civil service was provided for, and from 1952 to 1959 the Chief Counsel was appointed by the Secretary of the Treasury.

Chief Counsel reinstated as Presidential appointee.

After extensive consideration, the Subcommittee on Internal Revenue Taxation of the House Ways and Means Committee, under the chairmanship of Wilbur D. Mills of Arkansas, concluded that "the Chief Counsel should be restored to his former position as a statutory officer appointed by the President and confirmed by the Senate."

The Subcommittee noted that "the Chief Counsel occupies one of the top positions of responsibility in the enforcement of the internal revenue laws" and pointed out that the Chief Counsel "is the law officer for the Internal Revenue Service and should, therefore, be a statutory officer subject to confirmation by the Senate." The Advisory Group to the Subcommittee had previously said that the Office of Chief Counsel "is a post of severe and broad responsibilities, including major policy responsibilities, with a large and important legal staff in Washington and other legal staffs in branch offices throughout the country."

By Act of Congress, signed into law by President Eisenhower on September 22, 1959, the Internal Revenue Code was amended to provide for appointment of the Chief Counsel by the President, by and with the advice and consent of the Senate, thus restoring the office to its former status as a Presidential appointment.

Office of Chief Counsel.

The preceding paragraphs recount briefly the birth and growth of the appointive office of Chief Counsel during the first 100 years of Internal Revenue. Naturally, the brief statement oversimplifies the full experience of taxes and the law during those years. The history of legal counsel to the Commissioner is also the story of the legal staff of career internal revenue lawyers—a staff which as a continuing body over the years mirrors the dynamic growth of the American economy and attests to the increasing complexity of the tax laws.

In 1866 when the first Solicitor of Internal Revenue was appointed he counseled with respect to revenue laws when the nation had a population of 36 million. Today the population exceeds 180 million and annual tax collections total about $100 billion. The number of potential taxpayers, and thus also the number of potential tax disputes, has greatly increased. With such dynamic statistics as background, the need for constant innovation and occasional realignment in the Office of Chief Counsel is easily understood.

In 1913 a special division was created to prepare opinions interpreting the internal revenue laws. An official law library was authorized in 1917. Three years later, in 1920, with annual tax collections being counted in the billions of dollars, the legal office was organized into five specialized divisions, including one to handle civil litigation and another to enforce the criminal provisions of the tax laws.

A separate division was established in 1925 and given the function of representing the Commissioner before the U. S. Board of Tax Appeals (now the Tax Court of the United States). A legislative research section was created about 1928. Another division was organized a year later with the duty of reviewing cases involving substantial amounts of tax refunds.

The Legislation and Regulations Division was created in 1934 to assist in the development of tax legislation and regulations thereunder. Also, in 1934, a division was established to handle matters relating specifically to alcohol and tobacco taxes. And in 1942 a section was created to handle collection and compromise matters in bankruptcy and receivership proceedings.

Organization and functions today.

The Office of Chief Counsel at the centennial of Internal Revenue is a large and complex organization. It has a total working staff of 1,222 persons composed of 632 lawyers and 590 secretarial and clerical employees. Of the 632 lawyers, 246 are assigned to the National Office located in Washington; the rest are stationed in the nine regional and 23 branch offices over the nation.

Technical Divisions.

The Office of Chief Counsel performs certain functions that are of a technical nature. These technical functions fall into two general categories, each handled by separate divisions—the Legislation and Regulations Division and the Interpretative Division.

In fiscal year 1961, the Legislation and Regulations Division assisted in the formulation of the legislative provisions to implement President Kennedy's major tax revision proposals of 1961. The Division also assisted in the development and issuance of 74 Treasury decisions (regulations), 6 Executive orders, and 59 notices of proposed rule making, relating to tax matters, touching on issues of extreme importance and complexity.

During fiscal year 1961, the Interpretative Division disposed of 664 separate matters, many of which included legal review of important and significant revenue rulings published in the Internal Revenue Bulletin.

Litigation Divisions.

The Office of Chief Counsel represents the Commissioner before the Tax Court and advises him on other litigation, civil and criminal. Six divisions in the National Office are characterized as litigation divisions—the Tax Court Division, the Refund Litigation Division, the Joint Committee Division, the Collection Litigation Division, the Enforcement Division, and the Alcohol and Tobacco Tax Legal Division.

In a very real sense, litigation is a major function of the office. Of the total legal staff, national and regional, well over two-thirds work principally in the so-called litigation area. During fiscal year 1961, litigation personnel disposed of over 26,000 cases.

Tax Court Division.

This Division develops policies, programs, and procedures relating to the disposition of tax cases pending in the Tax Court, supervises and coordinates the defense and settlement of such cases to assure uniform treatment, and performs other legal duties.

In fiscal year 1961, taxpayers filed some 5,300 petitions with the Tax Court on top of a pending Tax Court caseload at the beginning of the year of around 12,600. Approximately 6,800 Tax Court cases were disposed of during the year. As of June 30, 1961, about 11,100 cases were pending in the Tax Court involving deficiencies and penalties in dispute of nearly one billion dollars.

Refund Litigation Division.

This Division performs all necessary legal service on behalf of the Internal Revenue Service in connection with taxpayers' suits filed in federal district courts and the U. S. Court of Claims for refund of taxes (except alcohol and tobacco taxes). It determines and coordinates the legal position of the Service in such suits and incorporates such determinations in recommendations to the Department of Justice with respect to the defense, acceptance or rejection of settlement proposals, and appeals for adverse court decisions in such cases.

The ultimate responsibility, however, in cases filed in the federal district courts and the U. S. Court of Claims is with the Department of Justice, and the ultimate control in matters of appeal is vested with the Solicitor General. By long-established custom, however, the Chief Counsel is called upon to make recommendations on these questions to the Justice Department and the Solicitor General.

During fiscal year 1961, the Refund Litigation Division received a total of over 1,300 new cases, and closed a total of 1,200 cases. As of June 30, 1961, there were over 3,000 cases pending in the federal district courts and Court of Claims which involved close to one-half billion dollars in taxes.

Joint Committee Division.

The Internal Revenue Code provides specifically that no refund or credit of tax in excess of $100,000 shall be made except with special review by the Joint Congressional Committee on Internal Revenue Taxation. To implement this statutory requirement, a separate division, known as the Joint Committee Division, reviews all proposed refunds or credits of income, excess profits, estate, gift, and miscellaneous taxes in excess of $100,000. If the proposed refund is approved, it also supervises the preparation of a report to be submitted to the Congressional Committee. A total of 723 cases involving overassessments of $372 million was reported during fiscal year 1961 to the Committee.

Collection Litigation Division.

This Division supervises and coordinates legal work of Regional Counsel on tax collection matters. It reviews certain offers in compromise, handles the legal work concerning certain Bankruptcy Act proceedings, and prepares or reviews recommendations to the Department of Justice on questions relating to appeal, settlement, and other miscellaneous matters in collection cases.

During fiscal year 1961, the Collection Litigation Division and Regional Counsel, Collection Litigation, disposed of over 10,000 collection matters.

Enforcement Division.

This Division handles and prepares for final decision criminal tax cases referred to the Chief Counsel by Regional Counsel or by the National Office. It considers cases in which a Regional Commissioner and the Director of the Intelligence Division of the Office of the Assistant Commissioner (Compliance) do not concur in recommendations of Regional Counsel involving prosecution.

A total of over 1,700 criminal cases, including headquarters and field cases, were disposed of during fiscal year 1961. Taxes and penalties aggregating almost $97 million were involved in cases with recommendations of prosecution.

Alcohol and Tobacco Tax Legal Division.

This Division handles the legal work arising in connection with the administration of laws pertaining to alcohol and tobacco taxes and various regulatory laws pertaining to alcohol and firearms, enforcement of which is vested in the Internal Revenue Service.

Over 4,600 cases involving alcohol and tobacco matters were disposed of during fiscal 1961.

Office of Regional Counsel.

There are nine Regional Counsels, one in each Internal Revenue region. The Regional Counsel, who operates under the Chief Counsel for the Service, serves as the principal legal advisor to the Regional Commissioner and to the District Directors within his region. He directs a staff of attorneys engaged in furnishing legal advice and performing legal services connected with the Tax Court, enforcement, collection litigation and alcohol and tobacco tax programs. The Regional Counsel, with the concurrence of the Regional Commissioner, settles tax cases docketed in the Tax Court, and represents the Commissioner in the trial of such cases before the Tax Court.

Chapter Sixteen

TAX ENGINEERS AND THE DEPLETION PROBLEM

THE AUDIT OR INVESTIGATION of information given in tax returns is ordinarily the responsibility of a revenue agent. He is a skilled and competent accountant and may indeed be a Certified Public Accountant or lawyer as well. Since a tax return is in reality merely a profit and loss statement, and where a balance sheet is involved a statement of net worth as of a given date, the revenue agent's examination entails primarily questions of an accounting or tax law nature.

However, some of the elements from which the profit or loss or net worth are derived are accounting features that involve engineering principles. For example, engineering principles are involved in determining which phases and costs of an integrated operation are mining and which are manufacturing. The distinction between the two must be made in order to arrive at the allowable depletion deduction under existing law. Similarly, engineering principles are involved in arriving at valuations and depreciation, which likewise are reflected in profit and loss statements and balance sheets. The Internal Revenue engineer acts, in a sense, as a professional consultant or advisor to the revenue agents on matters involving engineering principles.

A brief explanation is given in this chapter of some of the problems with which the tax engineers cope in enforcing the laws. The especially difficult and often controversial problems of the depletion deduction in returns of taxpayers with "wasting assets" like minerals, oil and gas, is treated at some length. The explanation throws light on a subject that challenges the understanding of the average taxpayer.

Engineers' contribution is vital.

On the employment rolls of the Internal Revenue Service are 40 engineers in the National Office and 130 field engineers who are permanently situated in 39 of the district offices located in major cities of the nation. These field engineers are specialists in five principal types of engineering: industrial, public utility, oil and gas, mining, and forestry. They are assigned to district offices largely on the basis of the industrial activity prevalent in the area or the volume of returns filed locally that contain engineering features.

The broad engineering activities engaged in by the five categories of engineers is brought out in the summary given below of the major problems with which they deal.

Apart from assuring taxpayers that their technical problems will receive competent, skilled, and qualified attention, the engineer makes a major contribution to the nation's overall tax enforcement program. He operates in a field that vitally affects the taxpayer and the Government's intake of revenue.

Advances in technology, automation, other mechanization, and the changing economic conditions in manufacturing and extractive industries give rise to an increasing number of problems requiring engineering knowledge. Though the problems center mainly on questions concerning depletion of mineral properties, the depreciation of equipment, and the valuation of all types of assets, the tax engineers make a valuable contribution to the prompt and efficient disposition of any problem entailing a knowledge of engineering principles.

Industrial engineers—problem areas.

Industrial engineers are located in the larger cities of the nation. They are primarily engaged with complex problems of depreciation or valuation arising from the high degree of industrialization in our economy. The most common specific problems involve:

–determination of the useful life and salvage value of all types of manufacturing machinery and physical property assets;

–proper tax treatment of repair, research and development expenditures;

–fair market value determinations in connection with the sale or liquidation of assets or for estate tax purposes;

–determination of the allowable amount of loss deduction for casualties, abandonments, demolition or obsolescence losses of property retired or about to be retired.

Public utility engineers–problem areas.

Public utility engineers deal with the technical tax problems involved in the communications, transportation, and power industries. Specifically, they are concerned with problems involving:

–the useful life and salvage value determination for railroads, electrical plants, television and radio facilities, and telephone equipment;

–proper treatment of repair and maintenance charges for these industries;

–fair market value determinations in connection with the sale or liquidation of assets and the establishment of basis from valuation and allocation;

–determination of allowable losses from retirement, abandonment, obsolescence, or casualty;

–valuation of intangibles–going concern value, goodwill, etc.–in the sale or purchase of capital assets.

Oil and gas engineers–problem areas.

Oil and gas or petroleum engineers are engaged with the multitude of tax problems that arise in the petroleum industry, mainly stemming from depletion provisions of the tax law, and the valuation problems that arise in the natural resources industries. They are most commonly concerned with such specific problems as:

–determining the proper depletion deduction, involving such details as allocating overhead, computing gross income, determining field price of natural gas, establishing existence of an economic interest, and oil or gas reserve determinations;

–establishing loss deductions involving the abandonment of worthless mineral interest;

–determining and defining intangible drilling and development costs for oil properties;

–proper treatment to be given to geological and geophysical expenditures made for the purpose of finding new sources of oil or gas;

–determining fair market value in the sale or liquidation of mineral assets as well as for estate and gift tax purposes;

–allocating purchase price and establishing basis for depletable and depreciable property. (Note that depreciable recovery is limited to basis, whereas depletable is not, increasing the importance of a correct determination here.)

Mining engineers–problem areas.

Mining engineers deal with problems similar to those in the oil and gas industry but unique to the mining industry. In addition to the problems generally outlined above for the oil and gas engineer, the mining engineer is specifically concerned with the problems of:

–establishing the proper cut-off point for mining versus manufacturing or processing operations of integrated producers, in order to properly compute the depletion allowance under the law.

–determining the proper treatment of exploration and development expenditures with the necessary consideration of the particular factors of mining methods, estimated costs and profits, etc.

Timber engineers–problem areas.

Timber engineers or foresters are engaged principally in depletion or valuation problems connected with the forest products industries. Special problems arise from capital gains provisions of the Internal Revenue Code together with questions concerning the basis of timber property. In addition, they must deal with problems involving the determination of the useful lives of logging equipment, sawmill machinery, and forest roads.

Tax Areas Involving Engineering Problems

Two broad tax areas involving engineering problems are treated briefly below: (1) Depreciation and determination of useful lives of assets; (2) determination of exploration costs of mines. A third area, depletion of oils, minerals, and other wasting assets, is discussed more fully beginning at page 176. The many problems involved in fair market determination are not mentioned, but from the problems implied in the three areas presented, it can readily be seen that the tasks of the tax engineer are formidable.

Reasonableness is stressed in approaching these complex technical problems. The Internal Revenue Service therefore tries to attract engineers who have good engineering qualifications plus an objectivity and facility of mind that permits them to see the taxpayer's side and the Government's side of the problems involved. Since this important field of tax law enforcement demands and requires the application of good judgment and reason, the Service has relatively high standards of qualifications for the job of tax engineer.

Depreciation and determination of useful lives of assets.

Depreciation may be briefly defined as the writing down of the cost of buildings, equipment, and other limited-life assets because of wear and tear from use or disuse, obsolescence, accidents, or inadequacy. Depreciation is loss of value; deterioration is loss of substance. In general, depreciation assigns to a fiscal period a portion of the original cost of the capital assets. This portion is computed in many ways depending on the type of asset, the nature of the enterprise employing the asset, and the financial needs of the enterprise. The various methods of arriving at depreciation are not pertinent to this discussion, though they are part of the knowledge of all tax engineers and revenue agents.

The tax engineer looks at depreciation as that element of value of production facilities consumed, representing the unit of original cost to be recovered by the goods or services produced and sold. The determination of production costs and the correct profit or loss of any business enterprise must consider this consumption factor to provide for the recovery of capital investment and the going concern nature of business.

Under the present law and traditional accounting concepts, the total depreciation over the life of an asset may not exceed its original cost or other basis. This reflects the view that the cost of a fixed asset is a prepaid expense and the deduction is for the purpose of measuring the annual conversion of the asset into cost in order to determine the profit or loss.

The engineering problems include the determination of the useful lives of assets to a particular taxpayer or, in simple terms, the length of time over which he is permitted to recover his cost. This determination is based on the actual use made of assets and experience evinced from the taxpayer's own operations. Useful lives are usually determined by actual records of use.

The new depreciation guidelines issued in 1962 have established useful lives for equipment that are much closer to the lives actually used by industry than the old depreciation schedule. The present guidelines also enable business to elect equipment lives as short as they are able to justify by actual replacement practices.

Determination of exploration costs of mines.

Under the law, taxpayers are permitted to charge mine exploration costs to expense up to $100,000 for any one year, and limited to four years, or $400,000 total cost. Further exploration costs must be capitalized, while all development costs may be deducted as current expense if development costs are not amortized.

Exploration costs are those incurred for the purpose of determining the existence, location, extent, and quality of the deposit. Development costs are those made to render the ore accessible when the mine or deposit could "reasonably justify commercial exploitation."

Depletion of Oil and Gas, Ores, etc.

Minerals, oil and gas, other natural deposits (including soil in place) and timber are wasting assets. Whenever any of them is removed from its natural position or native state, the original amount is reduced by just that much. This gradual reduction is known as "depletion," and to compensate for it the law allows an annual depletion deduction.

The theory behind the depletion allowance must be understood for a comprehension of why there is this legitimate deduction from income for tax purposes, and how it differs from a direct subsidy.

The subject of depletion, it will be seen, is fraught with problems, many of which have thus far defied solution.

Theory behind the depletion allowance.

Perhaps the best reasoning for the allowance of a depletion deduction was expressed by Mr. Justice Brandeis in U.S. v. Luday, 274 U.S. 295 (1917), where he said:

> The depletion charge permitted as a deduction from gross income in determining the taxable income of mines for any year represents the reduction in the mineral contents of the reserves from which the product is taken. The depletion affected by operation is likened to the using up of raw material in making the product of a manufacturing establishment. As the cost of the raw material must be deducted from the gross income before the net income can be determined, so the estimated cost of the part of the reserve used up is allowed.

Later the Supreme Court again likened the depletion deduction to the consumption of raw materials in manufacturing, when it stated in Anderson v. Helvering, 320 U. S. 404 (1940) that:

> Oil and gas reserves, like other materials in place, are recognized as wasting assets. The production of oil and gas, like the mining of ore, is treated as an income-producing operation, not as a conversion of capital investment as upon a sale, and is said to resemble a manufacturing business carried on by the use of the soil. . . . The granting of an arbitrary deduction, in the interests of convenience, of a percentage of the gross income derived from the severance of oil and gas, merely emphasizes the underlying theory of the allowance as a tax-free return of the capital consumed in the production of gross income through severance.

In essence, then, the depletion deduction is a matter of legislative action, enacted by Congress under the 16th Amendment, and which the Supreme Court of the United States has likened to the consumption of raw materials in a manufacturing process, the costs of which are deducted from gross income to arrive at taxable net income. The mineral producer is therefore allowed a deduction from his gross income for the severance of the minerals from their place in the earth.

With these broad principles in mind, many of the current specific depletion problems can be placed in better perspective. Most, if not all, of the serious problems surrounding this issue stem from a misinterpretation or misapplication of these fundamental concepts, together with a lack of reasonableness, sometimes, in approaching this complex section of the law.

History of depletion allowance reflects continuing difficulties.

The first income tax law under the 16th Amendment to the Constitution provided, in addition to an allowance for depreciation which had been present in prior acts, a deduction for depletion of ores and all other mineral deposits not to exceed 5 percent of the gross value of the output at the mine or well for which the computation was made. This provision was in effect a limitation of depletion based on cost and was not sufficient to recoup in some cases the cost of the natural deposit over the life of the property.

1916 Act. The Act of 1916 removed this limitation and provided that the total depletion allowable over the life of the property could not exceed the capital originally invested, or in the case of a purchase made prior to March 1, 1913, the fair market value as of that date. That law stated that the recovery of the investment or March 1, 1913 value for any year must be in the same ratio that the recovery of minerals for the taxable year bore to the estimated total recoverable reserves in the property.

1918 Act. The next change of any importance occurred in 1918 when, due to the demands made upon our natural resources by World War I, an effort was made to encourage their discovery and exploitation.

The law contained the provision "that in the case of mines, oil and gas wells, discovered by the taxpayer on or after March 1, 1913, and not acquired as a result of purchase of a proven tract or lease, where the fair market value of the property is materially disproportionate to the cost, the depletion allowance shall be based upon the fair market value of the property at the time of the discovery, or within 30 days thereafter. . . ."

This provision resulted in a great expansion in the exploration for natural resources, especially oil and gas. It brought with it, however, many administrative difficulties. In the first place, what were the limitations of the area of production which was discovered by one oil and gas well, or by the finding of a high grade mineral? In the case of oil and gas, it was finally decided that each well which was drilled on a location not proven to have oil at the time of the acquisition by the driller, and which produced in sufficient quantities to indicate a value disproportionate to the cost of acquisition, development and operation, would be considered to be a discovery well.

In the case of mines, there was no limitation as to acreage as long as the acreage belonged to the discoverer. Any mineral deposit discovered by a taxpayer, the value of which could be proven to be materially disproportionate to the cost of acquisition, development, and operation (that is, which could reasonably be expected to produce a good profit) was considered to have been discovered to the limit of the deposit within the acreage owned or controlled under the apex law by the discoverer. This, of course, necessitated the determination of the limitation of the mineral deposit or the valuable portion of it. It was often found that one tract or lease contained more than one deposit, each entirely separate from the others, which were therefore possible of independent discovery.

When, as was usually the case, there were many operators in the same oil and gas field, and in some cases, in mineral areas, taxpayers were inclined to question the correctness of the determinations of discovery value, since some discoveries were necessarily entitled to a much larger depletion unit than others. While such differences were easily explained to mining engineers and geologists who are familiar with the variations in value of properties lying side by side, they were not so apparent to the members of Congress. Therefore, when such discrepancies were brought to the attention of the lawmakers, they were inclined to question the work of the Internal Revenue Service and to look for some other method of reaching the desired result.

1926 and 1932 Acts. In the Revenue Act of 1926, discovery value depletion was replaced by so-called percentage depletion in the case of oil and gas. Under this provision, any producer of oil and gas or owner of an interest therein, such as a royalty owner, was entitled to deduct 27½ percent of his gross income realized from the sale of oil and gas but not to exceed 50 percent of the net income from the property. This 50 percent limitation was the same as that included under the discovery value depletion provisions. In 1932 this provision was extended to include coal, metals, and sulphur, but at the rate of 5 percent, 15 percent, and 23 percent, respectively, rather than 27½ percent of the gross income, all being limited to 50 percent of the net income from the property.

During the period from 1932 to the outbreak of World War II, there was very little interest expressed in the depletion provisions of the income tax laws. It was a period during which the new conceptions resulting from percentage depletion were being applied to limited sections of the mining industry without great awareness on the part of the rest of the producers of minerals. With the start of World War II, however, the demand for minerals in the United States was greatly expanded and it became necessary to encourage mineral production in many other categories than those already covered.

War and post-war enactments. The Revenue Acts enacted during World War II extended percentage depletion to include barite, beryl, ball and sagger clay, feldspar, fluorspar, flake graphite, lepidolite, mica, potash, rock asphalt, spodumene, talc, and vermiculite, all at the rate of 15 percent. It was the expressed intention of Congress to limit percentage depletion on these additional minerals to the period of the war emergency. However, on completion of the war, the right to percentage depletion was continued on these minerals; and was extended to include bauxite, bentonite, china clay, gilsonite, phosphate rock, pyrophyllite, thenardite, and trona, all at 15 percent.

By the time the 1951 Revenue Act was under consideration, many of the producers of other minerals believed that they were being discriminated against since their products were in competition with those that were allowed percentage depletion. As a result, 35 additional minerals were named as being subject to percentage depletion—16 at 5 percent, 9 at 10 percent, and the remainder at 15 percent of gross income, all being limited to 50 percent of net income from the property.

When the Code was re-examined and redrafted in 1954, discovery depletion was eliminated, and all minerals, unless they were extracted from the air, water, or similar inexhaustible sources, were made subject to percentage depletion. There are now 104 mineral categories set forth in the law and regulations.

Problems of percentage depletion.

While the computation of percentage depletion appears to be simple, it has given rise to many problems which so far have defied satisfactory solution. One of the principal difficulties is the lack of a precise definition of the various minerals, some of which may be entitled to 5 percent, others to 10 percent, and some to 15 percent.

For example, limestone, when used as a crushed rock, is certainly nothing more than stone which is subject to 5 percent depletion. Many times, however, limestone may be high in magnesium carbonate, which, while not sufficient to meet the mineralogical definition of dolomite, may be sold on the market because of its magnesium carbonate content. Both dolomite and magnesium carbonate are entitled to 10 percent. Should this same rock when it is sold as crushed rock be entitled to only 5 percent or to 10 percent?

The same question applies to limestone of chemical or metallurgical grade. The use of limestone for chemical purposes or in metallurgy is dependent to a great extent on its availability. Thus, a low grade of limestone may be so used in certain localities while a high grade of limestone may be used as crushed rock in other localities. The classification of the limestone under such circumstances determines whether the allowance shall be 15 percent or 5 percent.

Another example is gypsum, which was not specifically named in the 1951 Act. Many producers of gypsum wanted to deduct percentage depletion on the theory that it was a stone although it was not used as a stone. Others wanted it to be excluded from the percentage depletion provisions because they had discovered deposits which, under the discovery provisions, entitled them to larger depletion deductions.

Many other examples could be given, such as the difficulty of determining whether clay is ordinary brick and tile clay or refractory and fire clay, or whether thenardite should include other forms of sodium sulphate.

Problem of gross income is a difficult one.

One of the principal difficulties of applying percentage depletion is the determination of what constitutes gross income from mining. Many of the producers of minerals also market a product that is plainly not the result of mining, such as finished brick and tile sold by producers of clay. The specific words of the statute when taken out of context appear to justify the allowance of depletion on the finished brick and tile, since it is the first marketed product, but it is not the commercially marketable mineral product. The same problem arises in varying degrees in many other mineral deposits. As a result, the Internal Revenue Service has been faced with the difficult task of drawing a distinct line in each mineral industry beyond which the process applied shall not be considered mining, and the income from which shall not be entitled to percentage depletion.

The underlying principle on which Internal Revenue has based its regulations and its position before the courts has been that a miner is entitled to separate two minerals, to eliminate waste, to sort the product, such as in the case of sand and gravel, and to prepare the mineral for shipment from the mine or treatment plant.

The position of the Service as to particular minerals has been successfully challenged by taxpayers in a number of court cases, and Congress has in some instances authorized the classification of certain processes which go beyond the limits believed by the Service to be authorized by the general tax law provisions. The addition of many minerals to the list subject to percentage depletion in the 1951 Act, the complete elimination of discovery valuation, and the inclusion of all minerals under the provision for percentage depletion in the 1954 Code have presented the Service with a greatly magnified problem as to "ordinary treatment processes" necessary to produce the natural resource, the income from which is subject to depletion.

Rulings have been made in a number of instances concerning individual minerals, but subsequent experience has proved that some of these rulings were too hastily promulgated and without sufficient understanding of the industries' customs.

Other questions harass the Service and the taxpayer.

Since the depletion allowance is limited to 50 percent of the net income from the property, two additional questions are presented: first, what is the net income from the property, and second, what is the property?

What is the net income?

In the case of a mineral producer who does nothing more and has only one mine, the term "net income from the property" is relatively easy of application, since in the ordinary case there is no income from non-mining activities and there is no expense not applicable to mining. However, there are some instances where even such an operator may sell excess power or receive rent for the use by his neighbor of some of his mining equipment. The income from such activities is not income from mining and therefore both the receipts and expenditures relating to them must be excluded from the depletion computation.

In the case of those producers who process the minerals beyond "ordinary treatment processes," it is necessary to determine the portion of the operating expenses, as well as the gross income previously discussed, which is applicable to the mining operation. These costs, which must be allocated, include such things as officers' salaries and overhead, charitable contributions, taxes, etc. Such allocation is sometimes made in the ratio of direct costs of operation attributable to mining and subsequent operations, but other methods are sometimes more applicable, such as the time devoted by officers to the different activities.

What constitutes the property?

The problem of what constitutes the property has proved to be most troublesome. The question first arose in oil and gas, and the original decisions of the courts upheld the idea that the property was each separate tract or lease. Later, due to the development of the preferential treatment of capital gains, it became necessary to determine the period of ownership of property, and the date of acquisition consequently became very important. As a result, property was defined to mean each separate interest owned by the taxpayer in each mineral deposit in each separate tract or parcel of land. This definition was incorporated in the 1954 Internal Revenue Code.

At the same time, it was recognized that strict compliance with the definition was impossible in some cases. An election was therefore incorporated in the same section of the law, allowing the taxpayer to aggregate or treat as one property any two or more of such interests, provided they were within one operating unit. This election to aggregate must be made when the first expenditure after acquisition is made and is binding for all later years unless the Secretary of the Treasury or his delegate consents to a different treatment. His consent is not to be based on any tax consequences but on the facts of the situation; that is, are the properties which have been aggregated no longer operated as a unit or are those formerly in two operating units now operated as a single unit? Any properties which are not aggregated must be maintained separately, since only one aggregation may be made within one operating unit.

Many problems connected with this aggregation provision have yet to be solved. One of the principal difficulties is presented by tracts with multiple producing sands. In the case of such multiple sands it has been the custom, authorized by the regulations, to allow the different sands within one lease to be combined in computing percentage depletion, while under the new provisions of the 1954 Code, such a combination in the case of one lease would preclude a similar combination on any other lease within the operating unit unless the second lease was aggregated with the first. This results in compulsory aggregation of all the leases within an operating unit if the taxpayer wants to combine the various producing sands within each lease.

Another feature of the property question which has proved difficult is the determination of the operating unit within which an aggregation may be made. Such a determination must be made on the basis of the facts in each case. The distance of one lease from another certainly cannot be considered controlling. For example, two leases on opposite sides of a mountain or a deep valley might be very difficult to operate as a unit, even though only a mile or two apart, while leases or tracts in the plains area of the United States where transportation is easy might be operated as a unit even though separated by great distances. Some of the factors considered are interchangeability of equipment and labor, and common field supervision.

Determination of the character of an interest.

Any allowance of depletion depends on the ownership by the taxpayer of a capital interest which is depleted by the production and sale of the mineral. The Supreme Court of the United States has made it abundantly clear that this interest, which it calls an "economic interest," does not depend upon the legal niceties of the conveyancer's art but rather upon the economic consequences of the relationship between the parties involved.

Many situations still exist in which the determination of the character of the interest owned is very difficult. An economic interest may include that of operating owners, lessee, lessor, a net profits interest, as mentioned above, oil or mineral payments, etc. Under the original revenue acts, only the land owner was considered to be entitled to depletion, since he was the only one recognized as having title to the mineral in place. The Supreme Court held, however, that a lessee who had the right to reduce the mineral to possession also had title to a share of the mineral in place.

This concept was later broadened by the Supreme Court so that one who must look entirely to the recovery and sale of the mineral for the recovery of his investment would not be differentiated from one who had legal title to the mineral in place. As a result of this broadened concept, it is now possible to recognize the interests of anyone who has contributed to the acquisition, exploration or development of a producing property and who receives his income entirely as a result of the production and sale of the mineral as being a depletable economic interest, even though such interest has no responsibility for the production of the mineral.

This interpretation applies especially to geologists who contribute their services in exploration, to lawyers who contribute their services in the acquisition of the property, and to drillers and equipment dealers who contribute services or equipment in the development of the property without compensation other than the interest in the income to be produced. Any cost of such investors, even though it may be represented by equipment, becomes the cost of the economic interest acquired, returnable only through depletion.

Development stage and operational stage must be identified.

The basis for depletion, other than discovery and percentage depletion, is the cost, March 1, 1913 value, or value upon acquisition in certain cases. The cost of exploration has been recognized as capital cost and to the extent that it results in the acquisition or retention of properties, such cost becomes part of the depletable base of the property. Originally, the cost of development of mines was considered capital to be added to the acquisition and exploration costs to be recovered through depletion.

It was recognized to be impossible to determine with exactness what expenditures in a mine were development and what were operational costs, since development continues to occur to some extent throughout the life of a mine. For this reason, the life of the mine was divided into two stages, the development stage and the operational stage.

During the development stage, all expenditures in excess of receipts were considered to be capital costs to be recovered over the life of the mine after it reached the operational stage. The mine was considered to have passed from a development to a producing status when the major portion of the mineral production was obtained from workings other than those opened for the purpose of development, or when the principal activity of the mine became the producing of developed ores rather than the development of additional ores of mining.

After the mine had passed into the operational stage, expenditures were deductible, except that extraordinary development which benefitted ore which would be recovered over a considerable period in the future had to be deferred and recovered in step with the production of the ore so benefitted. It was not, however, included in the depletable base and was therefore recoverable in addition to, rather than as part of, percentage depletion.

Professional engineers can help management.

This brief recital of some of the problems faced by the Service tax engineers suggests that they are also the problems of the professional engineers, lawyers and accountants who serve the industries affected. The Internal Revenue people feel that the professional engineers can make an important contribution in this area by providing management with informed advice where engineering and tax law overlap.

Chapter Seventeen

INTELLIGENCE OPERATIONS AGAINST FRAUD AND CRIME

IN THE FORTY-THREE YEARS of its existence, the Intelligence Division has become known as one of the most dynamic and effective federal law enforcement agencies. Its agents have been popularly called "the giant killers" for their success in bringing to book on tax charges notorious violators of other laws, many of whom seemed at times to be beyond the reach of all authority.

The Division carries on a tax fraud investigation program, conducts coordinated raids against wagering tax violators, and investigates the tax affairs of major racketeers. These activities, with special attention to the tax aspects of the gambling business, are treated in this chapter.

How the Intelligence Division was set up.

The origin of the Intelligence Division as a distinct law enforcement agency is unusual and interesting. In 1919, six years after the enactment of the basic income tax law, many serious complaints reached the then Commissioner of Internal Revenue, Daniel C. Roper (later Secretary of Commerce), concerning alleged tax frauds and dishonest employees.

Commissioner Roper had previously served as First Assistant

Postmaster General and had become familiar with the work of the Post Office inspectors who investigate frauds in the use of the mails and occasional cases of dishonesty among Post Office workers. The Commissioner decided to create an Intelligence Division to make similar investigations in Internal Revenue.

On July 1, 1919, with the approval of the Secretary of the Treasury and the Postmaster General, six Post Office inspectors were transferred. One of these, the late Elmer L. Irey, was chosen to head the new unit. He became a famous figure in American law enforcement when his special agents later sent to prison many notorious gangsters, racketeers, and other criminals.

The Intelligence Division, grown from this small nucleus, now consists of approximately 1,600 trained technical employees, most of whom are either accountants, lawyers, or both.

An impressive record has been made.

Although approximately 1,600 special agents may appear to be a very limited force when spread over 62 different district offices throughout the nation, actually cooperation with other Internal Revenue divisions brings thousands more into the picture.

Intelligence works closely with the many Internal Revenue agents (Audit Division), Revenue Officers (Collection Division), and representatives of the International Operations Division, both here and abroad. Thus about 20,000 trained people cooperate and coordinate their examinations. This points up the risk anyone takes who willfully attempts to evade or defeat the payment of his proper income tax.

Responsibilities of the Intelligence Division.

The Intelligence Division is the enforcement arm of the Internal Revenue Service. Its jurisdiction includes the investigation of all alleged criminal violations arising under the internal revenue laws except for those relating to narcotics, alcohol, tobacco, and firearms. Such criminal violations relate to defrauding the revenue, the excise and occupational taxes on wagers, and interference with the administration of the internal revenue laws.

The majority of prosecutions involve willful attempted evasion of taxes. This includes income, estate, gift, excise, wagering, and withholding and social security taxes. Failure to file tax returns of all kinds constitutes another major portion of prosecutions. Other violations include willful failure to furnish required statements and information; willful failure to keep records; willful failure to pay or collect tax; filing false claims or statements; aiding and assisting in the preparation or presentation of a false document or statement; forcible rescue of seized property; conspiracy relating to the above acts; failure to obey summons; and concealment of assets.

The investigations are made to develop conclusive proof for presentation to the courts in criminal cases.

Duties of the Special Agent.

The primary functions of a Special Agent are identification of subjects for investigation, the gathering of evidence relating to such subjects by investigative procedures; the submitting of such evidence by written report; the recommending of appropriate penalty action, both criminal and civil, based on the evidence obtained and the established policies. They assist various government counsel in the appropriate criminal and civil courts and serve in many instances as the Government's chief witness at trial.

The investigation of fraud or other criminal violation cases may stem from information discovered by Internal Revenue Agents in the course of their audits and examinations; by Special Agents who have the responsibility of developing fraud cases; from surveys conducted for the purpose of identifying areas of evasion; through analyses of other cases; from information coming to the attention of other Internal Revenue employees. Investigations may also originate from information received from other government agencies, from banks, from newspaper items, and from the general public.

Steps taken by a Special Agent in a tax evasion case vary according to the particular case. Usually it will involve interviewing the taxpayer, third party witnesses, attorneys, and accountants; scrutinizing and analyzing the records of the taxpayer and those having dealings with him, including banks, brokerage houses, public offices; analyzing checks and deposits; preparing summonses for third party testimony and records and following through on enforcement; analyzing the tax returns of the taxpayer and his related interests; reconstruction of the taxpayer's financial activities or business, particularly where there are no records or books; analyzing the taxpayer's personal expenditures.

Willfulness is one of the crucial elements in attempted evasion or failure to file and involves a specific intent. Proof of the existence of intent is neither clear-cut nor easy. Congress and the Courts have not laid down any well-defined rule by which fraud can be conclusively identified or proved. Proof of intent is dependent on many circumstances surrounding the taxpayer's actions and business operations, and direct proof is rarely to be found. It is the Special Agent's job, through his investigation, to secure the evidence that indicates this intent, to compile facts concerning the taxpayer's actions bearing "badges of fraud." These badges of fraud are many. Some of the more usual are omission of specific items of income, unexplained increases in net worth, overstatement of deductions, alteration or destruction of records, keeping a double set of books, making false invoices, concealment of assets or covering up sources of income, making false statements in explanation of actions.

Activities of the Intelligence Division enabled the Department of Justice to obtain indictments against 1,484 individuals in tax fraud cases referred to it during the calendar year 1961.

In cases going to trial, 1,129 offenders were sentenced to a total of 271 years in prison, and to fines totalling $2.5 million. In addition, the federal courts imposed probationary and suspended sentences amounting to 2,274 years.

In initiating these investigations, Intelligence screened and evaluated almost 123,000 leads, or information items relating to possible tax evasion. More than 15,000 cases were actively investigated, of which 3,588 cases were completed, full-scale investigations.

Cases not deemed to warrant further action by the Intelligence Division were referred to other divisions of the Service for civil proceedings for collection of additional tax and penalties where applicable.

All categories are found represented in fraud cases.

Persons brought to justice for violation of Internal Revenue laws, while constituting a small minority of all taxpayers, include representatives of almost the entire range of professions and businesses, from steeplejack to gravedigger, doctor to undertaker, society matron to prison inmate. Important names in corporations, labor, politics, investments, and athletics, as well as the average wage earner and small business man, have come under Intelligence Division investigation and court action.

Several major cases in which the principals fell within the racketeer designation were prosecuted successfully in 1961.

The Government was successful in obtaining a number of convictions of employers who withheld income taxes from employees but failed to pay over these funds. Sentences in this type of case ran as high as three years imprisonment.

Omission from tax returns of dividends and interest was a factor in a number of prosecutions, as was failure to report "kickbacks."

Special agents also took a closer look at travel and entertainment deductions. In addition to convictions in the Bernard Goldfine cases which included this issue, the Intelligence Division in 1961 secured convictions in cases in which taxpayers failed to include reimbursement for travel expenses after taking the deduction.

Other cases involved corporations which used their expense account deduction for personal expenses of officers, and cases in which fictitious travel and entertainment expense was deducted or for which false statements in corroboration of the deductions were submitted.

A prison sentence was meted out to a son for filing a false return on the estate of his deceased father. In another case, a corporation and its manager received heavy fines for evading the tax on diesel fuel.

Other types of convictions show scope of fraud.

Another small sampling of cases suggests the variety and scope of tax evasion as practiced by the few who would defy the laws and the tenets of good citizenship.

A farmer and trucker who elected to serve a year in prison in lieu of a suspended sentence with rigorous probation requirements, after pleading guilty to failing to file returns for four years, was also fined $10,000.

A gambler who conducted a confectionery business as a front for a card game, was sentenced to three years in prison for failure to report his winnings.

Three partners in a public accounting firm received fines or prison sentences for a variety of tax derelictions.

A disbarred attorney and self-styled "tax consultant" was sentenced to two years in prison on charges of evasion of his own income taxes, and understating taxes of 22 clients.

Two brothers, operating four construction companies, were each fined $50,000 and placed on probation for evading personal and corporation income taxes.

A dentist was sentenced to 15 months in prison after pleading guilty to tax evasion through omitting professional receipts, padding deductions, and falsifying records.

The law behind the convictions is clear.

The sections of the Internal Revenue Code under which taxpayers are most frequently prosecuted in connection with violations of the laws are 145(a) of the Internal Revenue Code of 1939 and 7203 of the 1954 Code, relating to willful failure to file returns; and section 145(b) of the 1939 Code and 7201 of the 1954 Code relating to willful attempts to evade or defeat any taxes.

The crime of willful attempted evasion of taxes, defined in section 145(b) of the 1939 Code and reenacted in section 7201 of the new Code, is the principal revenue offense. A vast majority of tax prosecutions are instituted under this statute. Section 7201 of the Internal Revenue Code of 1954 provides as follows:

> Any person who willfully attempts in any manner to evade or defeat any tax imposed by this title or the payment thereof shall, in addition to other penalties provided by law, be guilty of a felony and upon conviction thereof, shall be fined not more than $10,000, or imprisoned not more than 5 years, or both, together with the cost of prosecution.

The law also provides for very substantial civil monetary penalties for fraud which are imposed in addition to criminal sanctions, or which may be applied independently where circumstances of a case preclude criminal prosecution.

The Gambling Business and Federal Taxes

In 1951, the Special Senate Committee to Investigate Organized Crime in Interstate Commerce (Kefauver Committee) reported:

> Organized criminal gangs operating in interstate commerce are firmly entrenched in our large cities in the operation of many different gambling enterprises such as bookmaking, policy, slot machines, as well as in other rackets such as the sale and distribution of narcotics and commercialized prostitution. . . .
>
> Gambling profits are the principal support of big-time racketeering and gangsterism. These profits provide the financial resources whereby ordinary criminals are converted into big-time racketeers, political bosses, pseudo-businessmen, and alleged philanthropists.

Wagering tax background reveals the problems.

In 1951, the House Ways and Means Committee was hard pressed to find additional revenue to meet the rapidly mounting government expenditures attributable to the Korean conflict. Expenditures of the Federal Government rose from $43.9 billion in fiscal year 1951 to $65.3 billion in 1952.

Having noted that organized gambling was a multi-billion dollar nationwide business which had remained comparatively free from either state or Federal Government taxation, the Committee recommended that wagering taxes be enacted. It estimated that these taxes would produce additional revenue of some $400 million per year. The Committee was convinced that the immunity of organized gambling from taxation was inconsistent with the need for increased revenue, especially when many consumer items of a semi-necessity nature were given new or additional tax burdens. Others in Congress supported the wagering tax because they believed it would hinder, if not prevent, this type of gambling.

The wagering tax laws were passed November 1, 1951. The collections from these taxes for each of the years since their enactment have been far short of the $400 million estimate.

Fiscal Year	*Stamps Sold*	*Revenue Received from Stamps*	*Revenue from 10% Excise Tax*
1952	19,855	$ 973,197	$ 4,371,869
1953	15,710	974,000	9,502,000
1954	13,583	1,008,000	8,550,000
1955	11,013	835,000	6,973,000
1956	9,562	639,000	6,385,000
1957	8,736	759,000	6,566,000
1958	8,121	628,000	6,311,000
1959	8,448	566,000	6,221,000
1960	9,356	560,000	6,084,000
1961	9,189	641,000	6,682,000
Totals	113,573	$7,584,197	$67,645,869

Intelligence work has increased without adding personnel.

The Internal Revenue Service, noting a very limited voluntary compliance with these laws, had originally requested 4,333 additional employees to administer and enforce these taxes more effectively. This request was rejected by both the House and Senate Appropriations Committees in 1952. No new enforcement personnel have ever been made available specifically to carry out the provisions of the wagering tax laws.

Internal Revenue's Intelligence Division was assigned the responsibility of investigating criminal violations of the wagering tax laws in addition to investigating criminal violations involving several other taxes. Without the resources needed to investigate all criminal violations of the tax laws for which it was responsible, it was compelled to allocate its facilities to perform each activity most effectively. From 3 to 6 percent of its resources were used to enforce wagering taxes, with the following results.

Fiscal Years	*Number of Investigations*	*Number of Cases Recommended for Prosecution*	*Number of Persons Convicted*
1955	1,119	957	724
1956	898	734	735
1957	706	603	399
1958	674	547	289
1959	634	514	278
1960	580	524	385
1961	890	781	503
Totals	5,501	4,660	3,313

Flagrant violators are investigated.

Initially, the Intelligence Division recommended prosecution for wagering tax violations in many cases where local law enforcement agencies had originally detected violations. This, however, did not produce the more significant violator type of case. Now, the Division's wagering tax enforcement efforts are primarily directed toward independent initiation and development of criminal cases involving important operators and situations in which there is widespread non-compliance. It does not generally investigate a violation involving an individual who has been convicted in a state court and who has received a substantial sentence if the federal violation involves substantially the same set of facts, unless the circumstances and the ends of justice require such action.

This policy, implemented by close cooperation with local authorities who are vigorously enforcing their anti-gambling laws, provides the most effective enforcement of the wagering tax laws possible within the framework of available resources. Duplication of effort is avoided, and highest priority is assigned to the more flagrant violations.

Surveillance-raid technique is generally used.

While no stereotyped procedure is used to investigate wagering tax violations, most cases involve a surveillance-raid technique. The suspected violator is kept under observation. If probable cause is established, a search warrant is obtained and served.

The major defensive maneuver employed by a wagering tax violator is to avoid having incriminating evidence on his person or on the premises under his control. Destruction of records, or their concealment, is commonplace. One interesting technique involves the chemical treatment of paper to convert its cellulose component into nitrate cellulose, frequently known as gun cotton. Paper so treated, when touched with a lighted cigarette or open flame burns very rapidly and leaves little or no ash. The element of surprise is the best counter-measure to these defensive tactics.

Property of violators is seized.

In its investigation of violations of the wagering tax laws, the Intelligence Division seizes for forfeiture property used by violators of those laws. The value of such seized property since 1956 is reflected in the following tabulation.

Fiscal Years	*Automobiles and Other Property*	*Currency*	*Total*
1956	$ 36,272	$ 58,417	$ 94,689
1957	129,004	104,841	233,845
1958	99,956	148,078	248,034
1959	116,335	209,198	325,533
1960	128,421	140,647	269,068
1961	175,383	400,795	576,178
Totals	$ 685,371	$1,061,976	$1,747,347

Two wagering taxes are imposed.

Two taxes on wagering have been imposed. The first is a 10 percent excise tax on gross wagers accepted, to be collected by each person engaged in the business of accepting wagers. It is imposed on those wagers of the type involving participants who are not present when the bets are placed or when the winner is selected and the prizes distributed. The second tax is an occupational tax of $50 per year on every person engaged in the business of accepting wagers either on his own account or in behalf of others. A tax of $250 per year is also imposed on any person who maintains a so-called "slot" machine, whether actuated by coins or not, on premises owned or occupied by him.

The wagering tax law specifically provides that payment of such tax shall not exempt any person from any penalty provided by a law of the United States or of any state for engaging in wagering, nor shall the payment of the tax prohibit any state from placing a tax on the same activity for state or other purposes.

Record-keeping is required for wagering tax.

Several record-keeping requirements are incorporated in the wagering tax laws, and penalties are provided for failure to comply with these requirements. Anyone liable for the 10 percent excise tax must keep daily records reflecting the gross amount of all wagers on which he is liable, as well as records of the gross amounts of each class or type of wager accepted on each separate event, contest, or other wagering medium.

Registration is required for occupational tax.

Those liable for the annual $50 occupational tax are required to register with the appropriate District Director of Internal Revenue. This includes disclosing the registrant's name and his place of business. If he is engaged in accepting wagers on his own account, he must also list the names and addresses of each person who receives wagers on his behalf. If he is accepting wagers for others, he must list their names and addresses.

The District Director of Internal Revenue is required by law to maintain for public inspection an alphabetical listing of the names of all persons who have paid certain "special taxes." This includes both the excise and occupational taxes on wagering.

The dilemma of the bookmaker is apparent. If he registers and pays the wagering taxes, he is generating evidence of his gambling activities which is available to local authorities. If he does not register, he exposes himself to the sanctions and penalties contained in the federal wagering tax laws.

Penalties are heavy.

A broad range of criminal sanctions and civil penalties are applicable for violations of the wagering tax laws. Those who attempt to evade or defeat the tax are guilty of a felony and upon conviction may be fined up to $10,000, or imprisoned not more than five years, or both. Similarly, for fraudulent declarations under penalty of perjury, the violater is also guilty of a felony, and upon conviction is subject to a fine of not more than $5,000 or imprisonment for not more than three years or both.

Willful failure to file a required return or to supply information is a misdemeanor, and upon conviction the offender may be fined not more than $10,000 or imprisoned not more than one year, or both. Anyone who engages in the business of accepting wagers without paying the special occupational tax may be fined not less than $1,000 nor more than $5,000.

Wagering taxes have been upheld.

The wagering taxes were unsuccessfully challenged soon after their enactment as an unconstitutional application of the taxing authority. The Supreme Court, in United States v. Kahriger, (345 US22, 735 Ct. 510) after reviewing the legislative history which indicated a Congressional motive to suppress wagering, noted that the tax did produce revenue and held that it was a valid exercise of the federal taxing power. The Court mentioned that the intent to curtail and hinder, as well as tax, was present in taxes imposed on paper money issued by state banks, colored oleomargarine, narcotics and firearms, and that all of those taxes had been upheld. It also stated that the tax was not invalid because the revenue obtained is negligible, and pointed out that the wagering tax had produced more revenue than narcotics and firearms taxes.

The registration provisions were found by the Court not to contravene the privilege against self-incrimination guaranteed by the Fifth Amendment. The privilege, it was pointed out, related only to past acts and not to future acts which might or might not be committed. Registration under the wagering tax laws was held to be required only if one wished to engage in the business of wagering in the future and did not compel confession about acts already committed.

In another case, documentary evidence from Internal Revenue was received in a prosecution for violation of state anti-gambling laws to show the petitioner's application for the wagering tax stamp and his return. The Supreme Court held the statute did not make such records of stamps confidential or privileged. On the contrary, it expressly required the name and place of business of each such taxpayer to be made public.

Investigations are becoming more effective.

Over-all, the Intelligence Division investigations of wagering tax evasion are becoming more effective. Of special value has been the technique employed from time to time of coordinated nationwide raids directed at syndicated bookmaking. Further, the emphasis on significant violators has resulted in the convictions of increasing numbers of major bookmakers on charges of evasion of wagering taxes or income taxes or both.

In its study of amendatory legislation, Internal Revenue has requested additional authorities for Special Agents similar to those of other law enforcement agencies engaged in comparable activities. During the 87th session, Congress enacted legislation along the lines of this request.

Chapter Eighteen

INTEGRITY THROUGH THE INSPECTION SERVICE

THE NATION'S WELFARE requires that the tax system be beyond reproach. Therefore, maintaining the integrity of employees, tax accountants, tax lawyers, and the general public in regard to administration of the tax laws is of vital concern to the Internal Revenue Service.

This concern for the integrity of the Service, together with vigorous adherence to the Civil Service merit system, free of political influences, was expressed by President Truman when he authorized the establishment of the Inspection Service within Internal Revenue. It was reiterated by President Eisenhower and by President Kennedy.

Criticism led to the Inspection Service.

The Inspection Service was created in 1951 in an atmosphere of Congressional and public criticism of Internal Revenue. Prior to the late 1940's the agency had enjoyed a reputation of high integrity and efficiency in the eyes of Congress and the public.

Immediately after the end of World War II, there were indications of malfeasance and nonfeasance among highly placed officials and personnel. The complaints gave rise to a series of Congressional investigations of an extent and scope rarely experienced by a government agency. In the early 1950's Congress publicly concluded that Internal Revenue was poorly managed in many respects and that a number of positive measures had to be taken to eliminate corruption.

As a result of Congressional criticism and resentment among the taxpaying public, steps were taken to reorganize Internal Revenue into a "Blue Ribbon" Service. Since 1951, the Inspection Service has played an increasingly important role in fostering this Blue Ribbon concept in the eyes of Congress and the public.

Prior to the establishment of a formal Inspection Service, there was no over-all supervision and coordination of inspection activities under a single office. The inspection program operated under the supervision of the several principal operating divisions. Investigations of the background of employees and of complaints against personnel were hampered not only by the lack of direction but by the fact that a number of key positions were not under the Civil Service merit system. This meant a sort of autonomy that frequently tied the hands of the Commissioner and other officials whenever efforts were made to correct deficiencies in operations or to discipline personnel.

Position of Director of the Inspection Service was established.

On July 19, 1951, Commissioner George J. Schoeneman issued a directive, approved by Secretary of the Treasury John W. Snyder, establishing the position of Director of the Internal Revenue Inspection Service.

This position was designated to "provide a uniform and thorough Inspection Service throughout the headquarters and field offices of the Internal Revenue Service with the objectives of maintaining high standards of conduct by all personnel, insuring continuing attention to improvement and efficiency in the operations of its offices, and the determination through inspections that such objectives are attained and such standards scrupulously observed."

From its inception, Inspection aimed at two principal objectives: (1) the independent review and appraisal of all Internal Revenue Service activities as a basis for protective and constructive service to management; and (2) the carrying out of a program for assisting management to maintain the highest standards of honesty and integrity among its employees.

The original concept of Inspection as an office merely to coordinate inspection activities and investigations of personnel was short-lived. On March 15, 1952, the Commissioner consolidated into the Internal Revenue Inspection Service all inspection functions, including the performance of all personnel investigations of applicants and employees and the investigation of charges of misconduct and irregularities on the part of Service officials and employees.

This action was a direct result of President Truman's plan, announced on January 2, 1952, to completely reorganize Internal Revenue.

The President stated that "this reorganization is part of a program to prevent improper conduct in the Service, to protect the Government from insidious influence peddlers and favor seekers, and to expose and punish any wrongdoers. . . . A strong, vigorous inspection service will be established and will be made completely independent of the rest of the Bureau. Through a comprehensive system of audits and inspections, this service will keep operations and management of the Bureau under continual scrutiny and appraisal. . . ."

Tax audit and financial statement were required of all employees.

In October, 1951, two new requirements were announced for Internal Revenue employees: (1) income tax returns of all officials and various enforcement personnel would be subjected to special examination; (2) all high grade officials and enforcement personnel must submit financial statements to reflect their net worth and account for their expenditures.

Both the tax audit and the financial statement requirements were the result of specific recommendations by the Subcommittee on Administration of Internal Revenue Laws of the Committee of Ways and Means which began the investigation of Internal Revenue in May, 1951. This Congressional committee had found numerous instances where the net worth of certain officials and employees was far out of proportion to known income.

In addition, the Congressional committee had found instances where Internal Revenue officials or employees had either not filed income tax returns or had filed patently fraudulent returns. The program for tax audits and financial statements, particularly the latter, was resented by some officials and employees. A few resigned rather than submit financial statements. However, the vast majority accepted these programs as necessary measures towards restoration of public confidence in the Service.

Assistant Commissioner (Inspection) replaced Director of Inspection.

In August, 1952, a further reorganization of Internal Revenue abolished the office of the Director of the Inspection Service. Inspection was given higher status by the establishment of the Office of the Assistant Commissioner (Inspection). In November, 1953, the Inspection field offices were consolidated into nine offices, each headed by a regional inspector. This is the basic structure of Inspection that exists today.

The regional inspectors' offices are located in the same cities as the nine regional commissioners' offices and have the same geographic boundaries. However, the regional inspectors do not answer to the regional commissioners. Instead, they are under the direct supervision of the Assistant Commissioner (Inspection) who in turn is responsible only to the Commissioner and the Deputy Commissioner. Thus Inspection is strictly a line organization. The autonomy of the regional inspector is, of course, essential to effective performance of both his internal audit and internal security responsibilities.

Internal audit and internal security function as two Divisions.

Both in Washington and in the field, Inspection is divided functionally into the Internal Audit and the Internal Security Divisions. The internal audit program provides an independent review and appraisal of all service operations as a protective and constructive service to the Commissioner and all levels of management.

The audit concept includes determination as to whether policies, practices, procedures, and controls at all levels of management adequately protect the revenue and are carried out efficiently and effectively. It is also responsible for the systematic verification and analysis of financial transactions and a review and appraisal of the protective measures and controls established at all operating levels.

Generally, all major field activities are audited and reported at least once a year. In addition, special audits are made when necessary. Inspection does not have the responsibility or the authority for correcting operating deficiencies. This is the responsibility of regional commissioners, district directors, and other management officials to whom the internal audit reports are furnished for constructive action.

The basic function of the Internal Security Division is expressed simply in a policy statement of the Commissioner. It reads: "An investigative service will be maintained which will assure the maintenance of the highest standards of honesty, integrity, loyalty, security, and conduct among Service employees."

The Internal Security responsibilities include the following principal functions:

—conducting character and other background type investigations of applicants for, or appointees to, all types of technical positions in the Service, all nontechnical positions in higher grades, and positions involving the handling of funds;

—investigations of complaints or information indicating criminal acts, violations of Internal Revenue regulations or other improprieties on the part of officials and employees;

—investigations of persons outside the Service where their actions involve corruption of, or attempts to corrupt or improperly influence, Service employees;

—background investigations of public accountants and former Internal Revenue employees who apply for special enrollment to represent taxpayers before the Service;

—certain tort investigations of alleged violations in Internal Revenue of the Government's policy of nondiscrimination in employment because of race, creed, color or national origin;

—investigations of personnel of certain other Treasury bureaus; and

—special investigations, studies or inquiries when requested by the Secretary of the Treasury, the Commissioner, or other officials.

Results of Inspection are salutary but not panacean.

Today, the over-all inspection program is considered an integral part of Internal Revenue's management control system.

The results of the inspection program are reflected in the current public image of the Internal Revenue Service as a government agency of high integrity. During the past several years, it has elicited the respect of Congress as an organization dedicated to efficient management and employee integrity. Since the reorganization of the Service in 1952 and 1953, which placed every permanent position under competitive Civil Service, there has been no valid basis for charges that Internal Revenue is politically motivated. In fact, such complaints have rarely been made in recent years.

Is the Service now free of improprieties? By no means. No prudent legislator, or government, state or municipal executive or judge, believes that enactment of stringent laws, improved methods of crime detection, or increased law enforcement personnel are the panacea of evil. Such measures may, and frequently do, serve as deterrents to crime but do not eliminate human frailties.

Since the days of the Internal Revenue scandals some ten years ago, standards and rules of conduct and demeanor for employees have become more rigid. (In fact, few agencies in the Government have as strict standards.) It has improved its internal safeguards and controls, and has increased and better trained its staff of specialists in the field of law enforcement and internal audit activities. Yet these measures have not completely ended bribery, embezzlement, and other crimes and misdeeds of employees.

A few convictions occur yearly.

The very nature of the work of some 30,000 employees of the Service who are engaged in examining tax returns, collecting taxes, and the like, is unique in the Government service with respect to the extent of authority vested in individual employees and the opportunities which exist for wrongdoing. Notwithstanding these factors, the Internal Revenue employees, by and large, have a remarkable record for integrity, impartiality, and devotion to duty. The number of cases involving bribery, embezzlement, and other serious crimes is minute in comparison to the entire Internal Revenue force.

During the past ten years convictions for criminal offenses in connection with performance of duty have averaged about 17 a year. This is only one out of every 3,000 employees on the rolls. A city with 3,000 employees on its municipal payroll, would not consider it shocking to find one employee each year prosecuted for misconduct in office.

Integrity of taxpayers and tax practitioners is watched.

While Internal Revenue is deeply concerned with maintaining the integrity of its employees, it is equally concerned with integrity on the part of taxpayers and tax practitioners.

In August, 1961, Commissioner Mortimer M. Caplin advised all employees of his increasing concern over attempts on the part of persons outside the Service to bribe Service employees. Repeating that the American tax system is one of self-assessment and voluntary compliance, and that its soundness is dependent upon the confidence of the public that the law is being administered fairly and impartially, the Commissioner stressed the importance of integrity among all persons who conduct business with Internal Revenue.

Ever since there have been taxes, some people have tried to buy immunity through bribery. This constitutes a constant danger to the Service's reputation for honesty. Any employee who is the subject of bribe attempts or bribe overtures is urged by the Commissioner to report the matter immediately to the Inspection Office in his region or district. Internal Revenue and Inspection have the ways and means to deal promptly and effectively with outsiders who attempt to corrupt its employees.

To a lesser, but equally serious extent, there have been cases where practitioners, and others purporting to be practitioners, solicit money from clients under the guise of having to pay off agents of Internal Revenue, when, in fact, no Internal Revenue employee has solicited any such payment. In some of these cases there was not even a tax matter assigned to any employee or pending before the Service. Although this type of shakedown is not presently a violation of any federal law, enactment of appropriate federal legislation is being sought. In the meantime, local law enforcement officials are investigating and prosecuting such complaints. Inspection has assisted local authorities in a number of cases which have culminated in state prosecutions.

Tax accountants and tax lawyers are held in highest esteem by Internal Revenue and its employees. In countless cases practitioners have brought to Inspection's attention cases involving attempts by practitioners, or those purporting to be practitioners, to corrupt Service personnel or to victimize taxpayers by shakedown attempts. The continued alertness and support of the tax practitioners to maintain integrity in all matters affecting Internal Revenue activities is of paramount importance.

Chapter Nineteen

CONTROL OF THE TAX PRACTITIONER

ONLY PERSONS ENROLLED to practice, who hold the so-called "Treasury Card," can represent clients as attorneys or agents before the Internal Revenue Service.

"Practice" includes all matters connected with presentations to the Service or any of its officers or employees relating to a client's rights, privileges, or liabilities under tax laws or regulations. Such presentations include the preparation and filing of necessary documents, correspondence and communications with Internal Revenue, and the representation of a client at conferences, hearings, and meetings.

Enrollment to practice is a privilege separate and distinct from a license to practice law or accounting. Also, admission to practice before the Internal Revenue Service does not give the right to practice before the Tax Court, and admission to practice before the Tax Court does not give the right to practice before the Internal Revenue Service.

By means of enrollment, tax practice before Internal Revenue is scrupulously regulated.

Office of Director of Practice exists for enrollment of practitioners.

The regulation of practice before the Internal Revenue Service is under the jurisdiction of the Director of Practice. He is appointed by, and is responsible to, the Secretary of the Treasury. His Office receives applications for enrollment from attorneys and agents, receives complaints and derogatory information relating to practitioners, and performs the duties necessary to carry out the provisions of Treasury Department Circular 230. This governs the enrollment and practice of attorneys and agents before Internal Revenue.

Preparers of tax returns need not be enrolled.

The preparation of tax returns does not constitute practice, and enrollment is not necessary for this assistance to taxpayers.

However, since 1959, preparers of tax returns, by blanket authorization, have been granted the privilege of limited practice without enrollment, before Revenue agents and examining officers in the Audit Division of the offices of District Directors. Unenrolled preparers who exercise this privilege must maintain ethical standards applicable to enrollees. Otherwise the District Director can place their names on a list of those ineligible to exercise the privilege of limited practice. A preparer whose name is placed on this list may present his grievance to the Director of Practice for review.

Need for regulation of practice is well established.

The need for control of practitioners was recognized by Congress as early as 1884. Congress authorized the Secretary of the Treasury to prescribe rules for the recognition of attorneys and agents, and to disbar or suspend any incompetent or disreputable person after notice and opportunity for hearing.

In the solution of any federal tax controversy, various statutory provisions relating to numerous procedural and substantive questions may have to be applied. Many of these provisions require a knowledge of such specialized matters as law, accounting, engineering, and economics. Thus, technical competence is highly important in practice.

It is in the area of controverted issues, as well as in tax planning and the preparation of tax returns, that the enrolled practitioner renders a valuable service. In innumerable situations, taxpayers are unable to determine their most advantageous tax course because of a lack of technical knowledge, training, or experience. They therefore seek the services of an enrolled individual to advise or represent them. Obviously, control of those claiming technical competence is required, necessitating inquiry as to their ability and integrity.

The enrolled practitioner fills the need of professional representation, and the Treasury Department, by its regulations, protects the public in denying enrollment to incompetent individuals and to those lacking good character or reputation. Likewise, competent and ethical practitioners are protected from the competition of incompetent and unethical persons. A similar benefit inures to the Internal Revenue Service.

Present regulatory system followed Congressional investigation.

The regulation of practice before Internal Revenue has become increasingly important over the years as the tax functions of government have expanded. In its early evolution, the enrollment and disbarment of practitioners was controlled by a Committee on Enrollment and Disbarment (later designated as the Committee on Practice) in conjunction with the office of Attorney for the Government. Matters pertaining to enrollment were acted upon by the Committee; disbarments and suspensions were the responsibility of the Attorney for the Government. This division of authority was a weakness in the regulatory system.

The need for coordination of all aspects of practice under one officer had long been apparent. It was pointed up in 1951 by the report of the Congressional Subcommittee on Administration of the Internal Revenue Service Laws. The investigation of the conduct of lawyers and accountants representing taxpayers before the Treasury Department led to several desirable changes, some of which are mentioned below. In addition, the committee system of regulating practice was abandoned in 1953, and Treasury Department Circular 230 was amended to consolidate both functions under one officer. The result of this consolidation was the creation of the Office of Director of Practice as it exists today.

One change brought about by the Congressional investigation related to the permanence of enrollments to practice before the Internal Revenue Service. The new regulations voided all existing enrollment cards as of March 31, 1952. They gave every enrollee an opportunity at any time during the first six months of 1952 to renew his enrollment card by filing a simple application, bringing up to date statements as to his tax status and any involvement in any criminal or professional disciplinary proceedings subsequent to his original application. This proved to be an effective house-cleaning method. By this means the roster of enrollees was swept clean of names of inactive, deceased, and unqualified persons. The number of enrolled practitioners thereby decreased from the accumulated total of approximately 97,000 to about 49,000 active, qualified persons.

The Subcommittee recognized that the honest and able practitioner performs valuable and vital services for the client, and that the incompetent and dishonest practitioner is a constant menace to the entire tax system. The Subcommittee was clear also in its reiteration of the well-settled rule that permission to practice before an administrative agency is not a right, but a privilege to be granted only to those worthy of it. The policy of the Office of Director of Practice reflects these conclusions.

Four categories qualify for enrollment.

Four categories of persons qualify for enrollment to practice before the Internal Revenue Service:

–attorneys, by virtue of their status;

–Certified Public Accountants, by virtue of their status;

–persons who demonstrate technical competence by experience or education together with a written examination; and

–former Internal Revenue employees whose conduct and technical experience have qualified them for enrollment without examination.

In addition, all categories of persons applying for enrollment to practice must show that they are of good character and of good reputation. In the case of attorneys and CPA's, the investigation is facilitated by virtue of the ethical requirements of their professions.

In considering an original application for enrollment, it is the policy of the Office of Director of Practice to grant an informal conference before the denial of an application, should there exist a question of an applicant's eligibility. If, after such a hearing, the decision of the Director of Practice is adverse to the applicant, a review of this decision by the Secretary of the Treasury is authorized.

Enrollment card evidences authority to practice.

Enrollment to practice before the Internal Revenue Service is evidenced by an enrollment card which becomes void five years after the date of issuance. Application for renewal must be filed with the District Director for the district in which the enrollee practices, during the 24-month period commencing 12 months before, and ending 12 months after, the expiration date of the card. The investigation of these applications for renewal serves as a moral fitness check-up of each active enrollee. Failure to file a timely application for renewal terminates the individual's enrollment.

The initial enrollment fee is $25.00, and a like fee is charged if an enrollee fails to renew his enrollment card during the 12-month grace period. When the application for renewal of an enrollment card is timely filed within the 24-month period the renewal fee is $5.00. Applications for renewal of cards are processed in much the same way as the initial enrollment.

Ethics of enrollees are continually under scrutiny.

The requirement for sound ethical practice on the part of the enrolled person is paramount. Technical competence is readily ascertainable and, once established, is likely to be a continuing factor. However, the ethics of practitioners, which affects their own character and reputation as well as their performance for their clients, is an area which continually is under close scrutiny.

All derogatory information received concerning enrollees is subject to investigation. If disciplinary action appears warranted as a result of such investigation, the enrollee is apprised of the charges against him. He is allowed to reply in writing, and to discuss the matter at an informal hearing before the Director of Practice. The charges are dropped if they prove unfounded, or a reprimand may be issued for proper cause.

When more serious charges appear and are proven, the Director of Practice may negotiate a resignation from practice, or the suspension of the practitioner's enrollment for a designated period. Or, finally, formal charges may be preferred. In that case, under the Administrative Procedure Act, the charges are heard by a Hearing Examiner, with the Director of Practice as complainant and the enrollee as respondent. The result can be exoneration, reprimand, suspension for a specified period, or permanent disbarment. The decision of the Examiner may be appealed to the Secretary of the Treasury.

Ethical canons of profession must be observed.

A fundamental duty of the enrolled person is that he abide by the canons of ethics of his profession. Apart from such canons, or even with them as a guide, the highest sense of rectitude is deemed vital in those who would serve the best interests of themselves, their clients, and the common good. Deviation from the standards of morality both required and expected of an enrolled person may cost him his livelihood, and cause untold damage to his profession. The most common ground for disqualification of a practitioner stems from questionable tax practices of his own or on behalf of his clients.

There are approximately 80,000 persons currently enrolled to practice before Internal Revenue. Relatively few of these persons have been charged with misconduct. Nevertheless, there is a constant stream of derogatory information affecting many persons. Some deviations from the required standards of practice set forth in Treasury Department Circular 230 occur honestly. They stem from lack of understanding or misconceptions which may be and are readily corrected. But the malefactor creates another problem. His questionable activities will not be countenanced by the Office of Director of Practice. The regulation of practice before the Internal Revenue Service must remain tautly bound to the highest principles of morality.

The Office of Director of Practice regulates scrupulously the practice of enrolled tax practitioners. Such regulation exacts and cultivates superior ethics, which benefits the enrolled practitioner, his profession, and our nation.

Chapter Twenty

CAREER OPPORTUNITIES IN THE INTERNAL REVENUE SERVICE

THE INTERNAL REVENUE SERVICE today offers opportunity for employment in more places than ever before in its one-hundred-year history.

The principal occupations in the Service are found nowhere else in Government. Hence, the Revenue Service develops its own qualifications and classification standards for its specialists, with guidance, assistance and review by the Civil Service Commission. The employees are recruited, developed, and utilized largely by Internal Revenue staff and line managers, within the general Civil Service framework, and subject to Civil Service Commission and Treasury guidelines, program leadership, and inspection.

In contrast to past years, when positions were filled by candidates who initiated job applications after routine announcements of examinations or vacancies, Internal Revenue now practices intensified and well-organized recruiting and training to obtain the specialists it needs.

Personnel have become more professional.

Within the past decade Internal Revenue has become proportionately more professional. Of the 57,000 employees on the roll at the close of 1962—all Civil Service career people except the Commissioner himself—about 60 per cent were in about 10 professional and semi-professional occupation specialties which are peculiar to the agency.

By far the most numerous group are the Internal Revenue Agents, who total over 12,000. These agents are professional accountants who examine tax returns and supporting records to determine compliance with the law. There are about 8,000 Tax Auditors and Tax Examiners, technical examining specialists with less accounting knowledge. About 6,000 Revenue Officers comprise the third largest group.

The Revenue Officers are also professionals and are concerned with increasing voluntary compliance with the payment and filing provisions of the tax laws, collecting unpaid taxes, securing delinquent returns. By utilization of *Mr. Businessman's Kit,* they aid new businessmen in becoming familiar with their tax obligations.

Other major Internal Revenue occupations are: appellate technical advisors (skilled accountants, lawyers or both) who handle taxpayer appeals from determinations made by District Directors; Special Agents who investigate tax frauds; Alcohol and Tobacco Tax Inspectors and Criminal Investigators, who enforce the tax laws relating to these closely regulated industries; Estate Tax Examiners; and Tax Law Specialists. Additional employees provide support in such fields as personnel, fiscal, administrative, and clerical.

As automatic data processing enters the operations of Internal Revenue, the proportion of professionals will continue to increase. ADP requires a high degree of professional skill; the extensive planning, research and improvement in ADP applications demand increasingly more skilled people. In addition, ADP in full operation will provide data leads which will in turn necessitate more taxpayer contacts, typically by Agents, Revenue Officers, and Tax Auditors. Thus the proportion of professional and technical specialists will increase correspondingly. Also, ADP will do much of the routine work formerly done by clerical employees, allowing them to be utilized in higher levels of work.

Recruiting program explains the opportunities.

Realizing its need for specialists and the competition for college graduates, the Service has greatly expanded its college recruitment program and has developed recruiting brochures, exhibits, and audio-visual aids to help explain the career opportunities available in Internal Revenue.

As late as 1953, employee careers in the Service tended to be compartmentalized into narrow organizational and occupational areas. Short-range operational needs were over-emphasized at the expense of development. The employee tended to remain with the same limited type of cases or narrow area of work which he had been performing over the years. When promotions did occur, they generally took place within his narrow subject-matter specialty, rather than between and over comparable functions. Planning for executive development was inadequate.

During the past decade, personnel and line management have cooperated in redesigning occupations and career ladders. They have recognized a continuing need to evaluate critically and not simply to describe and perpetuate the job patterns that exist. This critical review has led them to redesign job relationships, promotion procedures, and evaluations of individual employees. Management has seen and exploited the advantages of integrated systems for developing and utilizing employee skills.

Blue Ribbon Program establishes promotion opportunities.

The Blue Ribbon Program (page 201) is centered on high quality employees and their effective utilization. This program has stated and is achieving several personnel objectives:

(a) A recruitment system that brings into the Service employees who have potential for growth, as well as the ability to work at the entrance grades.

(b) A promotion plan which:

1. Moves all qualified recruits to journeymen levels within a reasonable period of time.
2. Identifies the most capable and moves them into higher positions within a reasonable period of time.

(c) A training plan that provides the specific training needed at each grade level.
(d) A supervisor selection and training program that provides:
  1. Arrangements ensuring that selections for first line supervisory positions are carefully made, and
  2. Training in the principles of supervision for the people who are selected to fill the positions.
(e) An executive development plan covering all positions from the first line supervisory level to the top-level positions within particular fields of work.

Personnel development program will apply to all categories.

Internal Revenue plans to expand and improve development programs for general as well as specialized categories of personnel. In addition, management is constantly alert to the possible revision of standards in selection, training, qualifications, and pay classification. These standards are never perfect, and are being refined continually.

People who make up the Internal Revenue Service have diverse individual skills and personalities. Internal Revenue planners recognize this factor of human individuality, with its manifestations in differing abilities, aptitudes, temperaments, and tastes. They seek suitable and promising combinations of these qualities in recruitment and in selections for assignment and training. They understand that quite often the needs of the Service can be met through meeting individuals' needs not only for recognition, but for growth and achievement as well.

Individual employees interact according to the interplay of their expectations with those of management. For example, they know that all reasonable consideration will be given them for promotion to journeyman levels and for opportunities to develop to higher levels. The Revenue Service has established an internal understanding of its attitudes toward performance and development, promoting mutual expectations which are clear and reasonable.

Training programs have been scientifically developed.

Because Internal Revenue does not have a labor market from which it can recruit persons with the knowledge of the Tax Code necessary to perform successfully in many of its occupations, and because many of its techniques are unique, it has a training program which is much larger and often more complex than that of many government agencies.

The training program, one of the oldest in government, was started in 1917. For three decades, correspondence type instruction predominated. Enrollment in the numerous tax accounting and tax law courses was required of new employees and was essential for promotion. As larger portions of the population came under income tax, correspondence courses were supplemented by lecture-type classroom training at times when there were spurts in recruitment or substantial changes in the law.

When decentralization of the Service occurred in 1952, it became apparent that if the Code was to be uniformly administered, personnel would require more sophisticated understanding of the provisions of law and of the policies and procedures established.

Beginning in 1956, successive Commissioners established training survey committees to study each major function of the Service. These committees laid the ground-work for comprehensive structures of training from recruit to specialists. Each committee included a distinguished non-governmental person from the field of tax practice and education and was rounded out with a senior official of the Service. Through this approach there was achieved a complete training plan for each of the Service's major activities, solidly based on identified employee needs and shaped by professional training experts.

Nearly all the training done by the Service today is conducted in classrooms or through carefully planned and supervised on-the-job training. To the extent feasible, trainees are placed in simulated situations structured to bring out the points the trainee will encounter when he is actually on his own. Instructors are carefully chosen, and are given training in instructional methods.

At the same time that technical courses were being developed, a management program was evolved for the progressive development of employees from the time of their original appointment to a supervisory position through the middle levels of management and on to executive positions.

Training takes employees up the career ladder.

The program is composed of approximately 50 separate and distinct courses designed to take an employee from recruit to full professional status in his activity and to provide training to the several specialist groups. In the 1960–61 year, the program involved the expenditure of about 1,250 man-years. In terms of instructor and student man-years, the program approximates in size and complexity that of any large university's School of Business Administration.

Everything that can be done is done to provide the training necessary to support career ladders within the Service. Under present policy, any recruit may aspire to become Deputy Commissioner. Every effort is made to keep the program lean and hard-hitting. Students consistently speak of the work as tougher and superior to their undergraduate instruction.

Since the development of the new program, practitioners have commented on the marked increase in employee competence. No course is established unless the line organization believes it will increase the effectiveness of the operation. Each course is consciously designed to advance good men and is part of the screening process before an individual is accepted for a service career. Every effort is made to utilize up-to-date practical techniques of instruction.

Facilities Management—a field with job opportunities.

The services performed by Facilities Management include transportation, communication, space, equipment, and records management, printing and distribution, physical security, and emergency planning. Its purpose is to provide quality tools for a quality Internal Revenue Service.

The facilities area has been frequently referred to as the "housekeeping" function of an agency. There was a time when this was a fairly accurate title, say in 1861, when all of Internal Revenue's office space was in the Treasury Building. No thought was given then to the scientific management of space, or the standardization of supply items.

Now Facilities Management works closely with the General Services Administration to provide the 57,000 employees throughout the nation with suitable plant, equipment, and services. This includes every kind of office supply, from pencils and paper to calculators and computers. The current inventory for some basic items indicates the size of the task: approximately 60,000 desks, 25,000 typewriters, and 15,000 adding machines and desk calculators.

The space problem is no longer a simple matter, either. At the beginning of 1962, Internal Revenue occupied space in 1,130 buildings in 901 cities and towns. These offices contained some 8,875,000 square feet of floor space, an area equal to a space six blocks square. Almost half this space is in federally owned buildings; the remainder is leased from private sources. Because Internal Revenue is a decentralized organization which can best do its job through continued close contact with the nation's citizens, its offices are spread throughout the country, from Fairbanks, Alaska to San Turce, Puerto Rico; from Lihue, Kauai, Hawaii to Presque Isle, Maine: 6,500 miles in each direction.

The location and condition of Internal Revenue offices, including facilities available to taxpayers and equipment available to employees, determines in large measure the quality of service rendered by the agency. For long years, tax practitioner groups had complained bitterly about inaccessible, crowded, antiquated Internal Revenue offices. At the same time, officials, themselves, became increasingly aware that these conditions led to inefficient operations and poor morale. This explains the stepped up program to obtain better space and equipment that has been so vigorously pursued in recent years.

While space and property management make up a large percentage of facilities work, these are by no means the only important jobs in this field. Printing and publications for the Service represents a massive undertaking. In 1961, Internal Revenue turned out 1,700,000,000 printed items, ranging from one-page tax forms to reports of several hundred pages. This material, if stacked in a single pile, would be 115 miles high. Distribution of this enormous quantity of materials to field offices and the public is also a Facilities Management job.

Record-keeping comes under Facilities Management.

As required by law, and in the interest of the public, Internal Revenue must keep a great quantity of records. It is the responsibility of Facilities Management to keep these records secure and complete, and as accessible as possible for as long as the law requires. The 1,350,000 cubic feet of records are stored in Federal Records Centers or their own records warehouses. This is equivalent to the area contained by a single building 100 feet on each side and 15 stories tall.

Automation has always presented problems to the Facilities Management area. Since 1919, when the Service first began to use punch cards for statistical work, Facilities Management has had to meet the requirements presented by the increasing complexity of technology.

Automatic data processing has given Facilities Management its share of challenges. ADP creates new problems in transportation and communication. In addition, over 2,000,000 square feet of specially designed space is required for the nine Regional Service Centers. New forms must also be developed, and old forms must be adapted to the requirements of the computers. Tax returns stored on tape present a need for new concepts in records management.

Progress is being made in the volume of records stored, however. Today most taxpayer data are stored on punched cards, but when the ADP system is fully installed the master file will be kept on tape. The master file on tape will require 125 cubic feet of storage area, equal to two average-size desks. The same records on punched cards would require 120,000 cubic feet, equal to a room 100 feet square and 12 feet high.

Fiscal Management is an area of employment.

Fiscal management is the process by which the Internal Revenue Service obtains and uses the money it needs to do its job. As tax laws change and the work of the Service increases, the cost of administering and enforcing the laws increases.

Internal Revenue has developed a Long-Range Plan for estimating its future work and the number of people and dollars required to cope with the workload. Through the financial management process, the Service asks Congress each year for an appropriation to pay the people needed, to provide space and equipment for them, to train them, and to meet all of the other expenses in printing, communications, travel, maintenance, and supplies involved in operating the Service.

Each year, the Commissioner of Internal Revenue appears before the House and Senate Appropriations Subcommittees to present these requirements for the coming fiscal year and to answer any questions the members may have on an appropriation amount.

After Congress makes an appropriation, an apportionment of the funds comes from the Bureau of the Budget. These funds are then allotted to the Regional Commissioners (and other plan managers) so that they may implement the work programs of the year. This distribution of funds is controlled and adjusted throughout the year as work plans and financial needs change. At the same time, because this is a continuous cycle, the plan managers submit their fund requirements to do the next year's work.

Internal Revenue constantly emphasizes the essential relationship between work management and financial management. Competent, carefully planned work programs are therefore prepared to justify financial requests.

Chapter Twenty-one

THE ROLE OF THE INTERNAL REVENUE SERVICE IN THE ALLIANCE FOR PROGRESS

At a White House reception for Latin American diplomats on March 13, 1961, President Kennedy proposed his *Alianza para el Progreso*. This program was presented as a 10-year cooperative effort of hemispheric development to lift Latin America's 200 million people out of misery. Land, tax, and other reforms were to be carried out to accelerate economic and social development and raise living standards. In outlining the terms of this Alliance for Progress of the American Republics, President Kennedy pledged financial aid and technical assistance from the United States and said that aid priorities would depend on "demonstrated readiness to make institutional improvements that promise lasting social progress."

At that time it was obvious that tax reform would be a major goal of the Alliance, but few people at Internal Revenue suspected that the Service would be called upon to play a significant role in the new program. However, during the series of inter-American conferences which followed, it became clear that tax administration reform would be a major factor in the over-all plan for social and economic development of Latin America.

Plan takes form at Punta del Este Conference.

After President Kennedy's announcement of the new program, a special meeting to implement the Alliance was held in Punta del Este, Uruguay, from August 5 to 17, 1961. At this conference the new plan took the form of a coordinated, all-out drive to achieve specific social and economic goals for Latin America in the next decade. All the Latin American nations except Cuba pledged themselves to make necessary institutional and fiscal tax reforms. The United States for its part, pledged financial and technical support to supplement Latin America's own efforts.

Self-help was a dominant theme of the conference. During the preceding year, Congress, in appropriating $500 million in foreign aid for Latin America, had stipulated that the United States should insist on self-help and social and economic reforms prior to aiding individual countries. At the conference, Douglas Dillon, Secretary of the Treasury and Chairman of the United States delegation, made it clear that before the Latin American countries would receive assistance from U. S. taxpayers, they would have to improve their own tax-collecting systems. Speaking to the assembled delegates, Secretary Dillon said, "To carry out these principles will often require difficult and far-reaching changes. It will require a strengthening of tax systems so that would-be evaders will know they face strict penalties, and so that taxes are assessed in accordance with ability to pay."

The Latin American delegates themselves emphasized the importance of self-help. One of the major goals affirmed in the Declaration to the Peoples of America was: "To reform tax laws, demanding more from those who have the most, to punish tax evasion severely, and to redistribute the national income in order to benefit those who are most in need . . ."

Thus, the Alliance for Progress was officially launched at Punta del Este, and tax reform, including tax administration reform, was made a condition for U. S. aid to Latin America.

Tax administration presents problems in Latin America.

As the Alliance began to gather momentum, it became clear that the Treasury Department would play a leading role in instituting tax reform in the Latin American republics. This meant that the Internal Revenue Service would be called upon to provide much of the technical assistance necessary to overhaul the Latin American tax collection systems. Consequently, in October 1961, Commissioner Caplin and Deputy Commissioner Harding attended the Inter-American Conference on Tax Administration in Buenos Aires, Argentina. While in South America, they also visited Chile and Brazil and conferred with their counterparts in those countries. These conferences provided an early opportunity for them to meet Latin American tax officials and gain some knowledge of what could be done to improve Latin American tax-collecting systems.

The job to be done is tremendous. A few of the Latin American Republics are making concrete progress in the field of tax administration. In some countries personal income taxes are inadequately administered. It is estimated that there may be as high as 50 percent non-compliance in several of the countries. Despite this, criminal fraud action is virtually unheard of. Furthermore, government employees engaged in tax administration are often untrained and poorly paid.

Internal Revenue is well qualified to help.

In many ways Internal Revenue was well prepared to offer the assistance needed in Latin America. It is one of the most progressive and best administered agencies in government and has been called by *Time* magazine "by far the biggest, most efficient and most successful revenue collection agency in human history." Internal Revenue's 57,000 employees possess a wide variety of training and experience in the various aspects of tax administration. Many of them have participated in the modernization of the U. S. tax system over the past years. Many have the language skills and aptitudes that make them valuable for overseas service or for training foreign tax officials in the U. S. Over-all, these personnel have considerable knowledge of tax systems and methods of administration that may be useful in the developing countries.

In addition, Internal Revenue has long been involved in many of the international aspects of taxation, in both operational and advisory capacities. The Service's organizational structure and administrative practices have served as the model for the tax collection agencies of several countries.

The experience of the Internal Revenue Office of International Operations, which administers the United States internal revenue laws in all areas of the world outside the U. S., is invaluable as a preparation for assisting the Latin American countries.

Personnel also have many years of experience in negotiating and servicing bilateral and multilateral tax treaties. Internal Revenue helped negotiate many tax treaties now existing between the U. S. and other countries.

Internal Revenue activities in the international field have not been confined to operations. In cooperation with the officials of the Harvard Law School International Program in Taxation, Internal Revenue has been conducting seminars and discussion programs for visiting foreign tax officials for a number of years. In addition, many foreign visitors have come to observe our tax system in action and to study the methods and procedures followed in administering our tax laws.

These activities have grown considerably over the years. Whereas five years ago an average of 80 foreign officials visited per year, in recent times the figure has almost doubled. From July 1, 1960 to June 30, 1961, the Service played host to 153 officials from 31 countries.

Technical tax assistance began with Chile, Peru and Brazil.

Prior to the Punta del Este Conference, the Internal Revenue Service had already begun providing tax administration assistance to Latin America on a modest scale. In July 1961, an Assistant Regional Commissioner (Administration) was detailed through the Agency for International Development (AID) to participate in their United States of America Operations Mission to Chile. His job there was to set up a tax administration school in Santiago to train Chilean personnel in administration and collection methods.

A few months later a Special Agent in the Service's Philadelphia District was also sent to Chile to help officials in that country establish an intelligence program to deal with fraud.

In January 1962, the Service received special requests from the governments of Peru and Chile for assistance with computer systems. To answer these requests, a Systems Analyst was sent to those countries. In cooperation with AID, feasibility studies were made of the two countries' plans to convert to automatic data processing.

The travel was not all one way, however. In January 1962, three representatives of the Brazilian Finance Ministry came to the United States to participate in IRS Revenue Agent training courses.

Program status is arranged for foreign tax assistance.

Late in 1961, when it became clear that the Service would be called upon more and more to furnish technical assistance and advice to Latin American countries, Internal Revenue's foreign tax assistance activities were given program status. The importance of this new effort was underscored when President Kennedy and Secretary Dillon determined the program to be essential to the foreign policy of the United States. Moreover, in November 1961, in an address to the 14th Annual Institute on Federal Taxation at the University of Southern California School of Law, Commissioner Caplin said of the new project: "I consider this program as one of our more important responsibilities. It is essential to help these countries with tax reform and improved tax administration if we are to halt the spread of Communism in Latin America."

Objectives of the program.

In furnishing tax administration assistance to Latin America, it will not be the aim of the Service to impose our tax administration methods and techniques on Latin American countries or try to mold their tax-collecting agencies into models of our own Internal Revenue Service. To attempt to do so would not only be inappropriate, but would also be poor tax administration.

This fact was recognized back in 1866 by a three-man revenue commission appointed to study internal tax revision after the U. S. Civil War. With rare foresight the Commission declared: ". . . A revenue system for a particular country cannot be framed theoretically or copied from any other, but must in every case be adapted to the resources of the country for which it is designed and the fiscal aptitudes and capacity of its people."

What, then, are the major objectives of the program? Basically, the program is designed to help the developing countries improve their tax administration so that their governments will have the revenue necessary to finance social and economic progress. Ultimately, this assistance will also serve the U. S. taxpayer. If these countries can attain a high degree of economic self-sufficiency, the U. S. foreign aid program can be substantially reduced.

A Foreign Tax Assistance Staff is created.

With burgeoning activities in providing direct technical aid to developing countries, it soon became apparent that some mechanism was needed through which international training and advisory services could be a normal part of Internal Revenue Service activities. Such a mechanism was also needed so that the Agency for International Development could call on the Service's resources and support in a systematic manner.

Consequently, on May 1, 1962, after several weeks of conferring with officials of the Treasury Department, the Agency for International Development, and the Organization of American States, Internal Revenue activated a new organizational component, the Foreign Tax Assistance Staff. This staff was placed directly under the Office of the Commissioner and was specifically created to carry out the foreign tax assistance program.

Under the leadership of the Treasury Department, which has the responsibility for aiding Latin American countries in tax policy reform, and under the general administration and coordinatoin of the Agency for International Development, the new staff serves as a point of contact for AID and multilateral agencies in drawing on the resources of Internal Revenue. Internally, it is the marshalling point for making available technicians and advisors for short and long-term assignments abroad.

To carry out the foreign tax assistance program, the staff performs two basic functions: (1) it provides the direct technical assistance requested by foreign governments for specific projects, and (2) it evaluates the progress and adequacy of these governments' tax administration reform achievements.

The staff engages in numerous collateral activities. Staff personnel conduct visitation programs, furnish manuals and other printed materials to foreign governments, help recruit specialized personnel, arrange training programs to meet the special needs of visiting foreign tax officials, and conduct surveys and studies for evaluating tax administration problems and programs of foreign governments. In addition, Staff personnel maintain liaison with Treasury officials on matters concerning foreign tax assistance.

The staff plans and organizes the tax administration aspects of the projects or missions involved. But the actual technical manpower is not available in this unit. Staff members discharge their functions primarily through personnel provided by other offices. Rosters of available technical personnel are maintained for assignment to tax administration missions abroad. Whenever possible, Spanish- and Portuguese-speaking technicians are placed on these rosters, and, when appropriate, language training is provided.

The program moves forward.

From the standpoint of implementation, the program is in its infancy. However, significant work is in progress.

A few Internal Revenue personnel are now participating in Agency for International Development missions to Latin American countries. In the National Office, staff personnel are engaged in planning and organizing for the job ahead. Rosters of Spanish- and Portuguese-speaking personnel are being drawn up and arrangements are being made for language testing and training. Staff personnel are currently furnishing tax administration advice and printed material to foreign governments.

While the Foreign Tax Assistance Staff is giving primary attention to Latin America at this time, plans are being made to meet comparable needs in other parts of the world. Hopefully, this office will become the point of professional leadership in solving the tax administration problems of developing countries.

Chapter Twenty-two

FEDERAL AND STATE TAX COOPERATION

UNTIL A FEW YEARS AGO federal-state tax cooperation consisted almost entirely of federal assistance to the states. By 1962 it had matured to an exchange that is mutually beneficial to the two levels of government.[1]

The Internal Revenue Service and the states have been making more extensive use of available information, the Internal Revenue Service through utilization of state tax records in fields other than the income tax, and the states through increased reference to federal audit findings and tax returns.

Further expansion in the cooperative exchange program will undoubtedly take place as new enforcement methods develop through the use of electronic data equipment by both the federal and state governments.

Exchange of tax records is not unreasonably restricted.

The exchange of tax records between the Federal Government and the states is not stringently restricted by the statutes or regulations of either level of government.

In the early 1920's there was some use of federal records by the states, but an explicit statutory provision for the inspection of

[1] Material in this chapter is largely based on Research Report 48, issued in 1962 by the Federation of Tax Administrators.

federal tax records was not introduced until the Revenue Act of 1926 became law. From that time on the Federal Government continued to open its records to inspection by state officials through a series of enactments dealing either with specific taxes or with the general availability of federal records. The present provisions of the Internal Revenue Code relating to the inspection of federal tax records by designated state tax officials were passed by Congress on May 28, 1938.

The Internal Revenue Code gives state officials access to returns for income taxes, estate and gift taxes, unemployment taxes, and motor fuel taxes among others. Federal administrative regulations have construed statutory authorizations broadly. Information for all taxes is generally available to the states with respect to both returns and audit adjustments.

Internal Revenue has restricted, however, the availability of information in cases in which fraud is involved. As a general policy, Internal Revenue has not divulged information which might affect prosecution or would relate to a settlement where a fraud penalty is agreed to. Under new coordination agreements, however, provision has been made for the disclosure of adjustments after the disposition of fraud cases.

State tax laws have given federal officials access to tax returns in several forms. A state tax statute may specifically open tax returns to inspection by federal officials, or it may accomplish this by excluding them from the effect of provisions requiring the secrecy of tax returns. In some instances, the authorization may be implicit by the absence of a statutory secrecy requirement.

Available information indicates that few states have statutory provisions which would seriously interfere with any program of federal-state cooperation. However, because secrecy provisions vary somewhat not only from state to state but from tax to tax within a state, there may be differences in the extent to which the states can enter into cooperation agreements.

State contact is with District Offices.

In the 1930's and 1940's, when taxpayer records were housed in Washington, transcripts of federal income tax returns of specific taxpayers were furnished to the states upon request. In addition, Internal Revenue prepared transcripts of federal audit adjustments for the states. For the year 1948, the Internal Revenue Service reported that the transcript service had been extended to 28 states.

Since Internal Revenue shifted taxpayer records from Washington to the district offices beginning in 1948, state tax officials have dealt almost exclusively with the district office in their use of federal records. Arrangements have been made mainly on an informal basis and have emerged from the working relationship existing between the district office and the state tax department. These relationships have varied among the states due to differences in tax systems and in administrative organization. Also, Internal Revenue has given District Directors considerable latitude in developing procedures for the state use of the federal records maintained in their offices.

States add revenue through audit adjustments.

States have added to their revenues through use of federal audit adjustment information. For the 13 states for which data are available, a report by the Federation of Tax Administrators shows that the tax change in one year aggregated $9.7 million. This includes adjustments for both individual and corporate income taxpayers.

For the four states which tax corporations only, or for which corporate data are available separately, the percentage of adjusted returns to the total number of returns filed ranged from 7.5 percent in Vermont to 13.7 percent in Pennsylvania. The average adjustment per return in the four states ranged from $144 in Rhode Island to $245 in Connecticut.

Various factors, other than the degree to which audit adjustments were used, are reflected in the differences in both the percentage of adjusted returns to total returns and the size of the average adjustment. Among these are the proportion of low-income taxpayers in the state's tax base; the extent to which back taxes for more than one year are included in the tax change; the proportion of adjustments resulting from office audits (which produce smaller changes than field audits), and the proportion of total adjustments attributable to corporate taxpayers. In addition, the revenue benefits from the state use of federal audit adjustments, as in the case of comparison programs, may be reflected in improved taxpayer compliance and thus in initial taxpayer reporting, rather than in the average adjustment for any one year.

Sixteen states compare federal and state income tax returns.

States which have reported programs for the comparison of federal and state income tax returns, either on a regular basis or as special programs, are: Alabama, Arkansas, California, Georgia, Kansas, Kentucky, Louisiana, Mississippi, Missouri, Montana, New Hampshire (intangible income only), North Carolina (self-employed only), Ohio (intangible income only), Oklahoma, Utah (self-employed only), and Wisconsin.

Among the 16 states, comparison programs are usually conducted annually as a routine aspect of income tax administration. Three states—Kentucky, Oklahoma, and Missouri—have compared returns on an occasional basis as special programs. Alabama photostated returns for the years 1946 through 1953, but dropped the procedure when it adopted withholding. North Carolina reported matching returns occasionally for corporations and regularly for self-employed individuals.

Louisiana and Mississippi make comparisons biennially, and in Wisconsin the program is routine, although conducted periodically.

What is included in a comparison program?

A state's comparison program usually includes all returns which show a state tax liability. Kentucky, Montana, and Wisconsin reported that the federal tax returns of all state taxpayers were examined. In Oklahoma, all federal returns were photographed, and those which indicated no tax liability were eliminated.

Programs conducted by North Carolina and Utah for the comparison of state and federal returns of the self-employed are continuous but not all-inclusive. Comparisons are made for different years for certain categories of the self-employed—lawyers, doctors, etc.

Limited data is available on results of comparison programs.

Data on the number of taxpayers who were subject to additional taxes as a result of the comparison programs and the amount of revenue involved are available for seven states. The states include North Carolina, which compared returns for the self-employed only, and New Hampshire and Ohio, which limit taxation to income from intangibles. Arkansas reported that it compared both individual and corporate returns. California, Montana, and Wisconsin compared individual returns only.

The largest amounts of added revenue derived from comparison programs for the year covered were reported by California, $3.6 million; Ohio, $740,000; and Wisconsin, from $450,000 to $500,000. From the comparison of returns of the self-employed, North Carolina reported additional revenue totaling $123,000 for the year.

North Carolina's comparison of returns of the self-employed resulted in adjustments of less than one percent of total returns, but yielded an average of $186 per return, the largest among the states.

Lists are matched in some states.

Several states that have not conducted comparison programs match lists of federal and state taxpayers. The purpose of this procedure is to discover federal taxpayers who have not filed a state return. It differs from programs which compare income, exemptions, and deductions reported on federal and state returns, in that it is concerned only with the names and addresses of taxpayers.

How Federal Government uses state records.

In a 1959 survey made by the Federation of Tax Administrators, virtually all states reported that federal revenue agents have access to state income tax returns, but request them only occasionally. Fifteen states reported that Internal Revenue district offices make use of information on adjustments resulting from state income tax audits. However, it appears that such use had been incidental and, except for one state, had had little revenue significance to the Federal Government.

In 1960, Internal Revenue estimated that it derived $10.6 million additional revenue annually from information furnished by the states. The savings to the Service from receiving this information from state sources, rather than by developing it through its own facilities, was estimated at more than $250,000. However, less than half of the added revenue was derived from information related to state income taxes. The largest dollar benefit came from state lists that were used in the enforcement of motor fuel taxes and the motor vehicle highway use tax.

Trend is to increase two-way cooperation.

Predominantly, federal-state tax cooperation has consisted of the utilization of federal tax returns and information by the states. Underlying this practice has been the recognition that tax compliance at the federal level has been substantially better than at the state level because of superior enforcement facilities, greater public awareness of the federal tax, and the absence of enforcement problems created by state borders. By referring to federal tax returns and audit adjustments, the states have been able to secure for their purposes some of the benefits of the Federal Government's more effective administration.

The effort to make federal-state cooperation a "two-way street" is a fairly recent development.

As recommended by a conference of federal, state, and local officials on intergovernmental tax problems, sponsored by the Treasury in April 1949, Internal Revenue began a pilot program for the routine exchange of abstracts of audit information between Internal Revenue district offices and state tax departments. The initial arrangements were made with North Carolina and Wisconsin on February 6, 1950. In the next two years, the test project was extended to include Colorado, Kentucky, and Montana.

Early reports indicated that the program was successful. The Treasury reported that in 1950, the first year of its operation, the exchange resulted in yields of about $500,000 for Wisconsin, and of close to $50,000 for North Carolina, where the program did not get under way until August 1950. On the basis of these results, the Treasury observed that, since neither the Federal Government nor the states could audit all returns, an exchange of audit findings permitted better coverage at both levels, "resulting in substantial increases in collections at minimum cost."

However, no further agreements were made over the next five years, and in 1957, when Internal Revenue entered into a cooperative agreement with Minnesota, a formal compact was drawn up which differed in important respects from the informal agreements of the pilot program. With the exception of the exchange with Wisconsin which had produced significant amounts of federal revenue, federal-state cooperation under the pilot projects had remained a "one-way street." The new form of agreement resulted from a reassessment of the pilot program and was designed to create a truly operative federal-state cooperative program.

The program initiated by Internal Revenue with its 1957 agreement with Minnesota formalized the areas of information to be exchanged and provided for substantial extension in the areas of cooperation. Since 1957, Internal Revenue has completed agreements with 15 other states. The states with which the agency has made coordination agreements, including the informal agreement with Colorado, are the following:

State	*Year*
California	1961
Colorado	1951
Indiana	1961
Iowa	1962
Kansas	1960
Kentucky	1961
Maryland	1963
Minnesota	1957
Missouri	1962
Montana	1960
North Carolina	1960
Ohio	1961
Oregon	1961
Utah	1961
West Virginia	1962
Wisconsin	1958

For four of these states—Kentucky, Montana, North Carolina, and Wisconsin—the new compacts represent an updating of the earlier agreements. Indiana imposes a gross income tax, not a net income tax. As previously noted, Ohio's taxation of income is limited to intangibles. Internal Revenue has reported that it intends to extend the new compacts on a gradual basis to other states where the administrative situation permits their practical operation.

Innovations are introduced in coordination agreements.

The new form of compact, termed an "Agreement of Coordination," is designed to encourage greater mutuality in federal-state tax coordination by several innovations. Unlike the earlier agreements, which provided only for the exchange of audit abstracts, the new compacts are tailored to the administrative circumstances in each state and, therefore, vary in detail. They are not limited to income taxation but provide for the exchange of information relating to other taxes—principally, death taxes, highway user taxes, and sales taxes—which many states have administered more intensively than income taxes.

The new compacts also open the way for coordination between the state tax departments and Internal Revenue district offices in areas other than the exchange of audit adjustments and returns, the basis for the earlier agreements. Notably, they provide a foundation for the beginning of a federal-state coordinated audit program by assigning to the states various classes of returns for which the states may conduct joint state-federal audits.

The compacts drawn up under the new cooperative program have been in operation too short a time to measure their revenue productivity. For fiscal 1959, Minnesota, which entered into its agreement in 1957, reported that it had obtained in excess of $800,000 in additional revenue as a result of information received on federal audit adjustments. Official Internal Revenue figures on the revenue obtained from action on state audit adjustments are not available.

However, in 1960, Dana Latham, the Commissioner of Internal Revenue, in reporting that the Service was deriving substantially more than $10 million annually from information furnished by the states, said that the estimated cost of supplying assistance to the states was no longer a significant burden. He stated that, while there was a period when the Service was concerned with the one-sided character of the information exchange program, since the extension of the program into areas other than audit adjustments, it had received new information from the states which had been of substantial value. In 1961, the Service reported again that it had found the new areas of exchange to be of value to one or both parties in the coordination agreements.

New Direction in cooperative relationships.

In his Economic Report for 1962, President Kennedy called attention to the need for the improvement and extension of federal-state cooperative efforts. In view of the President's statements in his Economic Report and the fact that the Service is confident that its program of administrative cooperation since 1957 has been a successful venture, the Commissioner of Internal Revenue has announced a New Direction for the program. In his address at the 30th Annual Conference of the National Association of Tax Administrators at Philadelphia on June 11, 1962, Commissioner Caplin announced a stepping up in tempo of the negotiations of agreements. "Experience with cooperative agreements entered into so far has shown beyond a doubt that both state and federal compliance stand to gain from mutual assistance provided for in these agreements. Substantial revenue increases have been obtained at low cost," said Commissioner Caplin.

In keeping with the increased tempo of the formal exchange agreement program, the responsibility of the field officials in the negotiations with state representatives has been expanded. Whereas previously the Service was ready to receive inquiries from states not participating in the program, field officials are now authorized to initiate meetings with responsible state tax officials to explore the potentialities of exchange agreements.

In the extension of the program to new directions, the Commissioner set out five points as guiding principles:

1. Development of mutually reciprocal and beneficial exchanges to the fullest extent feasible.
2. Coordination of audit activities with a view to maximizing combined audit coverage.
3. Design of new system developments based on electronic data processing to facilitate federal-state interchanges.
4. Development of agreements that embrace widest possible bilateral assistance, including available information from state agencies other than tax agencies.

5. Frequent and close consultation between state tax offices and Internal Revenue field offices in order to improve and expand exchanges.

Maximizing total benefits from the exchange.

Tested in the light of benefits received, the major dollar benefits of the program have accrued to the states by virtue of their access to the results of audits of federal income tax. However, Internal Revenue has not insisted on anything like an exact *quid pro quo,* but rather upon the receipt of qualitative information in a variety of tax areas. The benefits to the Service from access to state information concerning sales and excise taxes have been particularly impressive, especially in the area of highway vehicle use taxes. Additionally, large amounts of delinquency in the filing of federal income tax returns have been discovered as a result of access to various types of state data.

It is still too early, however, to measure the revenue productivity of the new agreements. Nevertheless, it is apparent that aggregate benefits of the agreements to both the federal and state governments have been impressive.

The slow and inauspicious beginning of federal-state cooperation with the income tax audit exchange program of 1950 and 1951 moved into high gear in 1957 when Internal Revenue adopted the expansive concept of cooperation. Since then the program has proved to be a valuable contributor to the goal of increased voluntary compliance. Its full potentials are yet to be realized, but forward progress is being made at an accelerating rate.

Chapter Twenty-three

COOPERATION WITH FEDERAL AGENCIES

THE INTERNAL REVENUE SERVICE has the clearly defined responsibility to administer the tax laws and collect the revenue. But Congress and other Government agencies share this responsibility to some extent. How these other agencies enter into tax administration and how the Internal Revenue Service cooperates with them are described here.

Congress controls basically.

The power of Congress to lay and collect taxes and determine the rates and the nature of taxes through the legislative process has been described in Chapter One.

Also of importance in tax administration is the budget control that Congress has over all government agencies. Additional personnel and new equipment requested by the Service must be approved through much the same channels as tax bills. (See page 4.) For example, the adoption of automatic data processing to handle income tax returns required Congressional approval of the necessary funds before it could be put into effect.

The Treasury Department directs the Internal Revenue Service.

Since 1789, when it was created, the Treasury Department has been responsible for the management of the nation's financial affairs. Its role in the area of taxes has assumed increasing importance as the United States has grown in size and importance in world affairs.

The Treasury Department prepares studies of expected revenue yields from existing and proposed tax legislation; examines the tax implications of administration proposals; supplies tax information and statistics to Congress; acts as spokesman for administration proposals; and directs the operations of the Internal Revenue Service.

Treasury also performs much the same function for the Executive branch of the Government as the House Ways and Means Committee and Senate Finance Committee perform for Congress. (See page 5.) The Secretary of the Treasury is the spokesman for the Administration on financial matters, and proposals for tax legislation flow from his office. Other Administration groups such as the Council of Economic Advisors enter into financial and economic matters, but Treasury is the working body, particularly on taxes, where policies are implemented.

Three staff offices in Treasury deal with taxes.

In the Treasury organization, three staff offices are primarily concerned with taxes: (1) the Office of Tax Analysis, (2) the Office of International Tax Affairs, and (3) the Office of Tax Legislation.

The *Office of Tax Analysis* is the basic tax study group for the Treasury Department and, in turn, for the Administration. It prepares reports on economic problems in the tax field and estimates the revenue effects of proposed tax legislation. These reports are made available to the President, other administration officials, the Ways and Means Committee, Senate Finance Committee, Joint Committee on Internal Revenue Taxation, members of Congress, and the public.

This Office projects over-all economic trends and estimates those levels of expected economic activity that are closely related to tax bases. These include personal and corporate incomes, and the sales levels of goods subject to excise taxes.

Estimates of the distribution of government receipts from taxes and other sources are made monthly by the Office of Tax Analysis for use by Treasury in its financing operations. This office also prepares monthly estimates of receipts from such specific taxes as social security and those earmarked for the federal highway building program so that funds can be deposited in these accounts.

The *Office of International Tax Affairs* conducts studies in the international tax field and handles technical details of international tax agreements. Its study areas include economic, legal, and statistical analyses of proposed tax legislation as they affect international investment and trade. The growth of the European Common Market, aid to underdeveloped nations, and such monetary problems as the international balance of payments, have given this office a key tax role.

The Office of International Tax Affairs also works with the State Department in negotiations on tax treaties with other nations. These treaties are designed to prevent double taxation and to remove possible tax barriers to trade and investment. It also reviews tax laws affecting nonresident citizens, aliens, and international transactions and participates in the Fiscal Committee of the Organization for Economic Cooperation and Development.

The *Office of Tax Legislation* analyzes and prepares reports on the legal aspects of proposed tax legislation and regulations.

Treasury participates in major IRS decisions.

Top Treasury officials participate in major decisions and actions taken by the Revenue Service since the Service is part of the Treasury organization. Matters involving the interpretation and application of tax laws passed by Congress frequently require this type of joint action.

For example, the major revision of depreciation procedures in 1962 (see page 150), stemmed not from a change in the law itself but from a change in the administration of the existing law. The new depreciation policy had a direct effect on Treasury operations since it reduced by a sizable sum the revenue that would be received by the Government from taxes starting with the year it was put into effect.

The Department of Justice handles prosecution of tax cases.

The Department of Justice is directly involved in tax administration since it is responsible for the enforcement of federal laws and is the Government's legal representative. Generally speaking, it handles all tax cases except those under the jurisdiction of the Tax Court, an independent executive agency. This latter agency tries cases involving deficiencies in income, excess profits, estate, gift and personal holding company surtaxes and has exclusive jurisdiction to review the Commissioner's determinations on claims for excess profits tax relief.

Two divisions of Justice handle tax work.

The Tax Division and the Criminal Division are responsible for most of the tax work in the Justice Department.

The *Tax Division's* chief duty is to serve as legal counsel for the Internal Revenue Service in certain litigation. It represents the United States in civil and criminal cases arising from the internal revenue laws with the exception of those pertaining to alcohol, narcotics, gambling and firearms. These are the responsibility of the Criminal Division.

Types of cases handled by the Tax Division include refund suits brought by taxpayers; title clearance questions; tax lien foreclosures; judgments against delinquent taxpayers, receivership or probate proceedings; and inter-governmental immunity suits where the United States resists attempts to apply state or local taxes to some federal activity or property.

Offenses within the jurisdiction of the Tax Division include attempts to evade or defeat taxes; willful failure to file returns and pay taxes; filing false returns and making false statements to revenue officials. In connection with these criminal offenses, the division supervises the institution of court proceedings and the U. S. Attorneys involved with the prosecution of these cases in the trial and appellate courts.

The *Criminal Division* performs a similar function for violations of alcohol, narcotics, gambling and firearms laws which are administered by Internal Revenue. Except for the alcohol laws, the taxes of these items are primarily regulatory rather than income-producing.

Social Security occupies a unique position.

Although it has no direct responsibility in our tax system, the Social Security Administration occupies a unique position. Employment taxes collected for the specific use of this agency comprise about 15 percent of all federal tax revenues.

Unlike other government agencies that receive funds from general revenues following due authorization and approval by Congress, the Social Security Administration receives its revenues from a fixed tax on personal incomes paid by employees and employers.

Increases in this tax rate since the inception of the Agency in 1935, and increases scheduled in future years under current legislation, have made this agency a growing factor in the total tax picture.

IRS Cooperation with Government Agencies

More than most federal agencies, the Internal Revenue Service today has relationships with many other departments of the Federal Government. With the Treasury, Justice, and Agricultural Departments, and with the Social Security Administration, there is a continuous liaison; with others, contact occurs upon special occasions.

Cooperation with Treasury Department is constant.

The Treasury Department is the supervisory authority not only for the Internal Revenue Service but for half a dozen other federal agencies. When matters of policy and major procedure are the issue, Treasury, working and conferring closely with Revenue's specialist personnel, determines the course of action.

The Secretary of the Treasury has a staff of top officials, to each of whom is delegated a specific set of responsibilities. The Under Secretary has the responsibility of general supervision of Treasury functions including Internal Revenue Service operations. Other top executives of Treasury also are concerned with phases of Internal Revenue operations, and all take part upon occasion in deliberations not only of the requirements that may affect tax collection but the effect that their action may have upon the Government at large and the public interest.

Actually, designated executive personnel of Treasury and Internal Revenue Service meet regularly one or more times each week to keep abreast of developments in the variegated tax field and to insure the continued close relationship that is necessary for effective tax administration.

When tax problems arise—as thousands do when there are millions of business and individual taxpayers—some are bound to apply to many other firms and individuals in similar circumstances. If the problem has wide enough range, a meeting of the top echelons of Treasury and Internal Revenue may be called to determine the proper application of the tax law to the circumstances presented.

Together, Treasury and Internal Revenue plan the annual submission to Congress of budget and operational matters. This, in itself, requires the most careful and detailed study, for explanations must later be presented of the extensive matters offered for Congressional consideration.

Enforcement activities are closely linked to several agencies.

In the field of enforcement, Revenue maintains close links with other bureaus of the Treasury Department, with the Justice Department, and with other agencies. The Office of the Chief Counsel of Internal Revenue maintains, of course, close and continuous relations with the Department of Justice, and the two work hand in hand on numerous cases of major tax importance.

Personnel of the agencies concerned with enforcement meet regularly in classes, and through special joint sessions, for members of each such agency must know intimately the type of work carried on by other segments of their group. Thus, personnel of Internal Revenue's Intelligence, Inspection, and Alcohol and Tobacco Tax Divisions receive instruction regularly along with enforcement employees of the Bureau of Narcotics, the Bureau of Custom's Investigation and Enforcement Division, and the Intelligence Division of the Coast Guard. Cooperation with the Federal Bureau of Investigation also occurs frequently.

In organized crime drives, several of these organizations may act jointly, and may, indeed, have the further cooperation of state and municipal authorities on matters of concern within their jurisdiction. When such activities are nationwide, they may well require the closest cooperation and timing to permit a coordinated campaign to be carried on simultaneously despite time variations in different parts of the country.

Closest connections are with Social Security Administration.

The closest connection of the Internal Revenue Service with any other major federal department is probably that with the Social Security Administration. The tax phases of Social Security operations are considered jointly by both agencies, and they work together in the collection of such taxes and in the regulation of numerous matters relating to them. The two agencies, in fact, frequently engage in joint campaigns to inform affected taxpayers of developments in which they and the agencies have a more than passing interest. Both agencies have a growing interest in the activation and ultimate expansion of automation in the filing of tax returns. Both are gearing for the demands of the future.

Relationship with Department of Agriculture is for farmers' benefit.

Another agency with which Internal Revenue has a continuing concern, which is highlighted early each year, is the Department of Agriculture. Farmers' tax returns vary in some degree from those filed by other taxpayers. Also, farmers file under somewhat different deadlines than the average taxpayer.

These considerations make it necessary for Internal Revenue and Agriculture to develop joint programs in which agents of the Service and county agents of the Department of Agriculture work together to acquaint farmers with tax facts of importance to them and to assist them with tax return problems.

Other agencies also get Service cooperation.

The Internal Revenue Service cooperates with various federal agencies that are concerned with national disasters, in assisting taxpayers who have been the victims of a catastrophe. Thus, the tax agency may grant extensions of time for the filing of returns by such taxpayers and give special consideration to refunds based on losses brought about by the disasters.

The tax agency works closely with the Small Business Administration to insure that the tax problems of the small businessman are fully considered and taken into account. Each year the Service prepares a new edition of *The Tax Guide for Small Business,* a helpful booklet that contains numerous examples of how typical tax problems faced by the small businessman may be properly handled in his return.

Starting in 1962, the Service jointly sponsored a series of tax clinics for businessmen with the Small Business Administration. Aim of the clinics is to help the owners and managers of small business gain a better understanding of the tax laws as they relate to their operations. The clinics are held as workshop sessions on college campuses with tax experts from industry joining with government leaders to conduct the discussions.

With the major overhaul of depreciation practices achieved in 1962, Internal Revenue has cooperated with both the Small Business Administration and the Department of Commerce in a program to explain these depreciation changes to business and industry. The Service has participated in the seminars held by these two government agencies on depreciation for businessmen.

The Internal Revenue Service maintains occasional contact with many divisions of the Department of Health, Education and Welfare; the Department of Interior; the United States Information Agency, and numerous others.

State Department cooperates in foreign tax assistance.

Each year, representatives of the tax departments of many nations come to study the tax system of the United States. In 1960, foreign visitors came from 31 different nations. Many of these foreign representatives visit one or more of the major installations of the Internal Revenue Service. Some of the visitors actually start out with comprehensive explanatory information at the National Office, and move on to regional and district offices, where they see the inner workings of our tax system. Many of them, indeed, spend days, sometimes weeks, in obtaining an intimate knowledge of the methods by which American taxpayers meet their obligations to the Government.

Some of the foreign nations, impressed by the modern-day operation of the Internal Revenue Service, have attempted, in greater or less degree, to base their own tax operations on it. Japan, for example, has modeled its tax system upon the United States system. In such instances, in addition to official consultations, Internal Revenue Service has provided the interested country with complete and detailed analyses, charts, tables of organization, and other data that might be helpful in constructing their own tax systems.

In recent years, conventions and conferences have been held in various foreign countries at which tax experts of several lands have met and talked at length with top tax men from the United States. Supplementing these conferences, Internal Revenue Service has provided many of the Latin American countries with representative libraries of its films and other informational materials. Also, in recent years, Internal Revenue has sent high-ranking officials to Latin American countries to give technical tax administration assistance in connection with the Alliance for Progress (see Chapter Twenty-one).

The arrangements which have brought about and made possible the friendly exchange of information have been carried on primarily through the cooperation of the Department of State. Specially designated representatives of the Service have worked closely with State Department personnel in planning and scheduling the visits from and to foreign countries.

Chapter Twenty-four

PLANNING AND RESEARCH FOR BETTER TAX ADMINISTRATION

THE FIRST ANNUAL REPORT of the first Commissioner of Internal Revenue, George S. Boutwell, dated January 13, 1863, recommended simplifying the revenue stamp system. Mr. Boutwell said it was expensive and cumbersome to have a different set of denominations of stamps for each type of tax. Wouldn't it be simpler to use the same set for all stamp taxes? It is this type of questioning that calls for planning and research.

Faced with countless small and large tasks, with mountains of documents, with endless questions of fact and law, with problems of personnel and supplies and budgets, a tax commissioner immediately starts wondering how to arrange his affairs so as to accomplish the most with the resources at his command. Also, as the taxpayer pleads for simplified forms and procedures and for less painful methods of compliance, the tax commissioner is impelled to seek remedies.

In Commissioner Boutwell's time, there probably was no single official or group designated to think up answers to tax administration problems. At that time, the mere task of creating a new tax office under wartime conditions undoubtedly kept all available hands busy doing the obvious first things. Between 1872 and 1913, the internal revenue system consisted primarily of alcohol and tobacco taxes and the problems were relatively small in number. With the advent of the modern income tax, later commissioners and Congress recognized the need for more planning—and for more facts to provide a foundation for planning. The present Office of Planning and Research is the formal planning organization that developed over the years in answer to this need.

First step was to organize statistical facility.

Soon after the 1913 ratification of the Sixteenth Amendment to the Constitution and the enactment of an income tax under it, Internal Revenue began collecting figures, not only on the number of returns, but also on the number in each category of income and the number in each of several size groups.

In 1916, this statistical work was formalized as the result of a request for more detailed information from the Senate Finance Committee. In fact, a specific direction to Internal Revenue to compile and publish such statistics was enacted into law in the same year.

Although some figures had been published as part of the annual report of the Commissioner of Internal Revenue, the new and expanded series of data was first printed as a separate document under the title of "Statistics of Income" to reflect the individual income tax returns for the income year 1916. These books, at least one for each year, have been published annually since then and have become standard tools for economists, tax technicians, and many other practitioners.

At present, the practice is to publish one set of volumes for individual returns and a separate set for corporation returns. Other periodic compilations cover estates, trusts, partnerships, and occasional special studies of other classifications.

Over the years, these volumes have provided a factual underpinning for planning and analysis in the tax field. Just as they did in 1916, the tax committees of the Congress use these figures in connection with designing and revising tax legislation. Similarly, in the Executive branch, the Secretary of the Treasury uses these tabulations in forecasting revenues, in predicting the consequences of proposed changes in the tax laws, and in evaluating operations of the law.

The Commissioner of Internal Revenue has additional uses for these statistics. Trained technicians analyze the statistics in order to pinpoint problem areas for enforcement or other administrative action. The data also provide guideposts for steering taxpayer assistance and educational activities, for improving forms and instructions, and for many other programs.

Other government agencies use them for a variety of purposes, notably the estimate of national income by the Department of Commerce. Industrial and investment counselors watch the tables for clues to business trends, marketing opportunities, etc. Similarly, universities and foundations find nuggets for their research and analysis programs.

The following summary tables illustrate some of the information disclosed with respect to individual and corporate taxpayers, revealing the changing character of these taxpayers over a period of years.

Early planning activities grew out of rising revenue needs.

Out of the statistical enterprise, a formal planning organization gradually developed.

The principal pressure for planning arose from the insatiable revenue needs associated with World War II. As the tax laws were broadened to extend the income tax from a "rich man's tax" to a general tax—multiplying the number of returns tenfold—and as many new and more complicated provisions were added, especially the excess profits tax on corporations, it became more and more necessary to modify the historical organization and methods of Internal Revenue.

A landmark in the planning history of Internal Revenue was the work done in designing a "pay-as-you-go" system for individuals in 1943 and simplified tax returns in 1944. Of course many other experts, both in the office of the Secretary of the Treasury and in non-governmental circles, also played major roles. But, when it came to nailing down the specifics of these plans, the Internal Revenue group was in the forefront.

This activity led logically to the establishment in 1945 of the first planning office, which was called the "Management Staff" and was directed by an Assistant to the Commissioner. Over the

Individual Income Tax Returns: Number of Returns and Sources of Income, 1956–60

Item	*Income year*				
	1960	1959	1958	1957	1956
A. Number of returns	*(Thousands)*				
All individual returns, total	61,028	60,271	59,085	59,825	59,197
Taxable	48,061	47,497	45,652	46,865	46,259
Nontaxable	12,967	12,774	13,433	12,960	12,938
Returns with itemized deduction, total	24,083	22,510	20,811	20,155	18,459
Taxable	22,185	20,761	19,054	18,569	16,973
Nontaxable	1,898	1,749	1,758	1,586	1,486
Returns with standard deduction, total	36,945	37,761	38,274	39,670	40,738
Taxable	25,876	26,736	26,598	28,296	29,286
Nontaxable	11,069	11,026	11,675	11,374	11,453
B. Sources of income	*(Million dollars)*				
All individual returns:					
Adjusted gross income, total	315,466	305,095	281,154	280,321	267,724
Salaries and wages	257,918	247,370	227,551	228,077	215,618
Business or profession	21,072	21,431	20,674	20,339	21,285
Dividends received	9,530	9,356	8,741	9,124	8,606
Interest received	5,057	4,395	3,659	3,319	2,872
Rents and royalties	3,312	3,235	3,227	3,259	3,344
Other income	18,577	19,307	17,304	16,202	16,000
Taxable returns:					
Adjusted gross income, total	297,152	287,775	262,188	262,169	249,551
Salaries and wages	244,063	233,804	213,043	214,187	201,837
Business or profession	19,754	20,222	18,900	18,596	19,176
Dividends received	8,876	8,789	8,257	8,627	8,201
Interest received	4,265	3,754	3,116	2,841	2,468
Rents and royalties	2,699	2,601	2,608	2,582	2,731
Other income	17,495	18,605	16,265	15,336	15,139

Corporation Income Tax Returns: Number of Returns and Sources of Receipts, 1955–56 — 1959–60

Item	Income year				
	1959-60	1958-59	1957-58	1956-57	1955-56
A. Number of returns					
All corporation returns, total	1,120,280	1,033,191	984,894	925,184	842,354
Active corporations, total	1,074,120	990,381	940,147	885,747	807,303
With net income	670,581	611,131	572,936	559,710	513,270
Without net income	403,539	379,250	367,211	326,037	294,033
Inactive corporations	45,715	42,251	44,369	39,214	34,822
Unincorporated businesses filing under section 1361	445	559	378	223	229
B. Sources of receipts	*(Million dollars)*				
Active corporations: Receipts, total	816,800	735,338	720,414	679,868	642,248
Business receipts	772,915	696,594	684,883	646,673	612,683
Dividends received	3,989	3,755	3,453	3,446	3,344
Interest received	20,893	17,938	16,893	15,058	13,207
Rents and royalties	7,711	7,471	7,068	6,830	5,875
Other receipts	11,292	9,580	8,116	7,861	7,140
Returns with net income: Receipts, total	719,416	632,343	625,621	614,857	584,975
Business receipts	682,186	599,576	595,602	586,109	558,996
Dividends received	3,879	3,638	3,286	3,352	3,303
Interest received	17,422	14,994	14,298	12,855	11,415
Rents and royalties	6,136	5,922	5,549	5,613	4,862
Other receipts	9,793	8,213	6,887	6,928	6,399

years this group frequently changed its name and organizational status. The present Office of Planning and Research, headed by an Assistant Commissioner of Internal Revenue, was created on May 19, 1958.

This organizational event was in recognition of the fact that the growth in scope and importance of planning in Internal Revenue called for specialization and adequate resources. Whereas one or two men could do a little planning in spare time in the 1943-44 period, the assignments now were so numerous and so complex that they had to be divided among teams of experienced technicians and professionals.

Four divisions operate in the Office of Planning and Research.

Under the new setup, four divisions were established with the following duties:

Plans and Policy Division develops and administers a system integrating the plans of all Service activities into a comprehensive Master Plan and monitors the implementation of the Master Plan. The Division participates in the formulation of the basic policies and organization of the Service; develops and administers systems whereby top management reviews and confirms current policies and organization and approves modifications thereto; and administers the internal management document system and reviews issuances for conformance to basic policies.

Research Division conducts advanced research into the federal tax system to develop new approaches to improve the Service's operations and to reduce the compliance burden on the taxpayer, within the framework of tax policy determined by the Treasury Department. The Division participates with the staffs of the Treasury Department and the Assistant Commissioner (Technical) in the preparation of legislative proposals and regulation revisions; designs and carries out surveys, polls, and other research to provide information needed for the formulation of operating programs and plans; and furnishes leadership and coordination for the program of federal-state cooperation in the field of tax administration.

Statistics Division conducts research and prepares statistics with respect to the operation of the income tax laws as required annually by the Internal Revenue Code to provide basic information for tax studies and legislation by the Congress and its committees, for administrative use by the Secretary of the Treasury and the Commissioner of Internal Revenue, and for the federal benchmark statistical programs on income, wealth, and finance; and performs other related research and statistical functions.

Systems Development Division is concerned both with electronic systems and other systems. It conducts a continuing program relative to the availability and capability of electronic data processing systems and other electronic or automation equipment and systems, the feasibility and adaptability of electronic equipment to specific Service tasks, and the development of special modifications for Service purposes. The Division reviews and coordinates projects of other offices involving the adaptation of electronic equipment and participates in the selection and installation of electronic equipment and systems. It also examines and makes recommendations for improvement of other systems and equipment applications.

Long-range planning is a major function.

Day-to-day planning for the various functional offices of Internal Revenue—such as those concerned with collections, audits, investigations, etc.—is of course done by those offices. It is in the long-range field of planning that the Planning and Research office contributes the long study and objective viewpoint that is so difficult to obtain from the officials who are "up to their ears" in more immediate problems.

In Internal Revenue, the first formal long-range planning of organization, manpower needs, and budgeting began with a study made by the Advisory Group to the Joint Committee on Internal Revenue Taxation in 1948. Although the study itself was made by a group of private citizens at the request of the Congressional committee, the Management Staff of Internal Revenue participated heavily in the research and factfinding aspects of the work. The study made it clear that Commissioner Boutwell's little band of tax collectors had grown to maturity and needed major resources of money and manpower to cope with its huge responsibility.

Also, attention began focusing on the organizational needs. The Management Staff, working with private consulting firms and others, participated in drafting the complete overhaul of the Internal Revenue structure, which was effected in 1952.

This was the reorganization that eliminated the political selection of all Revenue employees below the Commissioner, who is appointed by the President subject to confirmation by the Senate. The 1952 plan also created regional offices to supervise the 950 farflung field locations, and unified direction of field activities under the regional and district officials.

Numerous other organizational studies have been made since. This remains a major function of the Planning and Research office.

Another major function relates to forecasting manpower and budget needs. From the time that Congress broadened the income tax base in 1942, there never have been enough people and equipment in the Internal Revenue organization to do all the checking, auditing, investigation, and other processing and enforcement work that a prudent tax administrator would regard as being within his duty and responsibility. Even granting the premise that many of these tasks can be satisfied on a sample or spot-check basis, Internal Revenue found itself unequipped for such minimum standards.

The fundamental difficulty is that the Service's problems are so large and are so affected by changing population and economic factors that they cannot be dealt with adequately within the usual government cycle of one-year appropriations.

Therefore, a program was established in 1958 within the Planning and Research office to determine the long-range needs of the Service, with a year-by-year breakdown to provide a rational basis for its annual appropriations. Documented with detailed statistics of how and where the money and men are to be used, and the revenue results to be anticipated, these "brass tacks" analyses were instrumental in obtaining Congressional approval for substantial increases in enforcement manpower in each of the years in which the program has been in effect.

However, the plan is no mere foundation for money requests—although that is essential to achievement of Internal Revenue's operational functions.

Long-range plan is an action program.

In the larger sense, the long-range plan has become Internal Revenue's coordinated action program to eliminate operating deficiencies and to anticipate and prepare for future needs. The plan covers the following objectives:

—provision for the constant growth in tax administration workload, net of estimated increases in operating efficiency;

—expansion of the tax returns examination capacity to minimum levels of coverage needed to maintain an adequate level of voluntary compliance;

—expansion of the investigative efforts aimed at taxpayers guilty of tax frauds, especially racketeers;

—modernization of returns processing operations by installing an automatic data processing system;

—improvement of the system for detecting and securing delinquent returns. This requires additional enforcement personnel to conduct organized canvassing programs, and the development of a master file system, under automatic data processing, through which nonfilers will be identified;

—reduction of the delinquent accounts inventory to an operating minimum and keeping collection activity current with the increased workload generated by the proposed higher levels of tax enforcement;

—bringing into balance all enforcement-related activities, such as the Appellate and Chief Counsel offices, with the expanded enforcement programs;

—provision for modernization and improvement of space and equipment;

—provision for functional and geographical reorganizations that may be needed to maximize Internal Revenue's effectiveness.

Planning and Research investigated automatic data processing.

From its earliest days, the planning group devoted a significant portion of its energies to the search for mechanical methods of coping with Internal Revenue's mountain of documents and 90,000,000 accounts.

In those early days, it sponsored experimental installations of tabulating (punch-card) equipment in over a dozen offices. These tests demonstrated that high-cost mechanical equipment could be justified economically only if enough work was concentrated in one place to make full-time use of the machinery.

The next step was to establish partially mechanized service centers—one in Lawrence, Massachusetts, for the East; one in Kansas City, Missouri, for the Midwest; and one in Ogden, Utah, for the West. Within their limited assignments, these centers were extremely successful.

One of the first assignments of the new Planning and Research office, when it assumed its present form in 1958, was to explore the adaptability to Internal Revenue operations of the new large-scale electronic computer systems which had begun entering the business machine market.

The incredible speed and high capacity of the big "brains" were found to be ideally suited to the astronomical digit supply of Internal Revenue. A year of specifications writing, and many months of appraising manufacturers' proposals were to elapse before the present Automatic Data Processing System became a reality and implementation could begin. It is described in greater detail in Chapter Six.

Studies measure how taxpayers are complying.

A tax administrator has ready information on how many dollars are in the government till and how many returns are filed in his cabinets. But the big gnawing question is, "How many dollars and how many returns escaped?"

Therefore, another key program of Planning and Research has been to design measurements based on the study of scientific samples. The first major effort in this direction was called the "Audit Control Program." A representative sample of the 1948 individual income tax returns was set aside for special auditing and tabulation. From this study, it became possible to spot the most serious error areas (especially mistaken claims for dependency exemptions), and to estimate the additional tax that could be assessed if it were possible to audit larger proportions of the total crop of returns.

Later, a program was developed under the title of Management Information Reports to statistically analyze the results of the regular audit program. Then came a project to measure delinquency in filing various business returns (income, excise, employment) in sample geographical areas.

Out of these efforts grew a current plan to integrate such studies into a "Taxpayer Compliance Measurement Program." Its chief goals are to measure compliance in filing returns, in reporting income and tax, and to detect causes of noncompliance in these and other areas, including the causes of delinquency in payment of tax accounts. In other words, it will provide yardsticks for determining the adequacy of existing programs and suggest needs for future program changes.

Research often leads to proposed legislation.

Utilizing not only statistical methods, but also legal research, economic research, and general factfinding, the Planning and Research group engages in many other inquiries of importance to the improvement of tax administration.

Among such studies have been a number of related examinations of the problems in the taxation of dividends and interest. These studies include careful investigations of compliance—primarily by comparing dividends and interest actually reported by taxpayers on their returns with independent information from the payers of dividends and interest. As it became evident that large amounts (approximately $4 billion annually) of dividends and interest which are subject to tax and are not appearing on returns, other studies were made (in conjunction with the office of the Secretary of the Treasury) to design a system for withholding tax at the source on these kinds of income.[1]

In support of the automatic data processing program, another research project was to devise a system for assigning account numbers to all taxpayers to facilitate machine identification of their separate accounts. (See page 78.)

---

[1] Proposed legislation based on this study failed to pass in the 87th Congress. (See page 124.)

Research is varied; includes polling of people.

Another statistically oriented study was to analyze depreciation practices of business. Still another was to tabulate sample income tax returns to determine the characteristic patterns of filling in the returns (measuring, for instance, the frequency with which various lines and schedules are used).

Some of the research surveys involve polling of people in accordance with some of the modern opinion sampling techniques employed in marketing, election-forecasting, and similar activities. One example of such a survey involved questioning taxpayers to determine what kinds of assistance they needed in preparing their returns. Another interview-survey probed into the attitudes of taxpayers, practitioners, and officials toward the "informal conference" procedure for settling audit disputes.

Among a number of economic study projects was one to explore the basis for taxing corporations doing business in Latin America under the "Western Hemisphere Trade Corporation" provisions of the tax laws.

Planning and Research led in federal-state cooperation.

Since other Internal Revenue offices are very specialized in their functions, it fell to the Planning and Research group to utilize its Service-wide contacts and viewpoints to provide leadership in arranging for cooperation between federal and state tax authorities.

The opportunities for exchanging information and for avoiding duplicate investigations are very large. At first, these cooperative efforts were quite informal. However, after experiments in several states, it was found that a formal agreement would overcome some obstacles and stimulate a higher degree of cooperation.

Accordingly, the Planning and Research group undertook the negotiation of compacts with the states. Presently, signed agreements are in effect with 16 states, and an active program is under way to extend them to the remaining states. (See page 236.)

Primarily, Internal Revenue has a great deal of audit and investigation information that is invaluable to the states, particularly those that have state income taxes. On the other hand, the states can offer not only income audit data (on a much smaller scale than the federal program) but also much significant information from sales tax returns, motor vehicle registrations, and other local tax activities.

Various types of management activities are covered.

Mention was made above of the organizational planning activities of the Planning and Research group. A number of other management activities are conducted by this group. These include supervision of the internal management document system (consisting of a variety of manuals, handbooks, and other guides for internal operations) and coordination of the policy-documentation system.

The office also participates influentially in budgeting, location of service centers, merging of local offices, forms design, and similar activities.

It conducts many important contacts with organizations and institutions representative of taxpayers and their professional representatives. It is also a focus for contacts with universities and foundations.

Appendix

I. Letters to the Commissioner

II. Tables

Appendix I

LETTERS TO THE COMMISSIONER

THE INTERNAL REVENUE SERVICE undoubtedly comes into contact with more citizens than any other federal agency. Letters from taxpayers addressed to the Commissioner in Washington or to the District Director in the state where the particular taxpayer resides abound.

The letters reproduced in this Appendix reflect the sense of freedom to communicate both favorably and critically with Government representatives that is enjoyed in a democratic society. They show the tendency of the American taxpayer to express pleasure and satisfaction when a government employee performs his duties outstandingly and to complain when the quality of treatment falls short of rightful expectations.

Above all, the letters reflect the forthright character of the rugged individualist, the straight-from-the-shoulder, no-nonsense approach of citizens who recognize their obligations in a democratic society but who also expect their rights to be respected.

Part I

A LETTER TO TAXPAYERS AND SOME REPLIES

A Personal Letter to Taxpayers:

Oliver Wendell Holmes, one of our Nation's greatest judges, once wrote—"Taxes are what we pay for civilized society. . . ." Later, in saying he liked to pay taxes, he did not mention whether his enthusiasm included the filling out of tax forms.

But we all know that the forms as well as the taxes are necessary for the kind of orderly government which will preserve America and its way of life.

I therefore urge you to prepare your returns carefully and early. This will save you the inconveniences of correcting last-minute mistakes and obtaining last-minute information and assistance. Remember, the filing deadline is April 15.

Be sure you list all your income from every source—including dividends, interest and other earnings. List also deductions to which you are entitled, unless you are claiming them by the standard deduction.

After we receive your return, it is our duty to examine it for accuracy and completeness. In doing this, we may have to ask you to verify or correct some items. Most examinations are routine and should not cause concern to the overwhelming majority of taxpayers. If an examining officer indicates that additional tax is due, you will be given full opportunities for explanation and appeal if you do not agree with his conclusions.

Most taxpayers are able, with the enclosed instructions, to prepare their own returns. If, however, you have questions, you may telephone or visit the nearest Internal Revenue office. An employee there will be glad to help you.

Mortimer M. Caplin
Commissioner of Internal Revenue

St. Louis, Missouri

Dear Sir:

You have presumed to tell me how I should feel about taxes. In turn, I would advise you to apply yourself to your unpleasant occupation and let the taxpayer form his own opinions.

Yours,

Inglewood, California

Dear Sir:

I have just received my copy of the FEDERAL INCOME TAX FORMS FOR 1961 and have read with great deal of interest your message to Taxpayers.

Your message is human and simple. You are to be congratulated.

Respectfully,

Berkeley, California

Dear Sir:

In your personal letter to the tax payers your quotation from Oliver Wendell Holmes is a deceitful attempt to lull the tax payer into joyfully accepting his obligation to pay confiscatory 1961 Federal Taxes. The great chief justice died in 1935 long before our Federal Government placed almost unbearable burdens of taxation upon our people. If he had lived to see the Government spend our tax money on plans to send men to the moon and other equally worthless projects he would not have liked to paid taxes either.

Sincerely,

New York, N. Y.

Dear Sir:

I have just received my copy of the "Federal Income Tax Forms for 1961." I was very impressed with the Personal Letter to Taxpayers and feel that you should be commended for writing such a letter. I believe this letter typifies our democratic form of government. I especially like the informal manner of the first paragraph and the comment on Holmes' enthusiasm for filling in the forms.

I can't imagine any government other than ours that could approach its citizens, and have them like it, in your informal manner. We are all indeed fortunate.

I always wonder what a communist subject would think if his government could afford to treat him in this manner.

Congratulations on your job well done.

Yours truly,

Lawrenceville, Georgia

Dear Sir:

If we didn't have any more tax to pay, than Mr. Holmes did, we'd be happy about it too. I've just finished my "1040", and as usual I've not felt so civilized while fixing it. It was harder than usual to "find the pages."

This year's one, was "mixed in" like the commercials on some radio programs.

It always did aggravate me to have to work the back pages and bring the stuff to page 1. Can't you fix next years to work like a book, begin at the front, and go thru, like writing a letter? With the "answers" on the last page, instead of so much back forth, back forth turning.

On "Schedule D," we took the $50 off the stock on one page, then had to go to another page to take the 4% off. Can't you make a "compact model?" Besides the W2 short form?

The perforations wouldn't even tear off straight. I had to use scissors.

Yours,

Kansas City 23, Missouri

Dear Sir:

On receipt of Instruction Form 1040 (1961) I became very interested in paragraph one (1) page one (1) under heading "A Personal Letter to Taxpayers:", namely, as to why Oliver Wendell Holmes should have been chosen as an example.

I will not trouble you with the history of the life of Mr. Holmes or the fact that he may have paid Income Tax because he was a very wealthy man. I do however challenge the fact that he ever paid Income Tax on his salary. While the above mentioned paragraph does not say that he paid income tax on his salary it leads the average person to believe that he did. There are very few people in this part of these United States who will even bother to find out who Mr. Holmes is and fewer who actually have ever heard of him (with the exception of a few Harvard grads). While I did not graduate from any college and my education has been very limited I would like also to inform you that I greatly admire Mr. Holmes for the work he done for the State of Massachusetts for the work given the Federal Government and also the great amount of money he gave (without restriction) to the Federal Government upon his death.

I would be most pleased to hear from you. The information desired is for my own personal curiosity it will be used for no other purpose. If I had been looking for longer routes as a Democrat I could have written my Senator however the short route looked the best. I thank you,

Yours truly,

____

Dear Mr. ______________:

I have your letter of February 17, concerning my "Personal Letter to Taxpayers."

In quoting Justice Holmes it was not my intention to hold him out as a model taxpayer for others to emulate. I merely sought to draw attention to what he said about taxes being the price we pay for civilization—which I believe to be true.

As to whether or not Justice Holmes ever paid Federal income tax on his salary, I can state with certainty that he did in fact voluntarily and regularly pay such a tax during the period 1913-1919, as did the other Justices of the Supreme Court. During that time income tax on the salaries of Federal Judges was a much debated issue. In 1920 a test case (Evans v. Gore 253 U. S. 245) was brought before the Supreme Court, and the Court ruled that salaries of Federal Judges were not subject to the Federal income tax.

The decision, however, was not a unanimous one. Justice Holmes wrote the dissenting opinion, stating that:

> "To require a man to pay the taxes that all other men have to pay cannot possibly be made an instrument to attack his independence as a judge. I see nothing in the purpose of this clause of the Constitution" (Section 1, Article III), "to indicate that the judges were to be a privileged class, free from bearing their share of the cost of the institutions upon which their well-being if not their life depends."

Furthermore, his dissenting opinion was one of the bases for the Supreme Court decision in 1939 making Federal Judges' salaries subject to the Federal income tax.

After the 1920 decision, the Federal Government refunded the income tax Federal Judges had paid on their salaries. Justice Holmes received a refund of several hundred dollars, and, in a letter to a friend, confided that he spent it on prints.

I hope this information will be of assistance to you. I think it only fair to point out that the greater part of my message was an attempt to help taxpayers prepare their returns and to help them understand the Service's responsibilities once we receive the returns.

With kind regards.

Sincerely,

Mortimer M. Caplin
Commissioner

Part II

A CROSS-SECTION OF LETTERS FROM TAXPAYERS

Potlatch, Washington

Gentlemen:

Please furnish me with photocopies of all pages of my 1958 income tax return.

You have probably heard all the variations, but a puppy ate mine.

Thank you.

Respectfully Yours,

Pleasant Hill, Calif.

Our Dear Uncle Sam,

You sweet, generous thing. Imagine your sending us two refund checks each for $114.76. We cashed and used the first one immediately, needless to say, but rather wonder what to do about the second #72,113,938; May 10, 1962; to .... Not that we couldn't put it to beneficial use, and we do appreciate your generosity, but since we had to send you so much money last year in order to keep you going, we really feel that you probably need it even worse than we do, but let us know as soon as possible what you would like us to do with the check.

Your loving niece and nephew,

Anchorage, Alaska

Dear Sir:—

How are you? Please send me tax Form by next mail.

Good Bye From

Sirs:

This is the second inquiry as to my tax refund for 1961 I am forced to address to you. I submitted my return to you on Jan. 5, 1962. Some time later I pended a request to you for information. I have heard nothing from you.

I feel that you have had my return long enough to take action. Therefore in regard to your apparent slowness and lack of courtesy in acknowledging my request for information I am going to wait until April 1, 1962, for an explanation as to why this simple operation takes you over 60 days. If either my refund or a suitable explanation is not in my hands at that time (April 1, 1962) I intend to forward an inquiry to my congressman. I feel that such action is not really necessary and that it will only cause unpleasantness but you leave me no alternative.

Since I prepared and submitted my return, I have changed my address to the present one. Former address .... I realize that any communication from you to me may have been sent to the previous address but have faith that the U. S. Post Office can competently forward my mail, especially since I have only moved a block away and have the same postman.

As a taxpayer and a citizen I feel that I have the right to demand efficiency and courtesy from my government. I don't think I'm getting my money's worth.

Brooklyn, New York

Gentlemen–

I consent to your findings and apologize for lax,
In erring on my income tax,
Whatever the rebate "modern style,"
I wait abated, with a smile–
To enrich the locals with my hard earned jack–
'Cause eventually, you all will get it back.

TELEGRAM

DUE TO COMBINATION OF FLU AND PREGNANCY OF BOOKKEEPER UNABLE TO COMPLETE CORPORATION INCOME TAX RETURN. URGENTLY NEED A 90-DAY EXTENSION.

Dear Sir,

I'm writing you to let you know that I got my withholding check all right.

While with a drinking companion they hit me up for money to buy more drink with and I told them I didn't have it and said I was expecting my returns check and guess I would have to write about it. Just to put her off. I was afraid she had written so this is the reason. I am writing you now so if you should get a letter. *Please ignore* it as I got my check some time ago.

Respectfully yours,

(Following receipt of this letter, the taxpayer's wife telephoned that she had the check. She added that if his girl friend wrote to Internal Revenue, it should ignore the letter.)

Greetings:

I was thinking of filing an income-tax return this year, like I sometimes do, when I learned through an advertisement over the radio that in this country we have the "voluntary system of self-assessment." Now the only reason I have ever followed any system of self-assessment in income tax was to avoid being sent to prison, but since I have learned that this system is voluntary I shall simply volunteer not to assess myself at all.

Dear Sir,

I did not make any money this year.

P.S. I have relatives

Dear Sir,

On account of the recent freezing weather I will have a complete peach crop failure, and on account of deer and coons I had a complete failure on peas and watermelons in 1961. It is hard to buy fertilizer and work them. Then they eat them up. I want to know if a good coon dog would be deductible from my income. If I raise any this year, it will be necessary to have a dog, as it is for a farmer to have a good horse or bull. I lost last year between $300 and $500 by not having one. I don't know what I could plant that would be a profit, on peanuts and cotton that would be large enough for a profit. I think I know what your answer will be, but I had to ask.

Yours truly

Dear Sir:

Your letter of .... in regards to a coon dog I don't guess I made myself clear in my first letter, but can tell by your letter you are willing to give everything a person has coming. My intention was to buy a good stock dog, like a shepperd or collie and move him over to the watermelon and pea patches when they began to get ripe which I will have to stay with part of the time, until he learns to bark at things that come around. As far as hunting coons it is no pleasure for a man of my age, besides its against the law to hunt coons at nite where deer ranges. That is the reason there are so many here. I figure the dog will be cheaper than to put some one over there to watch. If I bought one and sold a puppy from her I'd be forced to show that on my income as a return. If a person were to operate a trading post or a kennel, would it be deductible like any other business?

Yours truly

Gentlemen,

I enclosed form 1040 simply to help you know I have not deceased.
Could I collect anything on my ex-husbands and my social security taxes before 1959?
Thanking you, I am

Very truly

Camden, New Jersey

Dear Sir:

This date the writer spoke to a young lady in your information department relative to a question relating to a loss under casualty—due to a sudden, unexpected and most certainly an "unusual" cause due to an invasion of a hostile agency. The case being so unusual, I was advised to write in for a ruling.

The home of .... was invaded by a skunk who sought haven in the cellar. The first knowledge of the invasion was the terrific smell through the house and upon investigation the "visitor" was found behind a corner cupboard.

For a full week egg traps and various other traps were set daily to no avail and in the interim appeal was made to the police of the Township for assistance. .... was told to contact the SPCA and from one day to the next Mr. Skunk held the "fort" spraying the cellar every time an effort was made to evict him (or her) until finally a week later, ..., armed with a shotgun waited until the skunk walked past the cellar window and shot the animal.

The family then proceeded to clear the cellar and due to the spraying of the skunk they were forced to destroy the corner cupboard—tables—clothing—jelly—preserves—floor covering, and in fact most everything in the cellar plus the clothing worn by .... when she made the first visit.

Damage is being claimed by the family in the amount of $300.00 which they say is a conservative amount and I would appreciate your advice as to whether this is a deductible item.

Awaiting your reply, I am,

Sincerely,

Camden, New Jersey

Dear Sir:

Reference is made to your letter dated .... wherein the question is raised as to the deductibility, as a casualty loss, of the damage caused by the entry of a skunk into one's home.

Generally, the Internal Revenue Code allows as a deduction losses of property, not connected with a trade or business, arising from fire, storm, shipwreck or other casualty, or from theft. The term "other casualty" is held to embrace losses of a character similar to those arising from fire, storm or shipwreck if occasioned by natural forces in an event due to some sudden, unexpected or unusual cause. It has further been construed that "other casualty" need not be limited to some act of nature.

The definition of "other casualty" excludes the progressive deterioration of property through a steadily operating cause. A casualty may proceed from an unknown cause or from an unusual effect of an unknown cause, where either effect may be said to occur by chance or unexpectedly. Where damage has been done by termites, such losses are generally disallowed because the damage was progressive and there is an absence of any accident, mishap, or some *sudden* invasion by a hostile agency. However, where it can be proven that the characteristic of suddenness is involved, even in termite cases, the argument as to a casualty could be offered.

Damage done by other insects or animals always present interesting situations. Damage to a fur coat by moths is not deductible as a casualty loss under the 1954 Internal Revenue Code, 800.167 (c)(3), since the element of suddenness is not present. Also, damage to a dwelling allegedly done by rats is not deductible as a casualty loss.

From the above, it is felt that the issue in the case which you present is the aspect of the "suddenness" of the destructive force which caused the damage. It is apparent that an animal of this type certainly would not be an invitee and therefore his entrance would necessarily be that of a sudden nature. Even the skunk's full week's forced lodging in the cellar of the home would not destroy such suddenness since there is no doubt that a forced eviction of this odorous animal was attempted. In view of this, a casualty loss may apply.

As to the amount of loss claimed through this incident, a deduction for a casualty loss, in the case of non-business property, should represent the difference between the value of the property immediately before and its value immediately after the casualty. Such amount is not to exceed its cost, or other adjusted basis, reduced by any insurance of other compensation received.

Very truly yours,

District Director

Dear Sir:

My wife and I are not incorporated. We're married. At your convenience, please forward to my residence at . . . ., a more appropriate tax return than the one herewith enclosed.

Very truly yours,

Dear Mr. Director:

Enclosed you will find my Income Tax Return for 1961 together with my check for the amount shown as due.

You will observe that I am paying $285. taxes for this year. As a taxpayer of substance I feel that I should be in a position to make a request as to the spending of my money and hope you will concur. Will you please see that the total money which I have paid goes to a "Friendly Nation."

Kodiak, Alaska

Dear Sir:

Concerning work and income. I have no forms from any employers. I been and I am sick.

Very truly yours,

Dear Sir:

Uncle Sam needs more citizens like me!

Every year I've owed money to the government when I've filed my income tax, and have cheerfully made payment. Again this year I paid cheerfully. But there was one difference.

I didn't owe anything.

I was entitled to a refund.

When the income tax accountant prepared my return, he informed me I would receive a refund of $19.32 this year. But the following morning when I addressed the envelope to forward the papers to your office, I absent-mindly wrote a check for the amount to be returned to me and promptly mailed it in the nearest mailbox. It was the next day before I suddenly realized I hadn't shaken the habit.

This is to call your attention to my error and alleviate further confusion. You may return my check.

On second thought, instead of being blessed, perhaps this country is decidedly fortunate there aren't more scatter-brains like this faithful taxpayer.

Dear Commissioner,

I love you, love you, love you! I knew it yesterday when I received you latest letter wherein you stated that I'd been selected for a pre-refund audit. It's like an engagement, isn't it?

True, we have only been penpals since sometime in March but I can't deny my heart.

The snows were still piled high in the roadways. The peaks were white all the way down their jagged slopes when I first went to place my dowry at your feet.

After a number of your letters I still was not about to be swayed by your reconsiderations. Like any woman I was only interested in how much you could give me.

You were adamant, relentless and still you pursued me and now you have won. I don't care one iota what you can give me. You see I am in love with you. I'm yours. Take me.

My days are magic and full of hope. I await the mailman with the 11 o'clock post;—my nights are only a little lonely because I know someone really cares—that's the glory of true love—my dearest.

I must run now, dear one, but keep your letters coming. Let's hope your father—what's his name—Audit Division—approves of our plans.

Love and Kisses

Appendix II

TABLES

NUMBER OF INDIVIDUAL AND CORPORATION INCOME TAX RETURNS FILED

Fiscal year	Type of return (In thousands)	
	Individual	Corporation
1962	62,326	1,231
1961	62,046	1,179
1960	61,260	1,072
1959	60,008	998
1958	60,793	971
1957	60,186	911
1956	58,640	869
1955	58,289	836
1954	58,673	745
1953	58,641	800
1952	54,681	756
1951	52,457	684
1950	51,876	666
1949	53,338	653
1948	54,984	611
1947	54,370	540
1946	46,547	591
1945	48,370	603
1944	43,069	621
1943	37,076	620
1942	26,369	660
1941	14,877	631
1940	7,914	547
1939	6,515	550
1938	6,655	553
1937	5,907	554
1936	5,010	565
1935	4,492	555
1934	4,098	519
1933	4,383	528
1932	3,724	532
1931	4,198	537
1930	4,445	540

Internal Revenue Service
Reports Division
May 1962

Table 1

COLLECTIONS ON INDIVIDUAL AND CORPORATION INCOME TAXES 1962—1863

Fiscal year	Type of tax (In thousands of dollars)	
	Individual	Corporation
1962	50,649,594	21,295,711
1961	46,153,001	21,764,940
1960	44,945,711	22,179,414
1959	40,734,744	18,091,509
1958	38,568,559	20,533,316
1957	39,029,772	21,530,653
1956	35,337,642	21,298,522
1955	31,650,106	18,264,720
1954	32,813,691	21,546,322
1953	32,536,217	21,594,515
1952	29,274,107	21,466,910
1951	22,997,309	14,387,569
1950	17,153,308	10,854,351
1949	18,051,822	11,553,669
1948	20,997,781	10,174,410
1947	19,343,297	9,676,459
1946	18,704,536	12,553,602
1945	19,084,313	16,027,213
1944	18,261,004	14,766,798
1943	6,629,932	9,668,956
1942	3,262,800	4,743,984
1941	1,417,655	2,053,468
1940	982,017	1,147,592
1939	1,028,835	1,156,281
1938	1,286,354	1,342,717
1937	1,091,777	1,088,100
1936	674,815	753,031
1935	528,074	578,678
1934	419,509	450,375
1933	352,574	394,218
1932	427,191	629,566
1931	833,648	1,026,393
1930	1,146,845	1,263,414
1929	1,095,541	1,235,731
1928	882,727	1,291,846
1927	911,940	1,308,011
1926	879,124	1,094,980
1925	845,426	916,231
1924	[1]1,841,759	([1])
1923	[1]1,691,090	([1])
1922	[1]2,086,918	([1])
1921	[1]3,228,138	([1])
1920	[1]3,956,936	([1])
1919	[1]2,600,784	([1])
1918	[1]2,852,325	([1])
1917	180,108	179,540
1916	67,944	56,994
1915	41,046	39,145
1914	28,454	43,128
1913	-	[2]35,006
1912	-	[2]28,583
1911	-	[2]33,512
1910	-	[2]20,960
([3])		
1872	[1]14,437	([1])
1871	[1]19,163	([1])
1870	[1]37,776	([1])
1869	[1]34,792	([1])
1868	[1]41,456	([1])
1867	[1]66,014	([1])
1866	[1]72,982	([1])
1865	[1]32,050	([1])
1864	[1]20,295	([1])
1863	[1]2,742	([1])

[1]Individuals and corporations were not shown separately.
[2]Excise tax on corporations.
[3]There was no tax imposed on individuals and corporations from 1873 through 1909.

Internal Revenue Service
Reports Division
May 1962

Table 2

EXCISE TAX COLLECTIONS

Fiscal year	Type of tax (In thousands of dollars)		
	Alcohol	Tobacco	Other excise
1962	3,341,282	2,025,736	7,385,158
1961	3,212,801	1,991,117	6,860,384
1960	3,193,714	1,931,504	6,739,522
1959	3,002,096	1,806,816	5,950,637
1958	2,946,461	1,734,021	6,133,786
1957	2,973,195	1,674,050	5,990,299
1956	2,920,574	1,613,497	5,470,124
1955	2,742,840	1,571,213	4,903,881
1954	2,783,012	1,580,229	5,153,992
1953	2,780,925	1,654,911	6,401,566
1952	2,549,120	1,565,162	5,690,023
1951	2,546,808	1,380,396	5,506,124
1950	2,219,202	1,328,464	4,757,232
1949	2,210,607	1,321,875	4,052,502
1948	2,255,327	1,300,280	3,856,057
1947	2,474,762	1,237,768	3,572,444
1946	2,526,165	1,165,519	3,344,615
1945	2,309,866	932,145	3,074,618
1944	1,618,775	988,483	2,237,118
1943	1,423,646	923,857	1,778,795
1942	1,048,517	780,982	1,593,583
1941	820,056	698,077	1,047,938
1940	624,253	608,518	784,479
1939	587,800	580,159	727,355
1938	567,979	568,182	733,999
1937	594,245	552,254	755,526
1936	505,464	501,166	706,843
1935	411,022	459,179	1,110,370
1934	258,911	425,169	1,005,135
1933	43,180	402,739	392,819
1932	8,704	398,579	46,268
1931	10,432	444,277	65,401
1930	11,695	450,339	98,662
1929	12,777	434,445	103,083
1928	15,308	396,450	144,117
1927	21,195	376,170	148,025
1926	26,452	370,666	345,561
1925	25,905	345,247	342,389
1924	27,585	325,639	498,229
1923	30,358	309,015	464,577
1922	45,609	270,759	654,745
1921	82,623	255,219	875,332
1920	139,870	295,809	911,328
1919	483,051	206,003	478,282
1918	443,840	156,189	194,814
1917	284,009	102,577	29,349
1916	247,453	88,064	50,590
1915	223,949	79,764	31,573
1914	226,180	79,816	2,461
1913	230,146	76,789	2,481
1912	219,660	70,590	2,783
1911	219,648	67,006	2,360
1910	208,601	58,118	2,278
1909	192,324	51,887	2,002
1908	199,967	49,863	1,836
1907	215,905	51,811	1,948
1906	199,036	48,423	1,644
1905	186,320	45,660	2,208
1904	184,893	44,656	3,355
1903	179,501	43,515	7,725
1902	193,127	51,938	26,803
1901	191,698	62,482	52,692
1900	183,420	59,355	52,541
1899	167,929	52,493	53,063
1898	132,062	36,231	2,574
1897	114,481	30,710	1,429
1896	114,454	30,712	1,665
1895	111,504	29,705	2,037
1894	116,674	28,618	1,876
1893	127,270	31,890	1,845
1892	121,347	31,000	1,511
1891	111,899	32,796	1,340
1890	107,696	33,959	940
1889	98,036	31,867	991
1888	92,630	30,662	1,034
1887	87,751	30,108	978
1886	88,769	27,907	227
1885	85,742	26,407	272
1884	94,990	26,062	449
1883	91,270	42,104	11,785
1882	86,027	47,392	13,674
1881	80,854	42,855	12,067
1880	74,016	38,870	11,631
1879	63,299	40,135	10,484
1878	60,358	40,092	10,648
1877	66,950	41,107	10,938
1876	65,997	39,795	11,445
1875	61,226	37,303	12,016
1874	58,749	33,243	10,514
1873	61,424	34,386	18,265
1872	57,734	33,736	25,864
1871	53,672	33,579	36,167
1870	61,925	31,351	52,511
1869	51,171	23,431	49,400
1868	24,612	18,730	104,865
1867	39,601	19,765	139,311
1866	38,489	16,531	181,980
1865	22,466	11,401	144,706
1864	32,619	8,592	55,329
1863	6,806	3,098	28,300

Internal Revenue Service, Reports Division, May 1962

Table 3

Fiscal year	Operating cost[1]	Collections	Cost of collecting $100	Population (Thousands)	Tax per capita	Number of employees		
						Total	National Office	Field
1866..........	$7,689,700	$310,120,448	$2.47	36,538	$8.49	4,461	221	4,240
1867..........	8,982,686	265,064,938	3.38	37,376	7.09	4,808	246	4,662
1868..........	9,327,302	190,374,926	4.88	38,213	4.98	5,393	251	5,142
1869..........	6,785,477	159,124,127	4.59	39,051	4.07	6,258	255	6,003
1870..........	8,241,514	184,302,828	3.92	39,905	4.62	6,266	252	6,014
1871..........	8,408,634	143,198,322	5.30	40,938	3.50	6,321	301	6,020
1872..........	6,522,774	130,890,097	4.36	41,972	3.12	6,141	301	5,840
1873..........	6,620,231	113,504,013	4.69	43,006	2.64	5,136	272	4,864
1874..........	5,948,478	102,191,017	4.40	44,040	2.32	4,784	264	4,520
1875..........	5,317,924	110,071,515	3.89	45,073	2.44	4,657	241	4,416
1876..........	4,775,000	116,768,096	4.71	46,107	2.53	5,184	241	3,943
1877..........	4,171,495	118,549,230	3.50	47,141	2.51	3,983	203	3,780
1878..........	4,056,410	110,654,163	3.75	48,174	2.30	3,729	203	3,526
1879..........	4,205,632	113,449,621	3.70	49,208	2.31	3,609	193	3,416
1880..........	4,505,641	123,981,916	3.63	50,262	2.47	3,405	193	3,212
1881..........	5,054,026	135,229,912	3.60	51,542	2.62	3,405	193	3,212
1882..........	5,107,481	146,523,274	3.50	52,821	2.77	4,002	196	3,806
1883..........	5,105,957	144,553,345	3.50	54,100	2.67	4,341	243	4,098
1884..........	5,100,452	121,590,040	4.20	55,379	2.20	4,126	243	3,883
1885..........	4,455,430	112,421,121	3.90	56,658	1.98	3,581	240	3,341
1886..........	4,299,485	116,902,869	3.60	57,938	2.02	3,292	195	3,097
1887..........	4,065,149	118,837,301	3.40	59,217	2.01	3,389	198	3,191
1888..........	3,978,283	124,326,475	3.20	60,496	2.05	3,295	193	3,102
1889..........	4,185,729	130,894,434	3.20	61,775	2.12	3,437	199	3,238
1890..........	4,095,111	142,594,697	2.82	63,056	2.26	3,741	201	3,540
1891..........	4,205,655	146,035,416	2.88	64,361	2.27	3,850	208	3,642
1892..........	4,315,046	153,857,544	2.80	65,666	2.34	3,938	208	3,730
1893..........	4,219,739	161,004,990	2.62	66,970	2.40	3,744	211	3,533
1894..........	3,975,904	147,168,450	2.70	68,275	2.16	4,339	207	4,132
1895..........	4,127,601	143,246,078	2.81	69,580	2.06	4,204	221	3,983
1896..........	4,086,292	146,830,616	2.78	70,885	2.07	3,991	198	3,793
1897..........	3,848,469	146,619,593	2.62	72,189	2.03	3,858	202	3,656
1898..........	3,907,011	170,866,819	2.29	73,494	2.32	3,832	222	3,610
1899..........	4,591,755	273,484,573	1.68	74,799	3.66	3,667	262	3,405
1900..........	4,653,688	295,316,108	1.58	76,094	3.88	4,003	277	3,726
1901..........	4,749,220	306,871,669	1.55	77,585	3.95	3,836	283	3,553
1902..........	4,603,888	271,867,990	1.70	79,160	3.43	4,111	317	3,794
1903..........	4,771,189	230,740,925	2.07	80,632	2.86	3,960	285	3,675
1904..........	4,619,310	232,903,781	1.98	82,165	2.83	3,834	262	3,572
1905..........	4,705,296	234,187,976	2.01	83,820	2.79	3,854	257	3,597
1906..........	4,727,170	249,102,738	1.90	85,437	2.92	3,703	259	3,444
1907..........	4,875,746	269,664,023	1.81	87,000	3.10	3,788	258	3,530
1908..........	4,830,699	251,665,950	1.92	88,709	2.84	3,872	259	3,613
1909..........	4,975,239	246,212,719	2.02	90,492	2.72	3,795	259	3,536
1910..........	5,044,503	289,957,220	1.74	92,407	3.14	3,844	258	3,586
1911..........	5,411,659	322,526,300	1.68	93,868	3.44	3,992	294	3,698
1912..........	5,509,984	321,615,895	1.71	95,331	3.38	3,838	272	3,566
1913..........	5,484,655	344,424,454	1.59	97,227	3.54	4,000	277	3,723
1914..........	5,779,330	380,008,894	1.52	99,118	3.83	3,972	277	3,695
1915..........	6,804,689	415,681,024	1.64	100,549	4.13	4,730	530	4,200

[1]Data represent "Expenditures" for 1866-1928 and "Obligations" for 1929 and thereafter.
[2]Excludes cost of Prohibition and Narcotic enforcement.
[3]Excludes the following Prohibition and Narcotics employees:

	Total	Nat. Of.	Field
F.Y. 1920..	2,592	450	2,142
1921..	2,671	503	2,168
1922..	3,678	604	3,074
1923..	3,382	687	2,695
1924..	3,319	688	2,631

[4]Excludes agriculture adjustment taxes.
[5]Excludes amount transferred to Post Office Department to cover cost of selling vehicle tax stamps.
[6]Excludes amount collected by Post Office Department for vehicles tax.
[r]Revised.

Internal Revenue Service
Reports Division
October 1962

Table 4

EMPLOYEES, AND THE U. S. POPULATION SINCE 1866

Report Symbol NO-D:R-2

Fiscal year	Operating cost[1]	Collections	Cost of collecting $100	Population (Thousands)	Tax per capita	Number of employees		
						Total	National Office	Field
1916........	$7,199,163	$512,723,288	$1.40	101,966	$5.03	4,718	560	4,158
1917........	7,699,031	809,393,640	0.95	103,414	7.83	5,053	524	4,529
1918........	12,003,214	3,698,955,821	0.33	104,550	35.38	9,597	2,245	7,352
1919........	20,573,772	3,850,150,079	0.53	105,063	36.65	14,055	3,090	10,965
1920........	[2]27,037,135	5,407,580,252	0.50	106,466	50.79	[3]15,848	5,462	10,386
1921........	[2]33,174,309	4,595,357,062	0.72	108,541	42.34	[3]17,470	6,493	10,977
1922........	[2]34,286,651	3,197,451,083	1.07	110,055	29.05	[3]17,710	6,671	11,039
1923........	[2]36,501,063	2,621,745,228	1.39	111,950	23.42	[3]17,613	6,552	11,061
1924........	[2]34,676,688	2,796,179,257	1.24	114,113	24.50	[3]15,884	5,759	10,125
1925........	[2]37,266,573	2,584,140,268	1.44	115,832	22.31	[3]15,568	5,584	9,984
1926........	[2]34,948,483	2,835,999,892	1.23	117,399	24.16	[3]14,333	4,536	9,797
1927........	[2]32,967,764	2,865,683,130	1.15	119,038	24.07	[3]13,211	3,801	9,410
1928........	32,599,845	2,790,535,538	1.17	120,501	23.16	12,914	3,661	9,253
1929........	34,377,083	2,939,054,375	1.17	121,770	24.14	12,273	3,584	8,689
1930........	34,352,063	3,040,145,733	1.13	123,188	24.68	11,979	3,448	8,531
1931........	33,997,786	2,428,228,754	1.40	124,149	19.56	11,833	3,461	8,372
1932........	33,870,904	1,557,729,043	2.17	124,949	12.47	11,716	3,407	8,309
1933........	30,031,723	1,619,839,224	1.85	125,690	12.89	11,524	3,383	8,141
1934........	28,826,226	[4]2,300,816,309	1.25	126,485	18.19	11,216	3,410	7,806
1935........	42,719,338	[4]2,773,213,214	1.54	127,362	21.77	16,523	3,756	12,767
1936........	48,065,039	[4]3,448,571,174	1.39	128,181	26.90	17,054	3,743	13,311
1937........	51,797,735	4,653,195,315	1.12	128,961	36.08	21,148	4,602	16,546
1938........	58,204,050	5,658,765,314	1.03	129,969	43.54	22,045	4,580	17,465
1939........	58,662,969	5,181,573,953	1.13	131,028	39.55	22,623	4,202	18,421
1940........	59,675,518	5,340,452,347	1.12	132,122	40.42	22,423	3,993	18,430
1941........	65,289,527	7,370,108,378	0.89	133,402	55.25	27,230	4,151	23,079
1942........	[5]73,805,704	[6]12,976,589,178	0.56	134,860	96.22	29,065	4,329	24,736
1943........	[5]98,568,512	[6]22,227,341,483	0.44	136,739	162.55	36,338	4,377	31,961
1944........	[5]129,416,848	[6]39,991,717,001	0.32	138,397	288.96	46,171	4,273	41,898
1945........	[5]144,786,970	[6]43,675,865,945	0.33	139,928	312.13	49,814	4,441	45,373
1946........	[5]174,055,640	[6]40,558,913,040	0.43	141,389	286.86	59,693	5,144	54,549
1947........	203,916,822	39,108,385,742	0.52	144,126	271.35	52,830	4,771	48,059
1948........	183,731,060	41,864,542,295	0.44	146,631	285.51	52,143	4,662	47,481
1949........	209,205,715	40,463,125,019	0.52	149,188	271.22	52,266	4,554	47,712
1950........	230,408,200	38,957,131,768	0.59	151,683	256.83	55,551	4,303	51,248
1951........	245,869,538	50,445,686,315	0.49	154,360	326.80	57,795	4,030	53,765
1952........	271,872,192	65,009,585,560	0.42	157,028	414.00	55,370	3,842	51,528
1953........	268,590,806	69,686,535,389	0.38	159,636	436.53	53,463	3,834	49,629
1954........	268,969,107	69,919,990,791	0.38	162,417	430.50	51,411	2,707	48,704
1955........	278,834,278	66,288,692,000	0.42	165,270	401.09	50,890	2,675	48,215
1956........	299,894,710	75,112,649,000	0.40	168,176	446.63	50,682	2,583	48,099
1957........	305,537,814	80,171,971,000	0.38	171,198	468.30	51,364	2,602	48,762
1958........	337,428,789	79,978,476,484	0.42	174,060	459.49	50,816	2,638	48,178
1959........	355,469,228	79,797,972,806	0.44	177,261	450.17	50,200	2,633	47,567
1960........	363,735,359	91,774,802,823	0.40	r180,676	r507.95	50,199	2,702	47,497
1961........	413,295,238	94,401,086,398	0.44	r183,742	r513.77	53,680	3,031	50,649
1962........	450,080,420	99,440,839,245	0.45	186,591	532.93	56,510	3,357	53,153
1963........								
1964........								
1965........								

	Total	Nat. Of.	Field
F.Y. 1925..	3,765	592	3,173
1926..	3,570	307	3,263
1927..	P. and N. enforcement placed under separate Bureau, effective Apr. 1, 1927 (Pub. Act No.751—69th Congress).		

Table 4 ***(cont.)***

Work flow in the Internal Revenue Service and the Courts
Fiscal years 1962 and 1961

	1962	1961
	Returns	
Tax returns filed, total	96,435,000	95,856,000
Individual income	62,326,000	62,122,000
Corporation income	1,231,000	1,179,000
Estate and gift	169,000	163,000
Employment	20,932,000	20,660,000
Excise	4,009,000	3,942,000
Other	7,769,000	7,790,000
Income, estate, and gift taxes		
Number of returns examined	3,278,000	3,274,000
Adjustments proposed by audit divisions 1/	2,100,000	2,187,000
Disposed of by audit divisions 2/		
Agreed, paid or defaulted	2,068,000	2,158,000
	Cases	
Total received in appellate divisions 3/	15,963	15,398
Disposed of by appellate divisions		
Agreed, paid, or defaulted	12,687	13,315
Courts of Original Jurisdiction		
Tax Court		
Total petitioned to Tax Court	4,749	5,368
Dismissed	228	330
Settled by stipulation	4,890	5,614
Settled by Tax Court decision	882	882
Decided by Tax Court but appealed	403	335
District Courts and Court of Claims		
Total filed in District Courts and Court of Claims	1,364	1,285
Settled in District Courts and Court of Claims	659	713
Decided by District Courts and Court of Claims	505	443
Courts of Appeals		
Settled by Courts of Appeals decision	414	261
Favorable to Government	268	174
Favorable to taxpayers	113	68
Modified	33	19
Decided by Courts of Appeals but reviewed by Supreme Court	6	8
Supreme Court		
Settled by Supreme Court decision	7	10

Table 5

The amounts of revenue involved at each level of the tax system
Fiscal years 1962 and 1961

	1962	1961
	(millions of dollars)	
Internal revenue collections, total	99,441	94,401
Individual:	50,650	46,153
Withholding	36,246	32,978
Other	14,404	13,175
Corporation	21,296	21,765
Estate and gift	2,035	1,916
Employment	12,708	12,502
Excise	12,752	12,064
Income, estate, and gift taxes		
Additional tax and penalties recommended after agreement in audit divisions	1,042	1,194
Additional tax and penalties determined after agreement in appellate divisions	146	178
Additional tax and penalties determined by settlement in Tax Court	63	92
Additional tax and penalties determined by Tax Court decision		
Defaulted or dismissed	4	8
Decision on merits	27	17
Additional tax and penalties in cases decided by Supreme Court and courts of appeals	12	39
Amount refunded to taxpayers as a result of refund suits	25	30

1/Includes deficiencies and overassessments recommended and claims for refund.
2/In 1962 there were 30,469 informal conferences held in which agreements were reached in 18,793. Corresponding figures for 1961 were 30,019 and 19,048, respectively.
3/Cases protested after audit division action and refund cases requiring review by the Joint Committee on Internal Revenue Taxation.

Table 5 *(cont.)*

Commissioners of Internal Revenue

Name [1]	State	Service	
		From—	To—
George S. Boutwell	Massachusetts	July 17, 1862	Mar. 4, 1863
Joseph J. Lewis	Pennsylvania	Mar. 18, 1863	June 30, 1865
William Orton	New York	July 1, 1865	Oct. 31, 1865
Edward A. Rollins	New Hampshire	Nov. 1, 1865	Mar. 10, 1869
Columbus Delano	Ohio	Mar. 11, 1869	Oct. 31, 1870
Alfred Pleasonton	New York	Jan. 3, 1871	Aug. 8, 1871
John W. Douglass	Pennsylvania	Aug. 9, 1871	May 14, 1875
Daniel D. Pratt	Indiana	May 15, 1875	July 31, 1876
Green B. Raum	Illinois	Aug. 2, 1876	Apr. 30, 1883
Walter Evans	Kentucky	May 21, 1883	Mar. 19, 1885
Joseph S. Miller	West Virginia	Mar. 20, 1885	Mar. 20, 1889
John W. Mason	do	Mar. 21, 1889	Apr. 18, 1893
Joseph S. Miller	do	Apr. 19, 1893	Nov. 26, 1896
W. St. John Forman	Illinois	Nov. 27, 1896	Dec. 31, 1897
Nathan B. Scott	West Virginia	Jan. 1, 1898	Feb. 28, 1899
George W. Wilson	Ohio	Mar. 1, 1899	Nov. 27, 1900
John W. Yerkes	Kentucky	Dec. 20, 1900	Apr. 30, 1907
John G. Capers	South Carolina	June 5, 1907	Aug. 31, 1909
Royal E. Cabell	Virginia	Sept. 1, 1909	Apr. 27, 1913
William H. Osborn	North Carolina	Apr. 28, 1913	Sept. 25, 1917
Daniel C. Roper	South Carolina	Sept. 26, 1917	Mar. 31, 1920
William M. Williams	Alabama	Apr. 1, 1920	Apr. 11, 1921
David H. Blair	North Carolina	May 27, 1921	May 31, 1929
Robert H. Lucas	Kentucky	June 1, 1929	Aug. 15, 1930
David Burnet	Ohio	Aug. 20, 1930	May 15, 1933
Guy T. Helvering	Kansas	June 6, 1933	Oct. 8, 1943
Robert E. Hannegan	Missouri	Oct. 9, 1943	Jan. 22, 1944
Joseph D. Nunan, Jr.	New York	Mar. 1, 1944	June 30, 1947
George J. Schoeneman	Rhode Island	July 1, 1947	July 31, 1951
John B. Dunlap	Texas	Aug. 1, 1951	Nov. 18, 1952
T. Coleman Andrews	Virginia	Feb. 4, 1953	Oct. 31, 1955
Russell C. Harrington	Rhode Island	Dec. 5, 1955	Sept. 30, 1958
Dana Latham	California	Nov. 5, 1958	Jan. 20, 1961
Mortimer M. Caplin	Virginia	Feb. 7, 1961	....

Note.—Office of Commissioner of Internal Revenue created by act of Congress, July 1, 1862.

[1] In addition, the following were Acting Commissioners during periods of time when there was no Commissioner holding the office: John W. Douglass, of Pennsylvania, from Nov. 1, 1870, to Jan. 2, 1871; Henry C. Rogers, of Pennsylvania, from May 1 to May 10, 1883, and from May 1 to June 4, 1907; John J. Knox, of Minnesota, from May 11 to May 20, 1883; Robert Williams, Jr., of Ohio, from Nov. 28 to Dec. 19, 1900; Millard F. West, of Kentucky, from Apr. 12 to May 26, 1921; H. F. Mires, of Washington, from Aug. 16, to Aug. 19, 1930; Pressly R. Baldridge, of Iowa, from May 16 to June 5, 1933; Harold N. Graves, of Illinois, from Jan. 23 to Feb. 29, 1944; John S. Graham, of North Carolina, from Nov. 19, 1952, to Jan. 19, 1953; Justin F. Winkle, of New York, from Jan. 20 to Feb 3, 1953; O. Gordon Delk, of Virginia, from Nov. 1 to Dec. 4, 1955, and from Oct. 1 to Nov. 4, 1958; Charles I. Fox, of Utah, from Jan. 21 to Feb. 6, 1961.

Table 6

INDEX

INDEX

D

E